D1345714

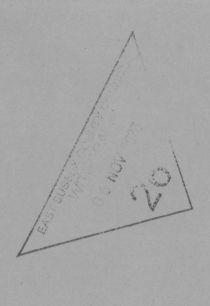

04740626

GROUNDING

Also by Lulah Ellender

Elisabeth's Lists: A Life Between the Lines

GROUNDING

Finding Home in a Garden

LULAH ELLENDER

GRANTA

Granta Publications, 12 Addison Avenue, London W11 4QR

First published in Great Britain by Granta Books, 2022

A CIP catalogue record for this book is available from the British Library.

1 3 5 7 9 10 8 6 4 2

ISBN 978 1 78378 697 8
eISBN 978 1 78378 698 5

Typeset in Calluna by Avon DataSet, Alcester, Warwickshire B49 6HN
Printed and bound by CPI Group (UK) Ltd, Croydon, CR0 4YY

www.granta.com

MIX
Paper from
responsible sources
FSC® C171272

For Mark, Albie, Isey, Charlie and Orla

Ground, v.

To lay the foundations of (a house etc.); to found; to
fix or establish firmly
　To set on a firm basis
　　To establish, settle
　　　To rest or rely upon
　　　　To alight on the ground

Ground, n.

The surface of the earth
　Soil or earth
　　Land of a particular type
　　　An area of knowledge or special interest
　　　　A basis for belief, action or argument
　　　　　A prepared underlying surface

CONTENTS

PROLOGUE

Some time ago there was a year that seemed impossible. My mother had died, following a long illness. Politics was fracturing, exposing fault lines many of us had wilfully overlooked. The world was waking up to the fact that we only had a decade to slow down climate change before catastrophe hit. That summer, when I felt unmoored in my grief and horrified by what was happening globally, we came home from a holiday to find a letter from the executors of our recently deceased landlord's estate. Our house – the place my husband, four children and I have called home for ten years now, which has seen sorrow, laughter, gatherings and sixty family birthdays – was going on the market.

At a dinner with friends that Christmas, someone told me, 'My aunt is buying your house.' I didn't know what to say. I looked online at house listings and found photographs of my children's bedrooms, the 'desirable garden' and 'interior in need of some modernization'. It was a humiliation to have our lives exposed like this. The prospect of relocating a family of six people, four chickens, a dog and a cat made me feel queasy. Over the weeks and months that followed, we struggled to find another house we could afford. The unsettledness plunged me into a blank despair. The house was caught up in a bitter probate dispute, and we were told there was a chance we might be able to stay, depending on the outcome. We had been evicted from a previous house, when I was pregnant with our second son, but back then it didn't feel as disastrous. Perhaps because we had only lived in that house for a few months, whereas this place truly felt like our home, the place where I'd allowed myself to imagine our four children growing up and us growing old, even though we were renting it. I swung between feeling utterly heartbroken and trying to be practical. Faced with prohibitive rents, we contemplated a move away from the area, which would involve finding new jobs and moving all the children to new schools. I realized there was another reason this potential move felt so difficult: it echoed the loss of a childhood home that I loved, which had reverberated throughout my life in the form of a continuous feeling of homesickness. And now the same thing was happening to my children.

When a plant is forcibly uprooted, or moved to a different environment, it may suffer something called 'root shock'. Its leaves curl and wilt, its limbs and twigs die back, its growth is inhibited, and the stress makes it more susceptible to injuries. It may even die as a result of the displacement. I was anticipating a form of root shock for myself and my family; and it was a familiar sensation.

In the disorienting, drawn-out limbo in which we found ourselves, waiting for the house to be sold – or not sold – I ignored the garden. What was the point of planting or tidying if we were going to have to leave? But my thinking slowly shifted. As estate agents and solicitors orbited our wary family unit, with no end to the uncertainty in sight, I was drawn back into the garden. I found myself digging, weeding, cutting and planting, in spite of our unsteady situation, allowing myself to imagine these seeds growing and flowering as the season turned. It was a modest and quiet act of defiance.

As I cared for the land outside our house, it also became an opportunity to look within: to explore the tensions between creating home and feeling trapped by it, to examine the different layers of my life as a daughter, a wife, a mother and a woman. Visiting celebrated gardens in Sussex, swapping cuttings with friends, collecting seeds and poring over bulb catalogues, I found inspiration and hope in the natural world. I discovered stories as porous as the chalk ground beneath the local landscape and as enduring as Sussex flint. My work in the garden – slow, intuitive, responsive – became a way to work out my changing place in my family, and to make sense of our precarity. I excavated in layers until I came to ground.

This is the story of a garden; of hope and home and living alongside uncertainty.

MARCH

1

CLEARING

Step out of the back door of our house and you'll find a long garden with a high, overgrown hedge on one side and an ancient brick wall along the other. Facing you is another old wall where a lilac bush sits beneath a rambling rose, the two caught in a perpetual tussle for the sunlight, all thorns and silken buds. The house is in the middle of a town, yet the garden feels like the countryside, and the traffic at the front slides past unseen. Over the side wall is a car park and behind the hedge a tall, ugly telephone exchange building. At the centre of the garden is a lawn, flanked along the sunny northern wall by flower beds and vegetable patches.

In March the fruit trees are in blossom, heavy and humming with bees. Behind the stooping plum tree, iced with tiny pink stars, four chickens scratch in their rubbly corner. I wonder if we will be able to take the chickens with us if we have to move. One of them is the only survivor of a group we bought with my mother, driving them home in an unnervingly lurching, crawking cardboard box. A fig tree – a fortieth birthday present given to me by a friend – squats near the lilac, still studded with last year's wrinkled fruit.

A small metal table and two chairs the colour of spearmint add to the greenness of the place. There are endless degrees of green: the deep, spinach green of the hedge; the vivid chlorophyll carpet of grass; the pale artichoke of unfurling leaves. It is not a grand or impressive garden, and I have only ever partially tamed it. Wildness pushes in from the edges – brittle piles of wood, brambles, ground elder, all creeping invisibly inwards. This March, I look out from my bedroom window over a garden bearing witness to a winter of neglect. I find myself noticing only the weeds and patchy grass, the rotting bike shed full of chicken feed and straw and bikes we never got round to fixing, and the encroaching hedge folding itself into our space. While I feel paralysed, the garden grows on.

Spring has come, and the equinox is approaching. This has always been a significant moment in the yearly cycle – the earth spins on its elliptical orbit, the sun directly over the equator, casting minimal shadow and bringing life into sharp focus. For the first time this year day and night are equal, a kind of tipping point in the chasing of the light. A suspended, tilting pause, a breath held for one moment of equilibrium, before we spill into the long daylight hours of summer.

All the planets in our solar system have equinoxes – it is a truly universal experience. At these points in a year, when the sun exerts its greatest pull on the earth, tides are more extreme. Sea waters are pulled strongly to the sun as it lies over the equator at its minimum declination, causing a tidal bulge. Powerful forces push the year onwards. Perhaps it is also a time when the membrane between different worlds is thinner, where stories of place cross between times and ages. There is a shift in energy that lends itself to 'spring cleaning', an awakening from the slumber of winter triggered by this movement towards light, and a desire to sort and beautify our surroundings. But this year, although I sense movement all around me, my instinct is to stay lizard-still; to freeze until I know where to begin. The garden, like the house, suddenly feels like an entirely borrowed space. What right have I to tend it? What point is there?

My daughter sits on the swing that hangs from the apple tree. Each of the children has swung there, until they got too tall and heavy and the branch stooped worryingly low. I follow her outside. As I fill a tub with chicken feed, she tells me she loves how 'wild' the garden is, but I take this as an insult, as if she were running a finger along a dusty shelf and saying, 'How lovely that you don't waste time cleaning.' Instead of responding with action – hunting for my tools in the eternal chaos of boxing gloves, bits of wood, tins of paint and old high chairs that fills the shed, I busy myself with indoor jobs. If we are to move, I need to start clearing, but I can't summon the enthusiasm for this, so I turn out my larder instead. Noticing the shoebox filled with garden seeds stored behind the jars of oats and rice, I sit down at the kitchen table and look through the envelopes and half-used packets. Some have gone out of date, so I set them aside. One contains ruby sunflower seeds given to me by a friend, collected from plants I had given her the year before; one, unopened, contains parsnip seeds that I didn't get round to planting last year; and another is filled with hollyhock seeds from my mother's garden. I collected them during her last summer, and suddenly I remember her garden diary. I rummage in a drawer and find the small, blue, cloth-covered notebook. Inside are notes of her garden activities over twelve years, entries organized by months, rather than chronologically. I turn the pages, looking for her Marches. Perhaps I can summon some inspiration from the tasks she was doing at this time of year.

*

*22 March 2004. Stormy, snowy weather. No veg sown,
but we're revving up for it. Daffs beautiful, Clematis
armandii flowering, including in willow tree for first time.
Purple clematis on holly tree also flowering. Mowed grass
once about two weeks ago. New bulbs under pear tree bit
disappointing. Hellebores excellent.*

*

I had found the diary a few months ago, on a snowy January
day at my mother's house, sorting through the remainder of her
belongings. My brother, sister and I had done a cursory tidying
away just after she died, because my stepfather, Tom, who is still
living in the house, found it too painful to see her knitting bag and
clothes. We took some things to the charity shop but put the more
evocative, heart-wrenching objects and garments in bags in the
attic, to deal with another day. Without her, the house feels dead.
It is old and jumbly, witness to many lives and deaths, with huge,
uneven flagstones in the kitchen – one has an ammonite curled
secretly in one corner, a spiral through time to this now-silent
room. A friend told me how she buried her parents' ashes beneath
the kitchen flagstones in her childhood home, and I had wished
we had somehow tethered my mother physically to this place.

On that visit we sorted through the remains of her time in this
world: the box of sticky birthday-cake candles, the out-of-date
spices, her sandals, pots of face cream, hair lotions, her drawings.
Strangely, what I found almost unbearably tender was the drawers

full of useless household objects, like dried-up Blu Tack and half-sharpened pencils. It seemed impossible that a life could be reduced to these quiet oddments. I felt a sudden and overwhelming wave of exhaustion. The dismal dirt and brokenness had me thinking about how ashamed I would be if I died unexpectedly and someone had to go through my house, picking through the gunk at the bottom of the fridge drawer or baulking at the basket full of odd socks. But then, in a pile of books in a corner of the kitchen, I discovered the garden diary. My mother had shown it to me some years ago, proud that she'd kept such a long-term record, inspired, I think, by a TV gardener whose hair she always wanted to copy. I thought it had been lost. And I realized that, of course, she was physically tethered here – in the scorch marks on a beam where she lit a candle too close to the ceiling, in the wood of the kitchen step, worn where she carried dishes from table to sink, in the brushstroke smears of paint on the bathroom walls, and, most vibrantly, in the plants still growing in the garden, six months after her death.

When she and my stepfather bought the house, it had fallen into major disrepair, and the garden was a daunting wilderness. For years previously the scrap-metal merchants who lived there used it as a junk yard, and it was a significant undertaking to turn it into a garden that would be productive as well as beautiful, and a fun place for their grandchildren to play. They made vegetable beds, a lawn and flower borders, and, to my mother's great excitement, they discovered an old well that still had water in it. As the years progressed, they were increasingly unable to do the heavy garden work, so they enlisted the help of two gardeners, called Mike and Mary, a few times per month. The ageing process is slowly tracked in the garden diary: Tom no longer digs the beds, and their enjoyment switches from working in the garden to looking at it.

Back in my kitchen, looking out on the daffodils and hellebores that are living echoes of my mother's garden, I turn the pages carefully. It is a straightforward account of jobs done and annual triumphs and disappointments. The seasonal notes are a mirror of my own garden journal. Her tasks are my tasks now. There is comfort in this practicality, labour and continuity.

*

It is difficult to imagine my garden in its full summer glory when I don't know how long we have left here. But I find succour in reading about other people's gardens and browsing nursery websites. I have always loved looking through catalogues – the gardener's overwintering hymn books that summon the spirits of the next season. While winter hurls its rain and storms at our gardens, we wait indoors, peeling back the pages full of promises. Although I've spent the past few months mired in grief and foreboding, it's not too late.

Out of habit, on each visit to my mother's garden, I have collected seeds and scattered them on her grave, or brought them home with me and slipped them into the seed box. Seeing how many little packets there are now, I am reminded that the weeks are passing, that I need to get back out into the garden. I have a strange sense of wanting to make it look beautiful for my mother. Some kind of tribute, I suppose – as if she were witnessing its outrageous, flamboyant aliveness from the nowhere place she now inhabits. As if she were somehow part of it – part of the tangible, thick, wet earth – and present in all the tiny buds that ripple in tender waves over branches and stems. I want to see her favourite flowers growing here in my chalky soil; and I want to see the autumn equinox here, to bookend the growing season and fill the garden with beauty that will return next year, and the years beyond that. The sun has tilted; now so must I.

*

I go to the town hall for the annual community seed swap, rifling happily through boxes of brown envelopes whose contents are marked in the handwriting of local gardeners. Dropping a small packet of my homegrown squash seeds into the box, I collect courgette seeds and cosmos in exchange, imagining the gardens and gardeners that grew them. I picture an elderly man bent over an allotment, breath rising in gentle clouds of steam, his gnarled hands scooping out seeds and airing them on a square of sacking. A woman is reaching up to remove a bunch of cosmos flowers hanging upside down in her potting shed, where they've been drying since the autumn. She taps the seeds carefully into an envelope, suddenly reminded of her children's fingernail clippings and bubble-filled baths.

Looking around at the gardeners in the town hall, I see a community tugged on a tide of forward momentum. The room is warm and thrumming with the energy of possibility. Back at home, I spread my little packets out on the kitchen table and begin to dream.

2

IMAGINING

AFTER A BRIEF WALK AROUND THE GARDEN TO OBSERVE SIGNS OF spring, I cut back the skeletal stalks of alliums and sedums that I've left over winter. My husband helps me dig out a stubbornly deep bramble root that I can't shift. He enjoys this kind of garden task – the brute-force jobs, or constructing chicken coops and log stores, but he leaves the rest to me, giving me free rein to imagine the garden however I like. He is a sunseeker, coming out here on hot weekend mornings to catch a moment's peace on the warm bench. I prefer the cold, fresh days of March when, as Dickens wrote, 'it is summer in the sun and winter in the shade'. I wash out a heap of plastic plant pots and leave them to dry in the weak spring sunshine. I fill a tub with compost and set the pots out in rows on the garden table.

In summer we eat out here, carrying plates and glasses from the cramped kitchen to the larger space outdoors. Usually, after a few short minutes eating together in the sunshine, some wasp appears and everyone bar myself and my third boy retreats grumpily back indoors. The two of us will stoically finish our meal, commenting on how food tastes better outside, flapping away the wasps and flies, and trying to ignore the sickly vape smoke that wafts over from the police station next door. In winter the table becomes a slime-creating laboratory, where my daughter and her friends assemble unseemly sludges that stick to every surface for weeks. I am still peeling gloopy strands of it from between the slats as I go about my task of readying. Now the table becomes a focal point for growing, a chequerboard of pots. I fill each one with crumbly, rich compost, creating a home for the seeds in my shoebox.

The progress I've made in the garden in the space of a few hours makes me realize just how little progress I've made elsewhere. In the wake of my mother's death, and with the threat of losing the house hanging over us, I am finding it hard to be creative. Words – my work – sink beneath an oily puddle of grief. Reading, usually a solace, seems impossible. I am unable to focus, repeatedly going over whole sentences without realizing it, running simultaneous conversations with myself as I skim across the page. My mind feels too full – too easily distracted – to be productive. Why is it that the need to be productive is so often our response to life? Sometimes we just need time to absorb what is happening around us. But I am not good at sitting still, particularly when loss folds its leaden arms around me. My instinct is to keep moving, to shake it off. Which is why the stasis of this winter has been so confounding. It is not my natural state. I am happier when I am busy, and the garden gives me a place to work and perform being 'productive'. Yet as I plan and potter, it also allows me space for reflection and day-dreaming. Perhaps this is why many writers and artists also love gardening – the powerful fusion of labour, craft and creativity.

*

Charleston Farmhouse, home of artists Vanessa Bell and Duncan Grant, where many of the Bloomsbury Group stayed, is near the village of Firle, set back from the busy Eastbourne road and skirted by a sweep of South Downs hills. It is only a few miles from my home and we were once offered a cottage nearby, as prospective tenants of the Firle estate. The house was charming but right on the main road, and I couldn't see how I could shepherd my four young children across the carriageway each morning, dodging lorries and speeding cars on our walk to school. I sometimes wonder how different our lives would have been if we had moved there – it is one of those haunting *never-weres*. In that dream life in the country cottage, my children grab their bags and lunchboxes, swinging their coats on and clattering through the garden gate. We cross the main road and then dodge the huge potholes in the lane up to Charleston. We chase dozy pheasants and make airplane runs into the oncoming wind. On past the dairy, with its whirring milking machine, and climbing the quiet lane to Firle. At night I would have seen the same outlines of curves and trees as the farm's inhabitants and their visitors. When the noise of the road subsided, I might have heard their ghosts wheeling and dancing in the moonlit garden. But instead we chose the town, this house. This story.

Despite turning down the cottage, whenever I visit Charleston I feel an instant sense of homecoming that I have never been able to fully understand. Perhaps it is to do with a yearning for the creative freedoms of the writers and artists of the Bloomsbury Group, unhindered by financial troubles or societal expectations – imagining myself making lunch for friends in the kitchen and writing quietly by the pond. Perhaps it is the cool, damp air that reminds me of my long-lost childhood home – also a farmhouse with low ceilings and thick stone walls.

Some years back, I ran writing workshops for schoolchildren in the old dairy at Charleston. They arrived on coaches, jostling and unleashed, horrified by the pervasive smell of cow dung. It was difficult to get these town kids to relate to the lives of the Bloomsburys, but I tried to encourage them to imagine life for the young people who lived there all those years ago, and to fill their senses with the place: the freedom to roam the fields, the cold water in the pond, the constant sound of the wind, the creatures passing through the landscape, and the people passing through the house. It is also difficult for some people to relate to the knotty love lives and complicated connections between the house's previous inhabitants. Living apart from her husband, Clive Bell, Vanessa Bell moved here with the man she was deeply in love with, Duncan Grant, and his lover David 'Bunny' Garnett, and the group was renowned for its unconventional approach to marriage and sex.

While I connected initially to the house's interior and its boisterous painted surfaces, as my interest in my own garden has grown, so my eyes have been increasingly drawn to the walled garden at the back of the house. On my visit today the weather is cloudy and a strong wind whips down from the hills, carrying the sea and salt over the land. Not wishing to follow a guided tour this time, I wander through the rooms: past the dining room, where the economist John Maynard Keynes, a friend and neighbour, would let off after-dinner fireworks; into the homely kitchen; then to Vanessa Bell's bedroom, with a bath in the corner and pictures of her beloved sons Julian and Quentin on the walls; through to Duncan Grant's beautiful studio, crammed with encrusted paint tubes and jars of brushes, poised as if the artist has momentarily left the room, and still smelling of turps and tobacco. And there, beyond the window, is the garden.

In the eyes of an artist like Bell or Grant, a garden becomes another world. There is an acute attentiveness to the light, to colour, sculpture and shape. Plants are selected not just for their performance in a border or pot, but for how they look when cut, how paint strokes might recreate their leaves and petals. This is how the garden at Charleston grew from a muddy potato patch with a few fruit trees into a celebrated artists' garden. In 1916, when Vanessa Bell moved here, it was a working farm, and the garden was rough and perfunctory. The new garden design at Charleston was rooted in the Arts and Crafts movement, and inspired by gardens in France and Italy, but Bell and Grant put a modernist, artistic spin on it. With the help of plans by the painter and critic Roger Fry, a friend of Vanessa Bell's, they laid out a new space, with a formal grid of paths and a lawn in the middle. Within this linear framework, the planting was loose, packing beds and borders with plants that provided colour and structure.

Over the years, the garden evolved and flourished under Bell's supervision. Like the Bloomsbury Group itself, it was a collaboration, with friends and family mucking in to help – Maynard Keynes is said to have weeded the paths and gravel with his penknife during his visits. What they created is, according to the Charleston guidebook, 'not a garden for gardeners. It's a garden for artists.' The diarist Frances Partridge, who was a regular visitor, wrote that 'Flowers seemed to grow larger at Charleston than any other garden', a reflection of the sense of abundance and profusion the garden generated. It was also a place of refuge, a place to live spontaneous, entangled lives away from society's judgemental gaze. Bell wanted to find a home and a landscape that could contain and shelter her friends. Charleston was ideal.

The garden at Charleston perfectly embodies both a defined,

functional space and an artistic vision. For Bell it was all about colour and form. She loved its riotous abundance, writing in a letter to Roger Fry that the garden was 'a dithering blaze of flowers and butterflies and apples'. In her son Quentin Bell's words, it was 'as though the joyous decoration of the interior had spilled through the doors'. As I stand on the threshold of the studio door, looking over the small piazza to the full glory of the garden, I imagine the picnics, children's treasure hunts, arguments, parties and creative endeavours that took place within its boundaries and that flowed over into other lives. The flowers look on knowingly, the secrets of the past carried on the wind that drives across the fields.

These secrets often had devastating consequences. Bell's daughter, Angelica Garnett, grew up believing that Clive Bell was her father and the discovery that she was, in fact, Duncan Grant's daughter caused great damage. After Bell told her the truth, Angelica took to wandering the garden, confused, devastated, alone. The garden was a sanctuary for this young girl caught in the eddies of her parents' choices, loves and shame. She had always loved spending her mornings out there. Inside the walled garden, she wrote, 'it was warm and sheltered, alive with the noises of insects and birds, which sounded different from those outside. In the early morning the sun shone through a milky mist, fragmented particles of blue and scarlet. As it vanished, the walls began to sing with warmth.' For her two brothers, the garden – but more often the surrounding spaces – offered freedom and scope for endless imaginative play. They rowed on the pond, moulded the rivulets from the spring-fed conduit into mud cities, played 'tennis' with quoits in the orchard, created 'ant palaces' and exploded gunpowder-filled canons.

*

The pond at Charleston is the first and last thing you see before going into the walled garden. After looking round the house, I sit on the bank watching throngs of great dark fish flicker beneath the surface. I pull out my notebook, close my eyes and tune my senses into the landscape. The quiet is immense. The peacefulness suddenly takes me back to a very different experience of visiting an artist's pond. Years ago, on a rather earnest Interrailing trip a friend and I took around Europe, we went to see Monet's garden at Giverny. In stark contrast with the tranquillity of Charleston, Giverny was teeming with tourists. As we slowly shuffled across the Japanese bridge, despite all the other people snapping photos of the famous water lilies, we experienced some of the same scents and sensations – light hitting water, wind rattling the willows – as Monet on his early morning stroll around the garden, stopping to watch clouds swim across the pond. I could literally walk in his footsteps, drinking in the colours and shapes he translated so beautifully into his paintings.

Monet and his family moved into the house in 1883 and he set about creating what he came to see as his 'most beautiful work of art': the garden. In his paintings, Monet plays with light to tell us the story of how colour changes the way the world looks. He asks us, 'What colour is life?' This love of tone and contrast extended to his vision for the garden and, like the Bloomsbury Group, he let his plants run fairly free. He was absorbed by the dance of light on leaves, the otherworldly reflections of the pond, and the constantly changing palette of his flowers. Visiting his garden, I felt myself transported back to the moment when the light hit the water at just the right angle, illuminating the wisteria and bouncing the sky back towards heaven, and an elderly painter with cataracts ripped off his bandages in a fury that the blues and violets he so adored have escaped him. The garden was his vision, in both senses.

There was a Monet print on the wall in my mother's bedroom. *A Corner of the Garden at Montgeron* (1877) depicts another pond, reflecting dappled sunlight filtering through the leaves of the trees behind it. In loose brushstrokes, Monet shows us dahlias, trees and a world concentrated in one small frame. All the beauty is there for us: eternal reflections and refractions; ripples. My mother's tatty-looking print had been badly framed, adding to the air of shabbiness and neglect that permeated the house. When we were sorting through her things, we had to pay attention to objects like this; things that had previously just existed as part of the whole. On the disused bed were piles of bedlinen that my mother had ironed and neatly folded all those months ago when she was well. I noticed a stippled Impressionist-print duvet cover and pillowcase that I had asked for as a birthday present as a young teenager, obsessed with Monet's work. The colours had lost their vibrancy over the years as various grandchildren were tucked in under the dabs and dots. I put it into my pile of things to bring home, and stood staring at a print in an empty bedroom full of memories that amassed like daubs of paint on a canvas.

Giverny is the perfect example of the imagination made physical, first embodied in the planting, and then transformed again through brushstrokes and globules of paint into another form. Just as water passes continuously through several states, never permanently in one, so an artist's garden and the art it inspires slips between materiality and imagination, provoking reactions in other people, firing something in their psyche that they might work into their own garden or creative life. As a child, I hated being dragged around stately homes or National Trust gardens, but now these visits feed my imagination, proffering ideas to take back home like warm pebbles slipped into a pocket on a beach.

For centuries, gardens and landscapes have been a vital source of creative inspiration. These real, lived places permeate art, music and literature, becoming characters themselves, haunting the pages or canvas, repeating like a refrain across bodies of work. I think of Georgia O'Keeffe painting the same stretch of road to her house, over and over again. Each time, she noticed something different in that pink-earthed landscape, found something different to say.

Frida Kahlo saw her garden at La Casa Azul, in Coyoacán, Mexico, as a work of art in its own right. She moved back to the house, her birthplace, following her mother's death, and settled there with her husband, the artist Diego Rivera. Kahlo blurred the boundaries between the interior and the surrounding landscape, painting the walls outside a cobalt blue that captured something of the Mexican sky, and bringing locally grown vegetables and fruit and flowers from her garden inside, until each space flowed back and forth into the other. Neither was 'finished'; rather, she saw them as works in progress. The garden space was laid out as a grid of courtyards, dotted with sculptures and objects she and Rivera collected on their travels or made themselves. She grew a range of plants, from tropical and native species, including orange trees, yuccas and cacti, to more traditional roses. These plants featured in her art, along with oleander, pomegranates, geranium, yam, guava, bougainvillea and plums. She also wore them, adorning her hair with floral garlands and crowns.

Her paintings often subvert traditional representations of fruits and flowers, creating complex and innovative responses to the natural world. In *Magnolias*, she captures the moments before magnolia buds unfold, and centres a short-lived pear cactus flower at the heart of the arrangement to show the fleetingness of life and the omnipresence of death. She also merges art and botany with politics to express her ideas about Mexico's national identity, often painting the dahlia, Mexico's national flower, or plants with connections to Aztec peoples. Trees and leaves create lush, textured settings for her portrait subjects and often take on a metaphorical significance. In her portrait of a horticulturalist, *Retrato de Luther Burbank* (1931), the figure has a man's torso but his bottom half becomes the roots of a tree, visible as if in a cut-away cross section, with a corpse decomposing below. She has chosen to portray a man who studies the natural world, who places an understanding of plants at the centre of his life, and she fuses his body with another living organism. She shows how nature inspires, preoccupies and nourishes us; and is then nourished by our bodies when we die.

This striking image of the circularity of life and death and life suggests a symbiotic and deeply enmeshed relationship between the land and those who tend it. You can see this most clearly in Kahlo's self-portraits, where the landscapes she cultivated and painted also become a form of autobiography. As a child, Kahlo suffered from polio, and as a teenager she was badly injured in a horrific collision between a tram and the bus she was riding on. The accident left her with terrible, lifelong pain. In her work, she combines elements from the natural world with the human body to represent this pain. Her painting *Tree of Hope* (1946) depicts two women, both Kahlo, in an arid, cracked landscape. The barren earth is gouged with fissures, and one of the women has cuts on her back – both these and the cracked earth are representations of the wounds she sustained during surgery on her spinal column. The visceral painting *Roots* (1943) shows Kahlo lying on the ground with vine roots emerging from her body and twining back into the ground. It has been interpreted as an expression of her love for her homeland, and her sorrow at not having had a child.

Kahlo's marriage to Rivera was complicated and often hurtful. In a vitriolic yet ambivalent letter to Rivera, just before surgery to amputate her leg in 1953, Kahlo wrote: 'I'm writing to you to let you know I'm releasing you, I'm amputating you . . . If there is anything I'd enjoy before I die, it'd be not having to see your fucking horrible bastard face wandering around my garden . . . Good bye from somebody who is crazy and vehemently in love with you.' It is interesting that it's her garden she wants to keep him out of. And it was to her garden she turned the following year, when she was dying, asking to be moved to a room where she could watch the summer blooms bursting against the blue walls and see the velvet magnolia buds she thought resembled hearts.

*

I always enjoy the moment of anticipation before stepping into the walled garden at Charleston. Each time I visit it is different, and on this spring day I am eager to tap into its energy. Turning my back on the pond, I walk back across the gravel.

Come with me.

Pass through the doorway in the wall, next to the house and near the pond. In the front border there are signs of the beginnings of the great hollyhocks that in early summer will nod as you walk past, their faces turned to the sun as they reach ever higher.   Gravel crunches beneath your feet. We will go straight ahead, along the side border crammed with tulips, wallflowers, honesty, irises, scilla, auricula and alliums, before we turn left at the back.   We pass the busts gazing outwards along the high wall, some of their faces disintegrating and smudged by time and weather.   Now we are standing in the piazza, a brick and mosaic area studded with broken household crockery, a less riotous spot, with pots for summer lilies and sweet peas, and an apple tree with a just-budding 'Bobbie James' rose twining up the trunk.   Through another gap in the wall, you can see the glasshouse and cold frames, where a busy volunteer works at a seed tray.   We can't go there.   In front: a grid of gravel paths and a small bed that will be bursting with herbs, vegetables and huge, alien-looking artichokes later in the year.   All this time the wind shakes the poplars and willows that keep watch around the garden's edge, enclosing the space with sibilant waves of sound.   Keep inside the walls; turn back to look up at the house, past the clotted box hedges, cut in undulating pillows alongside the lawn.   A straight path leads your eye back up to the house.   The wall behind you bounces the weak March sunshine onto your back.   To the right, another deep bed leads to the studio.   Imagine the hollyhocks, gladioli, dianthus, astrantia, helenium, delphinium, sea holly, sweet rocket and roses to come, ready to be cut, arranged and captured in thick smears of gouache and oils – a cartwheel of colour.   We walk up the path towards a vine-drenched pergola outside the studio.   Along the wall beside this path are espaliered pear and cherry trees.   We pause on the soft lawn that rolls gently – as if we were unfurling a grass blanket and flapping it onto the ground – to a rectangular pond with decorative tiling mirrored in the water and slick green lily pads.

Do you see it? Do you see why I love it?

*

The garden was not only a stage for the Bloomsbury Group at play (sometimes literally, as they dressed up and acted out spontaneous performances), it also provided food, which gave them a sense of plenty and independence, particularly during wartime and rationing. But it was also a place that witnessed darker moments. Within its walls, a bereft Bell wept for her son Julian, who was killed in the Spanish Civil War. We walk on the path Julian and his brother Quentin paced as they debated whether fighting in Spain was a good idea, a path where a different decision could have saved such suffering. But a lesson for me in the life of this garden is the sense of it, like the house, being an improvization, with no expectation that it was going to be for ever.

Despite negotiating a long lease, the Bells never actually owned Charleston. Like many wealthy middle-class people, they 'took' country homes as refuges for weekends and holidays, with none of the present stigma attached to renting property. The realization that they were always tenants prompts a shift in my thinking about our house. We have been putting off jobs like painting the dilapidated front door – what is the point if we are just going to be thrown out? – yet, as time goes on and we are still here, we are left with an increasingly scruffy house and a constant reminder that we may have to leave. Paint flakes from the porch, announcing to anyone who visits that this house is not properly cared for. I have become so used to its flaws that I do not really see them any more. Yet Vanessa Bell saw her rented home as something to embellish and celebrate, however temporarily. As I loop back round to the front of her house, where the pale-pink front door stands invitingly ajar, I start to see things differently. I find myself thinking about an apple-green front door and gate for our house. Living with uncertainty need not mean living dejectedly.

After Vanessa Bell's death in 1961, the garden was neglected, and by the time Duncan Grant died in 1978, it had become a mess of leggy perennials and grassed-over dullness. When the house was saved from a landlord's refurbishment by the Charleston Trust and turned into a place of homage and preservation of the Bloomsbury Group's heyday, the garden was also restored, and returned to a quintessential cottage garden. Photographs, diaries and Bloomsbury paintings offered the designer Sir Peter Shepheard sources for original plantings, while the head gardener, Mark Divall, emptied and dug over the beds three times by hand to remove the weeds, and spent years nurturing the garden back to beauty. It was archaeology of sorts, an uncovering of evidence that connected fragments of the garden's past to a vision for how it could look today.

For the present-day keepers of Charleston's house and garden, there are dilemmas about how much of the original planting should be reinstated, and which era or time should be recreated in a garden that spanned several decades and many stories. Today I find the head gardener dividing irises in one of the borders, and I seize the chance to ask such questions. We talk about how much each new gardener should be able to change the planting and increase diversity, how preserving and growing create an oppositional pull sometimes, a dance between the multiplicity of the past and the futures that await us. There is a tension, a need to find a sense of flow and progression, but also to take the visitor back to a particular moment in time. We talk about how to protect a garden without imprisoning it. Whose imagination do we permit to run free – the original creator's or the current inhabitants'? With a garden like this, there must be an evolution, a constant aliveness; the garden cannot die with its owners. It must embody the spirit of experiment, art, imagination – it's just a question of *whose* imagination will shape it.

Back home after my visit, I read a passage from a letter that Bell wrote to Angelica in 1940, which could be describing my own garden in this uncannily hot, dry spring: 'It has been such extraordinary weather. I hope you have had some of it. Only the garden is getting dried up. But the irises have rushed out and the tulips and wallflowers are ablaze.' A mother, sharing something of home, planting an image in her daughter's imagination. The echoes of familiar places creating a loop back in time. Doubtless the work of maintaining Charleston as a creative space for others constrained Bell's own art-making. Her role as both matriarch and muse must have come at a cost. The old cliché about the pram in the hall being the end of an artist's career provokes an uncomfortable feeling in me – I don't want to believe I can't be both a good writer and a good mother, but so far one always seems to be at the expense of the other.

In my garden, the early shade-loving hellebores and delicate snowdrops have made way for bolder bulbs, like a wave that builds as it rolls towards the shore. The relentless shifting seasons barrel on through the year, gobbling up the days and taking me further from my mother. Each month increases the gap between us. When she used to visit, she would ask for jobs to do, so she felt useful. Sometimes she would weed the garden, or mend things, happier when her hands were busy. Whenever I bend to snap off a dead flower head, I remember her fingers doing the same – pinching, twisting and collecting the faded bloom in one swift motion. As quickly as the flower is gone, so is she.

*

7 March 2005. Today I had my first weeding session.
Daffodils just out, hellebores lovely, peony just showing.

Last week amid great excitement the well was uncovered.
Deliberating over how to deal with it, but it's beautiful
and special whatever happens to it. Clear water and
amazing inner brick wall.

*

Over the following days, spurred by my visit to Charleston, I begin to plan my planting, allowing myself to dream a summer garden into being for the first time. I imagine sending a clematis coiling up the witchy old pear tree at the front of the house, to soften its ominous silhouette. In the back border, I will plant penstemons, which can compete with the fulsome salvias and self-seeding alliums, and *Alchemilla mollis* to tumble over the border edges, collecting raindrops like boiled sweets that will reflect the sky. Under the overgrown, oppressive privet hedge, I will weave more alchemilla and sweet woodruff amongst a slowly spreading *Geranium phaeum*. In front of the stump of an old elder by the back wall, I will plant a *Magnolia stellata* for its beautiful spring show. Nearer the house, in the side bed, two astrantias ('Roma' and 'Buckland') will echo the stars of the magnolia, while a few *Gaura lindheimeri* 'Whirling Butterflies' will add delicate, floaty tendrils. I will cut back the *Rosa* 'Madame Alfred Carrière' my mother gave my daughter on her second birthday, which has now bolted too high for us to fully appreciate, its curd-white flowers lost to the sky. In one bed I will replace the vegetables with a prairie area, lush with flickering grasses, verbena and a smattering of pink echinacea.

This is what I picture, in this strange springtime of waiting. I know from experience that these schemes will probably not turn out quite as I planned: common grass will likely overwhelm the clumps of pony tail grasses, leaving more a scruffy wilderness than a prairie; the shade beneath the hedge may prove too much for the alchemilla. But gardening sometimes rewards optimism and imagination. Poet Alice Oswald has it exactly right: 'If anyone knows how to bet on the future, it must be gardeners.'

*

12 March 2007. After very mild, wet winter, everything is very early. I mowed the very long grass last week. Tom has nearly finished digging the veg patch. Hellebores & snowdrops had extremely long stalks. Daffodils, hellebores, armandii, primulas beautifully spring-like. Pruned roses & clematises.

22 March 2009. Celebrated Mothering Sunday by mowing grass for first time. Bulbs, primroses, etc., all looking fantastic after sunny mild spell. Tom has planted potatoes and we've sown peas, beans, carrots, lettuce & onion sets.

*

For every artist's garden there are countless others, belonging to the 'unofficial' artist – the unrecognized, ordinary person who makes a living through hard toil and turns to their garden to express their vision and creativity. And many people conjure magic from the toughest situations. The writer Alice Walker describes how 'the artist that was and is my mother . . . adorned with flowers whatever shabby house we were forced to live in . . . Before she left home for the fields, she watered her flowers, chopped up the grass, and laid out new beds. When she returned from the fields she might divide clumps of bulbs, dig a cold pit, uproot and replant roses, or prune branches . . . until night came and it was too dark to see.'

Walker's mother created a veil of flowers that disguised the poverty she endured. With every move she started again, turning to the soil her forebears had been forced to work, to provide hope and show her resilience. Recent research by the Green Party shows that one in eight households in Britain doesn't have access to a private or shared garden, and of these people a larger percentage are from ethnic-minority backgrounds. Having a garden – whether as homeowner or tenant – is a privilege. Having the time to grow flowers rather than essential food for subsistence is a privilege. In speaking about my family's uncertain future, I am acutely aware of how fortunate we are to have a roof, food and a large garden to escape into. We live in a peaceful, prosperous county town, surrounded by fields, lark-filled hills, river and coastline. I count my blessings and am grateful for every year we've been here.

My children grew up scrambling in the trees nearby and making fairy houses in the roots, darting through wildflower meadows, playing spies in the woods, and learning to ride their bikes against the backdrop of the South Downs. After a morning of dawn breastfeeding, changing nappies, making dippy eggs, constructing Lego spaceships, reading a favourite book on a loop, and the constant sense that it *must* be later than it actually was, I would bundle the toddler into the pushchair and slide the baby into the sling, hoist one more small person onto the buggy board and ask the eldest to hold onto the side of the buggy. We spilled onto the street like a many-headed creature, making our way to the fields or a park. Being outdoors was essential for my sanity when my children were young. They would run in a pack until they had burned off their excess energy – 'Like puppies!' people would often say as we trooped home, children pouring off me like wax.

In those early years of our life here, raising the family felt like physical work, but as the demands of motherhood have shifted from the bodily to the emotional, I have turned more to the labour of gardening. As I fill pots with seeds and watch tentative green shoots emerge from their frozen slumber, I feel the garden working on my mood, my sense of belonging and my outlook on life. It is a reciprocal nurturing, an uncomplicated pleasure embodied in stiff muscles and muddy fingernails. I clear away more of last year's dead growth, making space for the light to get in and for new life to flourish. I try to find a sense of agency within our seemingly powerless situation. The garden keeps on turning, and I can make something beautiful in the time we have left.

*

1 March 2008. Mowed grass for first time. Have pruned, manured and mulched roses, clematis, caryopteris. Mild early spring – snowdrops nearly over, masses of primroses and clematis.

18 March 2011. Tom steadily dug over all the veg patches. I manured the raspberries & today we planted the first potatoes. Ceanothus (itself a replacement) nearly dead after v. cold winter. Spring flowers lovely – I should mow any day now. Second contorted willow to be cut down on Monday.

*

As we await the next twist in the probate wrangling, I retreat further into my imagination. Over the last few weeks, I have dreamed up a garden that is unmistakably mine – a place that will nourish my family and my soul, and, little by little, I sense it coming into being. Beneath the soil, out of sight, spring is beginning, working its way into roots and rhizomes, spreading warmth and energy along ancient tunnels and into the chalk and flint beneath us. I love the way a garden works invisibly, growing through the night, some changes so gradual we don't notice them happening. Instead we must tune into its song, listen to the music of this motion. As land artist Andy Goldsworthy said, 'The real work is the change.'

The unhappy peach tree (that has never produced a single peach) is in blossom. Every year I get excited by the promise that it won't return to its usual wizened state, and this spring the unfurling leaves look encouraging. Ground elder has sprung up everywhere, but I decide to mow the lawn so I can see the bare bones of the garden before I get properly started on weeding and planting. A sweet chlorophyll tang mingles with the smell of fresh washing, and I feel, for a moment, that all is right in the world. At this time of year, you can see the spaces between the plants and branches, spaces that capture light and movement and start to tell a story of the garden to come. Without all the foliage and fullness of the growing months, you can sense the life that is going on unseen below the soil.

I buy more seeds and bare-rooted plants with money I should have been saving for the move. In battered trays, I sow sweet peas, *Daucus carota*, *Ammi majus* and cosmos, imagining a floating foam of white rising above the borders, dotted with Monet's flecks of colour. The pond is covered with a glaze of algal gloop. Next to it I plant a geranium and some irises, with roots like fat, dead fingers. I tie a climbing 'Snow Goose' rose grown from a cutting against the metal trellis that stands in for windows in the shed. Now just brown woody stems and jagged thorns, I can picture the pale white puffs of flowers that will soon emerge from this skeleton. It is perfectly named, this rose, with its pillows of feathery blooms that cover the shed in their sweet-scented down. Next to this, hiding the rusty corrugated-iron cladding, is a honeysuckle, now tangled and collapsed. I secure it in place, trying not to snap the sinewy shoots. A few stray daffodils have appeared, as well as columbines and the saucery leaves of the hollyhocks my mother transplanted from her garden and brought here in pots filled with the claggy clay of her home soil, so different to the friable earth into which I firmed the plants. A jar of soil – collected from her grave when we planted it with bulbs and geraniums and a rose cutting from her garden – stands on my desk, a constant reminder of her return to the earth. The soil has become greyer, the clay drying out into a crumbly humus. Sometimes I unscrew the lid and inhale the dank smell, trying not to think about how her body is decaying deep in that clay and whether her dress has already dissolved.

The old apple tree is in blossom – not as abundantly as last year, but it has good years and bad years, and I just let it be. The plum tree I planted, which now yawns over the chickens' fence like a neighbour leaning in for a chat, is also covered in delicate buds. I plant *Achillea ptarmica* 'The Pearl' and *Achillea* 'Summerwine', purple hesperis, and ox-eye daisies. I pot up echinacea roots, which may in fact be dahlias – I can't remember and am hopeless at marking things, never having the right pen or a label handy; somehow I persuade myself that I will recall what each pot contains, but I usually have to wait until some identifiable leaves start to emerge.

The hours I spend out in the garden are a salve. When I can't cope with the uncertainty of the house sale, when I feel sorrow or prickling anger or just need a respite from the demands of family life, I pick up a trowel or my secateurs and I quietly, determinedly set to work. My fingers needle into the earth, plucking out stones and weeds. I pick a handful of chard in an exchange of energy that transmutes form into force, releasing captured light into the bodies of my children as we eat. My muscles stiffen and ache as my body answers the questions I am asking of this place: *What is the use?* I demand. *Wait and watch*, it replies. It is enough to press seeds into the soil, to water them and look for them.

3

UTOPIA

MY GARDEN IS A GENIE MY GARDEN IS THE PULSE OF A SLEEPING CAT
my garden is a gale's breath my garden is outside of time my garden
is dripping my garden is the heavy tread of a workman's boot my
garden is waiting but not waiting my garden is a plump belly my
garden is the soft crackle of a fire my garden is earthbound my
garden is the smell of summer and of everything.

What do I mean by my 'garden'? At first, it seems obvious: the
boundaried space behind our house. But I mean more than this. The
soil, flint, detritus, roots, trunks, seedlings, plants, trees, bushes,
pond, stone, bricks and creaturely inhabitants are all connected
by this place but also the spaces beyond. Some have intertwined
their limbs, growing up and around and into each other. Some
spread their roots underground, reaching out to other places
outside the walls and hedge, communicating with plants far away.
Others drift across the air, existing in light and wind until they
settle somewhere else. Scrawny foxes and neighbours' cats appear
then disappear, fleet-footed in their nocturnal visitations. A family
of hedgehogs nest invisibly in a wood pile, yet I occasionally catch
a glimpse of one, or have to rescue what appears to be a panting

ball of grass from beneath our dog's hesitant, curious paw; and then it is gone again. I found a dead hedgehog on the lawn once; no obvious signs of injury, just a crumpled, prickly lump halfway between the safety of the hedge and the open grass.

My garden is a defined place, but it is also more than that. It is a noun, a verb, and an ideal. It exists in its own time, where climate, season and sunlight create spirals of moments that occur, repeat and end. It is all the people who have inhabited or passed through it. It is a living organism, a community of beings, lifetimes of layers. It is star dust and bones and silica.

The notion of a garden is an ancient yet surprisingly ambiguous concept. The Persian word *pairidaeza* comes from *pairi*, 'around', and *daeza*, 'wall', describing an enclosed space and giving us our word 'paradise'. In Old English, *geard* means 'fence', indicating the garden was also a defined, separate area. And in the Hebrew tradition, a garden was a place of protection and shelter, a place of otherness that would keep you safe. The Christian Garden of Eden is a paradise, and this thinking of gardens as utopian, idealized spaces has had to coexist with a need for usefulness – as spaces for growing food and medicine or as places of healing. This tension was played out after the English Civil War of 1642–5, when flowers were considered frivolous vanities, and a law was proposed to enforce the planting of fruit trees in an attempt to create the 'Garden of God'.

Some of us continue to wrestle with this duality today, wanting our gardens to look appealing but also to serve a purpose. The Mojave words *Ich chuuvawve* (often translated as simply 'a garden') describe not just a place, but more the activities that occur within it – the practices of planting and tending. And there is emotional work being done here too. As I dig out ground elder, needling down for its roots, and tip bags of rotted manure over the vegetable bed, I am also aware that my mind is beginning to break free of the loop of worry and grief that has become habitual. Sometimes I am caught up in daydreams. Sometimes I am thinking of nothing but the work. Sometimes I am thinking of nothing at all. In these moments I begin to understand how the act of gardening can be concurrently a tangible and a spiritual activity.

*

9 March 2014. At last, a dry sunny spell. I mowed the grass, pruned the roses & manured them. Daffodils, primroses, hellebores all looking beautiful. Spring has sprung.

*

I order four dahlia tubers, lavender ('Munstead'), another *Astrantia* 'Roma', a polyanthus, two *Gypsophila* 'Rosenschleier', a helianthus, an eryngium (to replace the one I tried to grow last year) and two rudbeckias ('Goldsturm' and 'Cherry Brandy'). The bright flowers will go in the cutting patch, at the moment just a mass of feathered tansy seedlings, creeping bindweed and dandelions. I uproot a clump of tansy for a friend who loves yellow plants. This vigorous, highly scented plant has an interesting history. Its name is rooted in the Greek word *athanaton*, which means 'immortality', possibly due to its long flowering time, and it was traditionally grown for its medicinal properties. Herbalists prescribe tansy to treat intestinal worms or for compresses on inflamed joints. It was also rubbed on corpses and used to prepare embalming linens in order to stop worms working their way into the flesh, as well as being used to dye wool.

My patch of tansy occupies a relatively unloved area of the garden, bringing a useful buttery brightness amongst the old plant pots and paint-peeled shelving behind the shed. I do have to keep it in check, so giving some to my friend serves a mutual purpose. We often exchange seeds or cuttings, or help each other out with weeding when things get unmanageable; and, as the less-experienced gardener, I learn much from her. She is better at research, less seat-of-her-pants, than me, and as a result her garden is beautiful and orderly without being overdone. When we visit each other, we usually begin in the gardens, looking at what is happening and swapping success stories and tales of disasters. Just after my mother died, she came to help in my garden, tackling overgrown beds while I wept, overwhelmed by all there was to do. One of my favourite photos is of the two of us standing on her lawn, both heavily pregnant, bellies touching, surrounded by her glorious daffodils. Our babies were born within days of each other, and daffodils always remind me of that anticipatory spring. In winter, indoors, we knit together – hats for the babies, a shawl for my mother; and the rest of the year we garden, swim and walk together. Ours is a friendship twined together with tansy, tomatoes, sweet peas and salty swimsuits dripping on the line.

When the lavender arrives, I plan to plant it behind the paved area, under the back wall. I start to imagine it with some purple sage and a clematis clambering skywards, but my budget and a realistic look at what I can achieve curtails these more ambitious ideas. Instead, I set to work with what I have. The raspberries have grown into a thick and tangled sprawl, so I uproot around one third, enlisting my husband's help with the heavy digging. Another friend comes round to collect my rejects, keen to plant them in her allotment. She has the same landlord as us, and is in a similarly precarious position, so we exchange the latest news over a cup of tea in the garden. She leaves with pots full of spiky raspberry canes, as determined to plant hope as I am. I cover the newly exposed earth with cardboard and a layer of horse manure, hoping this will rejuvenate the soil and quash the weeds that have run free beneath the hairy raspberry stems. This will be a new vegetable bed, if we are still here to plant it.

A gap in the side border seems perfect for the packet of nigella seeds I discover in my old shoebox seed storage, so I scatter it straight onto the ground and hope for the best. In pots and trays I sow peas, broccoli, *Lagurus ovatus* 'Bunny's Tails', and hollyhocks. The pear and peach trees need staking; the pear is growing at a strange angle, like a broken bone. My husband helps, driving a thick piece of wood into the ground next to the tree, and clipping it to the narrow trunk. I worry that we have damaged the tree's roots and should have shored it up as soon as I planted it, but I didn't know any better then. The tree is straighter, more 'proper'. This simple adjustment suddenly makes the whole garden seem neater.

More online shopping: this time seed potatoes ('King Edward', introduced in 1902, so fitting for our Edwardian house – plus they are delicious), shallots ('Gourmet') and French beans to go in the new bed I have cleared of raspberries. Some self-seeded chard is about the only thing growing in the existing vegetable bed, apart from a couple of leeks that I forgot to dig up last year, and a few stray onions. It is a dispiriting sight, a reminder of my failure once again to grow anything like enough food to be self-sufficient, but it also makes me determined to try again, to be better this time.

A peacock butterfly lands gently on a chard leaf before wheeling away. Behind the chard sits the fig tree, with its narrow wrists and curled fingers reaching upwards, claw-like. I cut it back hard last year, worried it would grow too large and damage the wall next to it. But it is back, as strong and vigorous as ever, replacing its lost limbs in its inexhaustible growth. To tend this garden is to engage in a constant struggle not to be overwhelmed.

*

29 March 2014. Just before going to Crete we put in a row of potatoes. Battling with celandines but everything looking lovely, specially primroses. Picked lots of flowers for Mothering Sunday posies as we'll be away till mid-April.

4

BELONGING

In the course of my life so far, I have lived in twenty different places (the average is around seven in a lifetime). Between each place, I carted the same boxes of painted milk-bottle vases, wooden stepladder shelves and unread books, surrounding myself with familiar objects. I shed friends, lovers and broken relationships, the flotsam of each failed new start ending up in skips, charity shops and rubbish bags. I packed up and moved on, wanting to put down roots but always searching for something else, trying to feel at home.

In Australia, living with my now-husband on what was supposed to be a four-year adventure overseas, I didn't miss one particular thing; rather a collage of 'home' began to form in my mind. It was a jumble of sensory experiences – smells, feelings, tastes – that in word form looks like this:

Moss
Cold churches
Grey sky
Frost-stiffened grass crunching underfoot

Self-deprecating greetings
Marmite
A hug from someone who has watched me grow
Miss Marple on TV
Drowsy, dreamy English gardens in summertime

The vast, bleached, bold place I found myself in was never going to fit with my sense of what constituted home. I became pregnant, and the longing for home intensified. I felt unable to be a mother so far from my own. Returning to England with a six-week-old baby and nowhere to live was not the smartest of moves, but I was too scared of raising a child away from everything I knew. The problem, I realized, was deciding where to land next. Since spending much of my childhood in Bristol and Wiltshire, my heart has always pulled me westwards. I love the honeyed stone and gentle hills, the rolling burr of the accent. But we ended up in Sussex, and, after fifteen years at the foot of the South Downs, I find myself more deeply rooted in this landscape than I had thought possible. Driving home from a sea swim, salt pricking my skin, I gulp in the late-March countryside, awash with blackthorn blossom bedazzling the hedgerows. Such pure white before the fiery jewels of summer take over. This place, now, is what happiness tastes like. But do I belong?

Despite living here for one third of my life and birthing two (and raising four) children here, there are people in this town who would challenge the idea that I belong. For them, if you were not born here, you can't claim to be 'from' here. But surely belonging is more than just a chance of birth? What of the opposite form of 'othering' experienced by many people of colour who *were* born in a place, but are told to 'go back where you belong'? The concept of belonging is weaponized by racists in acts of violence and microaggressions and we can find echoes of an unpleasant nativism in the horticultural world. We talk of 'invasive' and 'alien' species, whilst also selecting some of these non-native plants to represent Britishness. Take Kent, for example, named the 'Garden of England' for its historic orchards. Yet the apple is not a native British fruit, hailing in fact from Kazakhstan.

Whilst there are undoubtedly problems with introducing vigorous species that can affect local biodiversity, some so-called invasive species actually have very little impact on the habitat in which they grow. And conversely, by over-domesticating plant species, we can actually damage their resilience and local diversity. Lilac is thought to have come to Britain from Ottoman gardens, and was taken to America by colonial settlers, where it became a popular garden plant that represented respectability and well-cared-for neighbourhoods. In her poem 'Lilacs', Amy Lowell describes this assimilation into New England's landscape; she tells the lilac, 'You have forgotten your Eastern origin'. Gardens teach us the folly of investing in origins; if we track back far enough, we tend to find an incomer that has simply been embraced for its blooms or scent and made itself at home.

And the fact is that, despite being settled here, a feeling of unbelonging runs quietly in my blood, surging at times like this when a move seems imminent. I never know how to answer the question *Where are you from?* It is as impossible to answer as *Who are you?* Identity is so bound up with place that an uprooting loosens this sense of self. It is left to our imaginations to create an idea of home, somewhere secure and safe; somewhere to belong.

A limpet's shell moulds itself to the contours of a particular rock, and it returns to that exact indentation where it fits perfectly.

'Placeness' is malleable, like the limpet's shell. It is particular. I need somewhere to simply 'be', to hold less tightly to my imagined ideas about 'home' and instead think in a more supple, generous, expansive way about how to belong in this fragile world. A garden can offer this kind of space, a landscape to alter and nourish until it is unclear where it starts and we end; limpet-like, we fit together. It is, to paraphrase Virginia Woolf, rooted but flowing. It knows the transformational nature of uncertainty. But am I ready to accept this? I am still too angry, too panicked. The life choices we have made brought us here, but much about my family's situation is beyond my control, and the systems around us have created a precarious housing market and tenancy agreements that favour the landlord. The word 'precarious' is connected to the Latin *precarius*, meaning 'obtained by prayer'. I try to find a prayer in our unsettledness. As the days get longer, my sense of urgency grows – I need to strengthen my roots before it is too late. Woodland flowers like wood anemone, muscari and common dog violets know that they must flower early, before the canopy closes in above them.

*

10 March 2015. First sunny spring-like day I've been free to start gardening. I pruned the roses & clematis while Tom pottered & sat in the sun. Spring flowers & bulbs looking gorgeous. Must mow grass again soon.

*

The morning light is milky-soft, sweeping away the fleeting dew. I stand by the back door drenched in the sounds of spring. The garden seems to contain all the seasons at once – green shoots hint at summer beauty, fruit-tree buds hold autumn's abundance, and the skeletal stems of last year's growth remind us that winter, though just ending, will come again. Inside the trees the sap is rising, flooding the awakening trunk, branches and uncurling leaves with water and sugar. Beneath my feet their roots are drawing up deep, hidden water and talking across their subterranean world.

Mother's Day comes. The first without her. I channel my rage and grief over her absence by savagely cutting back the brambles that enmesh the rambling rose along the back wall. In contrast to all the planting I have been doing recently, right now I want to destroy things. I want to feel the sting of the barbs in my flesh; to feel *something*. My hair gets knotted in the ranging rose stems, making me feel the bush is consuming me, ready to grow over and around my body, like a spider spinning a shroud for its prey, until I have disappeared and all that remains is my sadness dripping onto the ground below. There is a myth that tells of how the blood of a dying dragon seeped into the ground and rose up as sap in *Draco dracaena*, the dragon tree. Thorns snag my arms and hands, tearing my skin to reveal the red sap within. And then, suddenly, it is over. I am spent. I retreat indoors, rinsing my cuts in the sink and nursing my bruises. I do not know how to reconcile being permanently disconnected from my original home – from her.

As the spring clock-change approaches, it brings the promise of longer days outside. March marks the passing from darkness into light, and I notice how this shifting of daylight is mirrored in the movement of shadows and sunshine in the garden. When we arrived here, I should have spent a whole year watching the way the light moves across the place, planning my planting around this. But instead, with little experience, a knack for impatience, and a large area to corral into some kind of order, I began with small sections, planting sunflowers that we could see from the house, and carrots in what seemed to be a vegetable bed. I slowly built the garden around what I thought would look good. It was intuitive, mostly, but I could also work from the previous tenants' loose structure of beds along the sunny side. I am still learning the importance of setting plants in the right place, and not presuming they will be happy just because I have decided I want them in a certain position. Through many failures and disappointments, I have discovered the need to work with what I've got, rather than the idealized version in my head.

What I've got is an imbalance. The left-hand side of the garden is shady, dominated by the overgrown hedge and a large elder tree, behind which loom blank windows and blocky concrete lines. As you move away from the hedge, you find increasing sunlight tracking across the lawn and beds, culminating in the brick wall that captures warmth and throws it back onto the border beds. There is a flow from dark to light, but I need to somehow soften or blur this division. Light and dark are almost equal in this space – as in the equinox – but it feels too binary. I decide to leave a swathe of grass near the hedge unmown, with curved edges to moderate the lines and create a sense of movement between the two areas.

The days continue to swell with the growing light. I find myself tuning in to the frequency of yellow. On walks I see primroses beaming from verges, and the anthers of wood anemones like yellow pins pressed into a white pincushion. In the garden, fat white-tailed bumblebees weave with invisible threads from blossom to blossom, unzipping the air in slow burrs of mustard and black. The daffodils are still yellow, but beginning to brown at the edges, leaves thinning to paper and heads bowing towards the ground. I remember my mother mowing down the daffodils once they've gone over, but I can't bring myself to inflict this drastic violence on them. Instead, I tie up their leaves and let them slowly drop back into the earth.

I want to find out about a type of daffodil that bears the same name as our house, and I reach for my mother's huge RHS *A-Z Encyclopedia of Garden Plants* for inspiration. There are over seven pages of daffodils, showing fifty species, from starry-faced narcissi to classic trumpets. A square piece of cloth falls out of the book. She must have been using it as a bookmark in the middle of some sewing project. A few pages on, I find a cutting from the *Observer*, dated 1998, explaining how to choose plants for an east-facing wall. This was not long after they moved into their last house, and she must have been planning the garden. I remove the yellowing paper and go back to the daffodils. There is something in the origin of the name 'narcissus' (from the Greek word for 'numbness', due to the bulbs' toxicity) that speaks to my grief-flattened state of mind. Buying more of these plants feels like a way to cement my hope that we will be here next year to watch their golden faces push up from the soil.

A clump of sunny celandine has appeared by the pond, the glossy petals looking as if they would squeak if stroked. My son dug out and made this pond by himself last year, in a sudden burst of enthusiasm and desire to improve the garden. Next to it are two miniature Easter Island statues, to mark the faraway place that has my husband's heart. The blackbirds in the garden are busy building nests, the males' yellow beaks trilling their arrival. My daughter and I are trying to learn the songs of different birds, and each evening we replay a selection and try to guess what they are. We can recognize the blackbird, singing its welcome for spring with high, clear notes mixed with throatier chirrups. 'The birds still remember what we have forgotten, that this world is meant to be celebrated,' writes the conservationist Terry Tempest Williams – a prompt to listen for the joy in these songs rather than simply tick them off our list.

I try to listen to this garden, too, to the stories of this plot of land buried in the understory or within the plants reaching skywards. Instead of inoculating myself against the threatened eviction by focusing on all the negative things about the house, I must instead create a dialogue with this place. I think back to our joy at moving here – the understairs cupboard the children thought was like Harry Potter's bedroom, the high ceilings and breathing space, the garden. We filled the space as the children grew, our clutter and clamour fitting like limpet shells to our home place. What of us will remain here when we leave? What of this place will we take with us? Some Australian Albert's lyrebirds are said to have produced a rhythmic imitation of an Aboriginal corroboree, echoes of the eighteenth-century tongue reverberating into the twentieth century, after the indigenous community had been destroyed by white settlers. The bird's song contained an archive of lost human sounds and speech. For as long as I am able, I want to be in conversation with the garden, to put my ear to the ground, tune in to its voices and whisper back what I discover.

APRIL

5

UNFURLING

Let me leave the clatter of my life indoors. I want to show you the way a leaf gives up its scent when rubbed, or the whistle of a pigeon's wings as it passes. I want to bring you beside me as I work: sowing seeds at the garden table – more sweet peas (the first batch didn't germinate), squash, kale, purple sprouting broccoli, leeks; observing the weather (a drought, the sky squeezed dry); biding my time before moving tender seedlings outside (trays balancing on the bathroom windowsill and potatoes chitting behind the TV); kneeling amongst the ground elder, filling buckets with uninvited greenery (hands red and sore, legs creaky).

There is still no rain. After a deluge that began in October and ended in February, we have had weeks of whitewashed sunshine. The winter grass was a squelching morass, but is now yellowing and crisp, as if its life force is slowly evaporating into the air. It feels strange to be watering the garden in April. This was the month my daughter was born, my only spring baby. Over the years, it has rained, snowed and been baking hot all beneath April's fickle skies. We have held birthday parties in the garden, hiding treasure and making pretend horses out of broomsticks and socks for small girls to gallop around on; we have arranged birthday Easter-egg hunts up on the Downs when it was so hot a gaggle of children sheltered in the shade of a spindly tree. April can catch out the novice gardener like me, who gets excited by the first whiff of warmth and moves pelargoniums back outside, only to see them wilt and wither under a late frost.

Another strangely, worryingly dry day of hard sunshine and bleached skies. I step outside after supper, seeking rest after rising early to try to work before the house awakes. The traffic washes past, the sounds squeezing through the gap between the garden wall and the police station. I count eight surviving tulips in the pot by the back door (one fell victim to a football, the others were dug up by the dog). They are always something of a surprise, as I can never remember which variety or colour I planted back in the middle of winter. I love watching their coy heads emerge on matchstick stems, and trying to work out what they will become.

It is odd to think how carelessly I plant tulips now, when back in the seventeenth century they were so highly valued that a single bulb could be exchanged for gold or houses. Dutch growers were at the centre of the tulip trade, which stretched across Europe and as far as Turkey, making enormous fortunes from these flamboyant plants. Tulips take seven years to develop from seed to flower. Their tricksiness, instability and unpredictability heightened the desire amongst collectors for years. But then, suddenly, 'tulipomania' dissipated like the dew, leaving tulips to become simply, as Michael Pollan writes, 'mass-produced eye candy'. My mother never liked tulips – she said they were 'too corporate' and made her think of roundabouts. They are, I think, perfect signifiers of spring, a taste of the fire and exuberance of the new season after the greyness of winter. I like layering them in pots with irises and narcissi in

November, each bulb a nugget of hope for the return of the light and longer days.

The two tallest tulips by my back door have begun to unfold, revealing a peach-striped-with-green outer layer and pinky-yellow inner folds. Delicate filaments of colour, watercolours smudged with rain; a pursed mouth; their leaves rising modestly, pinched in halfway up the stem, creating a curved funnel to send water down to their roots. Each one is different. I haven't noticed this before, just accepted their bold sweeps of colour as uniform. But when you *really* look, you see a refinement that is lost in the blocks of bright colour in mass-planted, roadside flower beds.

Tulips are at their most beautiful at exactly this moment – on the cusp of opening, offering a glimpse of their tender insides. Above me are whips of sunset clouds, the same colour as the tulips – shades of orange-pink both above and below me, as if the world itself were simply a glass surface. Tonight is the Pink Moon of spring, also poetically called the Hare Moon, Sprouting Grass Moon, Egg Moon, or Super Moon. In this soft, luminous, burgeoning evening, it feels like life is a hot spark falling softly onto dry tinder.

*

19 April 2004. Spring here with warm, sunny, showery weather. Most veg sown, lettuce & onions doing well. Still eating spinach & chard though next lot sown. Lilac & pear tree out, damson & cherry coming. Tulips everywhere, daffodils nearly over. Pulling up weeds by the trugful along the long border. Grass green but mossy – needs scarifying & treating.

*

Indoors my cosmos seedlings need potting on; they have grown too leggy and frail, sulking and drooping over the edges of their small containers. It is time to give them more space and harden them off outside. Holding them carefully by their cotyledons (their first leaves rather than their true leaves), I push beneath their roots with a pencil and gently ease them out of the soil. It seems impossible to imagine these pale stems supporting the flurry of blooms that I hope will come in the summer, but this is part of the dance of gardening – these leaps of imagination, projecting ahead as well as focusing on the here and now. Or perhaps I should say, travelling around the curve of a circle, rather than 'projecting ahead'; it is the same circle we have looped before each year and will loop again. I am careful not to tear the seedlings from the soil, to avoid root shock. Instead, I pry them slowly from their warm earth homes and firm them into bigger pots.

One morning, I receive an email containing the news that the house has been taken off the market. It is a huge relief. But the executors are still fighting over it, and our fate will be decided by who wins. This latest development feels like a temporary truce. Frustrated by just waiting around for events to unfold, we look at another house, in the countryside, with a big garden filled with potential. It is lovely, but my heart is not in it. In fact, it feels as though I have nothing more of my heart to give: it has already been divided into parts that I have left elsewhere. One part is here, in this crumbling, homely place; another thuds mutely at my mother's graveside; one part belongs to my children, pulsing alongside their own; and another lies on the riverbank next to a house that I loved and lost, like a fish flopping on the shore.

6

CHILDHOOD

Cooking, cleaning, school runs, shopping, folding washing, family admin, work. The daily rituals and labour of motherhood. This month there is planning for Easter, birthday-party invitations, visits to relatives to add to my list. I have to snatch moments to attend to the garden, sometimes accompanied by my daughter and always by the dog. I enjoy working silently out here, but I also love the times when someone is with me. I have tried to encourage the children to help, offering them space to grow their own vegetables, but they prefer to play in the garden, rather than work in it. Usually, I can entice my daughter to join in a specific task if I make it sound exciting enough. Today, we're picking lilac and rhubarb to make a syrup (to add to gin for the adults, and to pour over pancakes for the kids). Dusky pale buds and delicate open flowers release a warm, powdery scent like the inside of an older woman's handbag; or a paper roll of sweets; or a foreign summer; or a mouthful of syrupy medicine. She selects the best blooms and I snip them into a bowl. We watch a fly crawl away from a stem, and she lifts the lilac to her nose, saying it smells of ballet. We smell some more plants: the nepeta, woodruff, columbines, and I remember the writer Tove Ditlevsen's words, 'Each childhood has its own smell.' I wonder what my daughter's childhood will smell of, will taste like, when she looks back on it.

My children are connected to this garden, despite spending less and less time in it as they grow. It is where they learned about their relationship with the natural world, and where they implanted memories of their physical interactions with a place: crawling through the hedge behind the trampoline into a secret den, climbing the apple tree to help with an autumn harvest, skimming leaves off the pond's surface with a fishing net, digging down into the earth with a shiny new beach spade. It has been a place of imagination, away from adult supervision or structured play, whilst my husband and I were at work or inside doing chores; it is still a place of privacy, with the potential for adventure. When they were younger, at some point in the day the energy in the house would erupt into chaos and I would turn them all outside, playing highly competitive games of swingball or badminton with them.

Our happiest family times in the garden are when we have friends over for barbeques, all the children piling onto the trampoline in a health-and-safety nightmare tangle of limbs, footballs and weapons. The paint pots and strips of butcher's paper I have stuck to the concrete under the kitchen window for art activities are mostly ignored, and instead they make a beeline for dangerous games. The grown-ups sitting at the table, the children eating on picnic blankets in little huddles, the dog banished inside so she doesn't steal anyone's sausage – the garden is filled with life and laughter. I hope they remember it like this, as the backdrop to our family life. I hope I've planted a small seed of love for the natural world, so that they care for it and feel part of it as they grow. Revising for exams on the grass, practising new-found bike-riding skills, jumping into the paddling pool, waging war on each other with plastic bullets: the garden has been a formative space in their childhoods. The *feeling* of it – perhaps its boisterous untidiness and abundance – will reverberate in some way through all the gardens they inhabit and create.

My daughter has had enough of picking lilac and heads back inside to finish her game of 'schools'. I am alone again. The seed-swap cosmos seedlings are ready to plant out, though they seem very short. I also transplant *Ammi majus*, zinnias, one scabious and two nicotiana, teasing them gently from their first home and pressing their pale roots into richer soil. They take their place amongst the chorus of other plants in the borders, awaiting their turn to perform. This stage in the growing process is always nerve-wracking. I worry about whether they will survive the snails and slugs; wonder if they have enough space, light, nourishment, water; fret over whether I've moved them too early. It reminds me of my children's first days at school, leaving them in the care of others, their faces pressed to the window so they can wave at me as I go. Have they got the right PE stuff? Did I remember their packed lunches? Will they stop crying when I am out of sight? Will someone rub their knees if they fall? Are they ready for all this?

*

In creating a garden, part of us is trying to recapture something of the dreamlike quality of being a child outdoors. The grooves and neural pathways are worn deep. In Shetlandic, the word *bonhoga* means a spiritual or childhood place, and it consists of memories and images, or even something intangible, like a quality of light or a sensation, as well as the physical space. There is a similar Welsh word, *cynefin*, which encapsulates the idea of somewhere where youth and place collide; a place to which we can never return but that exists as a memory imprint of a heartland. The Welsh notion of *hiraeth* refers not to a specific place but to a longing for that place where we felt we most belonged. A safe space. Home. It is this place that creates us, and this place that haunts us. *Hiraeth*, I think, is what I experience when I think of our lost house, and what I want my children to be spared if we are evicted from here. But part of the lesson I am learning is that I can't shield them from all pain or fix every broken thing.

Home is not always a safe space. For some, the idea of feeling nostalgic for a childhood place is an alien concept, dripping with sentimentality, that ignores the challenges many people spend their lives trying to leave behind. I was fortunate. My ghosts are mild and pliable; they allow me to sleep soundly, to love freely and to look backwards as I walk. But I respect those who have no wish to tread old paths and I am sorry for their pain. I cannot speak their stories, but I want to acknowledge them here, on this page. I want to acknowledge the dangers of nostalgia as a trick of the mind. And yet I want to allow the girl who dreamed of a return – who pined for a long-lost house, and who is now trying to capture something of that place and magic, something of the essence of it, in her children's home – to glance back.

On my flights back to the past, often triggered by something as simple as the vivid juice of a scrunched up dock leaf, or the smell of straw as I clean out the chickens, I remember the intimacy of childhood gardens and landscapes. Being down at ground level, feeling the scratch of stubble on my legs, holding a worm up close, twisting grasses around my fingers. And it is these memories that are sifted to the surface as I work in my garden. From the age of two to eight I lived in Bristol, in a long, curving terrace high on a hill. Every house backed onto one huge communal garden that ran the length of the whole street, and we children poured out of our houses, along the stone terrace and down the steps into the wilds. There were lawns, flower beds and a steep muddy slope, nicknamed the Death Slide. When I wasn't dangling my brother over the edge of this perilous clay precipice, I was trotting around the lawns on a pretend horse, scrubbing for woodlice (or 'freddies', as we called them) in the roots of a giant copper beech tree, or racing my bike along the terrace. This place represented freedom, exploration and the space to play however we liked.

Our next house was a Wiltshire farmhouse, the place I lost that created a blueprint for my future ideas about home. You'll find the house crouched in a valley on the edge of a small village. Turn left at the scrubby triangle of grass where we caught the school bus, then continue down a narrow lane. Follow the lane round a slight bend, a lazy river to your right, a steep bank of trees to your left. When you reach the stone bridge you'll see it, an L-shaped honey-stoned house with a barn along its flank. If you stand there on the bridge, you might hear the water rushing over the weir, the crack of crows high in the trees, and the whisper of the willows along the riverbank. What else might you hear if you really listen – 'Listen with the ear of your heart,' as St Benedict urged? Perhaps the shouts of a mother calling her children in for tea; the clop of a horse's hooves as its owner leads its home from the paddock; or the voices of men coming in from the fields, hot and dusty from the harvest. There are stories within that landscape, older than mine.

As was fashionable in the 1970s, my parents had left the city in search of the rural 'good life'. They found the old farmhouse, in a state of disrepair, but with land and outbuildings and in a beautiful position. Before the place was ready for us to move in, my father and I drove out there at weekends, from our house in Bristol. My main job was picking out the sedimented chicken droppings from between the cobbles in what I hoped would become a stable for a much longed-for pony, whilst he hammered and painted and occasionally electrocuted himself. We (my parents, myself and two younger siblings) moved in with much excitement, and for three years we lived what I thought was a perfectly happy life.

The garden blended into the surrounding fields and riverbanks. There was a fence at the edge of our land, but it was not a real boundary for us. Our horizons expanded beyond our home and into a small valley. The spooky wood, with hundreds of broken bottles and hidden tunnels to the nearby town; the gravel pit layby, strewn with old porn magazines and condoms, which became the scene for spy adventures; and the Roman road, with pothole puddles to cycle through. I was allowed the pony I had wished for, and together we explored far and wide, mapping our routes by fallen trees, hills and streams. I moved through, over, within these spaces as comfortably as the sparrows inhabit my hedge.

What do I remember about this place? Perpetual summers, punctuated by one very snowy winter when there was a power cut and the villagers brought their dinners over on sledges to cook them on our coal-fired stove. My bedroom, with its purple-and-beige patterned wallpaper and Bucks Fizz posters. The heat-and-milk smell of the cows accompanying us up the lane as we walked to catch the school bus, heaving their swollen udders up the hill to the dairy. The sharp cold of the river water as I dangled my feet off the bridge, and the illicit slime of weeds as I stepped along a rusty pole buried beneath the water.

These fragments of memory don't fully encapsulate how entirely at home I felt there. I loved the stone of the village houses and walls; I swam in the river; I dug for buried treasure and climbed for the views stretching between the earth, water and sky, all the while feeling a complete sense of belonging. Yet when I look more closely at that feeling, I have a sense that something is missing. What I remember as an idyllic childhood must, in reality, have been difficult. My parents were separating, and my father had grave money troubles. My mother never really fitted in with the conservative villagers, her only friends being an artist who lived at the top of the lane and a few fellow churchy folk. She was envious of my best friend's mother, who, I made clear, was better at cooking and more fun to be around. I spent as much time as possible away from the house, perhaps picking up on the tensions between my parents. And maybe this is what gave me that connection to the landscape – a feeling that inside the walls of 'home' things were uncomfortable, but outside I was free.

My parents split up, my father went bust, and we had to move out. When we left that house, my family was splintered, my mother struggling to cope, and an unfamiliar, quiet rage began to boil inside me. Our new home was in the middle of town, on a busy road, and held none of the romance of the old farmhouse. I morphed into a clichéd teenager, lolling in my attic bedroom and smoking out of the window as I gazed intensely at my James Dean poster. I expressed my disconnection and dislocation through unconscious rituals and patterns – I tapped the sides of my head on my shoulders, making sure not to do more on one side than the other, and I placed my fingers down on surfaces in a particular order, starting again if I touched one finger down more frequently. If I did not do these rituals properly, something bad would happen. I twitched and tapped my way into adolescence, a restless pupa crunching my way awkwardly out of my cocoon. How could I belong anywhere?

In our new house, I rarely went into the garden, but over my exam summer I sunbathed and revised on the back wall, baking my skin into the stone. My mother was now a working single parent with little time for gardening, so this was a rather wild, unruly place. The garden sloped away to the left, down towards the river, and was bordered on three sides by low walls. There were two terraced areas, one with a pond and one that my mother wanted to plant as a vegetable garden. I helped her dig it over, but I don't remember her harvesting much produce, so I think she didn't manage to get it going. My great-aunt used to prune things drastically when she came to stay, leaving a stark, barren expanse in her wake. A tree grew through the wall into the lean-to conservatory at the back of the house, and the grass was always uncut.

At this point in my life, the natural world offered freedom in a different way – space for furtive fumbles with my boyfriend, the sensations of the itchy long grass making more of an impression than his insistent fingers. Or practising inhaling cigarette smoke up through my nostrils like the French exchange students, under a tree in a field. It is all there, layered beneath the sediments of young adulthood, ready to excavate if needed. When I was fifteen, my mother remarried, and a year later we left the area completely, adding to my sense of homesickness.

When I revisit the farmhouse in my head, I revisit the emotions embedded there all those years ago that wait, like a seam of natural gas, to be released. I see now that the sense of dislocation that manifested in my physical tics echoes still within my bones. For years I dreamed of the house and plotted ways to get it back. As a young adult, living in a different part of the country, I would persuade friends to drive for hours in the middle of the night so I could sit by the river near the house, dunking my toes in the icy water I had spent so many hours playing in. Whenever I saw a house in similar Cotswold stone, I would feel a pang of longing. At university, I experienced nervous exhaustion – by which I mean I would start shaking uncontrollably, repeatedly. For a time I was unable to function, retreating to my mother's house to be looked after until the shaking receded beneath the surface. I wonder now if these were earth tremors, shock waves emanating from a lost home and working their way through my body. Like magnetized minerals always seeking their pole, my body hummed with the pull of that place.

*

1 April 2006. We came back from Mexico to a cold not-spring, but this week at last it's warmer & there are lots of daffodils. Mowed the grass today for the first time. First potatoes, carrots & onions in this week. Hellebores beautiful.

*

Charles Darwin also experienced the reverberations of a childhood garden. His early years at The Mount, in Shrewsbury, sparked his yearning to explore, observe and experiment with the natural world. This boyhood emotional ecology, rooted in one place, started him on a course that would change his life, as well as the scientific discourse of his time.

Science and art are both fed by the natural world. The mid-twentieth-century American artist Anne Truitt describes an epiphany that inspired her paintings: 'What did I know? What did I love? What was it that meant the very most to me inside my inner self? The fields and trees and fences and boards and lattices of my childhood rushed across the inner eye as if borne by a great, strong wind. I saw them all, detail and panorama, and my feeling for them welled up to sweep me into the knowledge that I could make them.' Just as Truitt brought these places to life through brushstrokes and pencil markings, their shadows made from memories of light-fall, so planting a garden offers us a way to manifest aspects of our past lives and places we carry within us. They give us the chance to create our own utopias and arcadias, gathering up all the gardens we have loved and scattering pieces of them to fall into a new form – a living, breathing bricolage in the image of our idealized garden. We are back to the idea of gardens as paradise.

When our adult home is elsewhere, those traces of early outdoor spaces and landscapes are psychic, held in our heads and experienced as a yearning for our various lost lands. They exist only in our imaginations. For Roald Dahl, this *unhoming* occurred when his family moved from their home in Llandaff, Cardiff, a place with a garden where the young Dahl used to climb up into the trees to write. His house was sold after the death of his younger sister and his father, so the loss of a beloved home was irrevocably bound up with grief. Dahl spent the rest of his life yearning for the place he felt was his true home. Echoes of Llandaff ripple through his work and his final home, Gipsy House, in Buckinghamshire, where he created a playful garden and grew prize-winning vegetables. In recognition of his love of gardening, visitors put onions on his grave.

Rudyard Kipling felt such a strong attachment to his aunt's house (a place that offered a respite from the foster home he dubbed 'the House of Desolation') that when the building was demolished, he asked to keep the bell that had hung on the gate. He wanted every visitor to his house to feel the same sense of welcome and safety he'd experienced whenever he rang that bell and walked up the garden path. Houses, gardens and landscapes are always made up of absences and presences. As an adult, I didn't get interested in gardening until moving to our current home, and so all the places that came before inform this place. I have created an unconscious memory map of my homes, a psychogeography of connections that forms the blueprint for my visions of this garden. There is no starting from scratch – if we have to move, I will carry this place with me, alongside all the others, and plant it in another landscape.

*

As the weather is still dry, I mow the grass, wielding the power cable as if controlling a flighty horse. The repetitive movements of the mower – up and down, back and forth – create a rhythm that reminds me of jiggling a pushchair to try and lull a child to sleep. None of my children took naps in their beds; instead, I rocked them to sleep outside, often using the lip of the house's threshold to add to the motion. I would peer down through the transparent panel on the pushchair canopy, hoping to find the child asleep, but was often confronted with a pair of big, wide blue eyes staring up at me. My eldest son had a particular sound he would make before falling asleep: a kind of quiet drone, like a yogic *om*. When I heard it, I knew I could nearly stop pushing. Once they were asleep, I parked them next to the sitting-room's French window so I could do the hoovering and see their legs kicking when they woke up, or

I sat talking nearby with mum-friends in the garden, rows of small pink feet peeping out from blankets. Sleep, then, was an obsession. It was a rarity, a luxury, a distant simplicity. Now I am often the first awake in the mornings, padding around a quiet house after a sleep interrupted only by my own wakefulness. I forget those wrung-out, stretched-out days and nights, when all I could think about was having a bath and lying down for a few hours. To say I miss the sleepless years would be ridiculous. But I do miss the drowsy blue dawns with a baby in my arms, their doughy fingers kneading my chest and their eyes locked on mine. It seems to me that the state of motherhood involves part of you always wishing you were somewhere else.

I stop push-pulling the mower. The cut grass collects in the blades and I turn it over to release it. The smell is summer, the future. I leave the grass cuttings to rot down so the grass can feed itself with nitrogen and other essential nutrients, improving the soil structure and releasing water back into the ground. Winding up the extension lead and pulling the mower back to the shed, I inspect the pots on the garden table. Instead of fussing over young children, my attention is now on growing and protecting my tiny seedlings. I watch for any signs of life, and then I coax them upward with water and sunlight.

7

EXILE

THE RASPBERRY CANES ARE FILLING OUT WITH LEAVES, CREATING A busy canopy that in a few weeks will be as tall as my daughter. In the vegetable patch, a leek is going to seed. There is nothing of much use for eating yet. I place the early 'King Edward' potatoes in their trench alongside the cutting patch. I prepared the ground using the no-dig method, which perfectly suits my inability to commit a large amount of time to digging the garden, and my curiosity about alternative ways to cultivate plants. With this approach, you simply cover the ground with a thick mulch (I used a layer of cardboard topped with well-rotted horse manure) and wait for the weeds to suffocate and the nutrients to filter down into the soil. The theory is that digging actually damages the structure of the soil, and this method has been shown to produce great results. We will see.

The seed potatoes look gnarly and puckered. Despite their unpromising appearance, I am excited for the magic of digging up potatoes in a few months' time. There is something so beautiful about plunging a fork carefully into the soil and slowly uncovering the golden free-floating orbs. The Finnish author Tove Jansson shared my love of these most basic of vegetables, giving one of her Moomin characters the words, 'I only want to live in peace, plant potatoes and dream.' Soon there will be broccoli, beans, peas, courgettes – simple feasts, but so much tastier for the work I've put in. For now, vigilance and patience.

The history of many peoples is inextricably connected to the land they once nurtured, and to the food they grew. Food is one of the things we use to recreate a sense of belonging, but we rarely think about the person who grew or made it – a person who perhaps cuts sugar cane on land where their ancestors were held captive, sugar that I make into a cake using my mother's favourite recipe; the rice farmer in Bangladesh whose meagre living is obliterated by floods caused by climate change, rice that thousands of miles away fills a steaming bowl along with beans, sweetcorn and the tastes of childhood. The same systems and calamities that uproot people also strengthen the symbolic significance of plants and landscapes, creating a complex interconnectivity.

In my garden, it is easy to forget this sometimes, in the simplicity of digging up potatoes or picking ripe plums. As well as revealing the imbalance and inequalities of our food systems – who gets to eat what, and why – there is something reassuring about food that reminds us of 'home', transcending physical borders and time through the complex sensations of smell and taste, creating potent layers of memory. This thought is like applying a dock leaf to a nettle sting – it soothes my fears of displacement. I can grow food somewhere else, and it will still taste like home.

Back in the kitchen, washing the mud out of my fingernails, I catch a fragment of a radio programme about an allotment-holder who grows beans that originated in plants he brought over from Jamaica as part of the Windrush migration. Just as gardens haunt our memories and our present, so plants provide a means of connecting the two. Often, this is most heightened with edible plants. We can recreate the tastes and smells of a long-lost homeland in a new place, and we can continue meaningful traditions through the food it provides. Forced from their land by European settlers as part of the 'Indian-removal' process in 1838, the Cherokee people began the terrible 'Trail of Tears', marching from their rightful home under threat of violence from 7,000 armed troops. Their homes were looted and destroyed, and they were permitted to only take a few essential possessions. Climbing beans were said to be among them. Many people didn't survive the journey – it is thought that over 5,000 Cherokee people died of disease and starvation on the way – so it is miraculous that some of these beans did survive and were cultivated on the new reservations.

Plants contain histories and traverse time. Take the pea seeds buried in Tutankhamun's tomb as fodder for cattle in the afterlife. Those peas were plundered from the tomb by Howard Carter in 1922 and given to Lord Carnarvon, who propagated some at his garden in Hampshire. In defiance of death and decay, the peas were brought back to life, nearly 5,000 years after their burial, and seeds collected from these plants continue to produce 'Tutankhamun' peas today. The afterlife, as gardeners know, is all about seeds.

Throughout human history, when migrants or refugees arrive in a new place, they bring seeds or plants that connect them to their homeland, hoping the soil in their new place will nurture these talismans of home. One such community were the 150,000 Hmong refugees who left Southeast Asia after centuries of persecution to make a new start in the USA in the mid twentieth century. As an ethnic group, the Hmong people never had a homeland of their own and so were perhaps better equipped than some to adapt to a new environment. But they retained strong traditions and practices that often clashed with the Protestant American world. The Hmong culture is deeply ritualistic, with a fundamental belief in spirits and souls, as well as traditional shamanistic remedies. Although the Hmong families who settled in the USA were able to cultivate the plants they had grown in their homelands, they found themselves unable to practise many of their rituals to ward off evil spirits. Many of the previously healthy young men started dying suddenly in their sleep. It is said they died from homesickness, struck with a fatal terror at being somewhere they could no longer keep the spirits at bay.

Homesickness is a potentially devastating feeling. Experimental autopsies examining the brains of French soldiers who died from hypothermia in the nineteenth century proclaimed 'nostalgia' as the cause of death. Some countries forbade the singing of national songs because it caused such sorrow amongst troops. Of course, there is no equivalence between being forcibly displaced, or fleeing one's homeland to escape violence, or leaving to fight a war, and experiencing the loss of a family home. But even a small-scale house move can feel like a painful severing of familiarity and comfort. The author Charles Lamb, whose wife Mary had nervous breakdowns after every house move, wrote in 1827 of his unwanted departure from a beloved home, 'You may find some of our flesh sticking to the door posts. To change habitations is to die to them, and in my time I have died seven deaths.'

The nature writer and poet Ronald Blythe records the enforced sale of farms in his Suffolk village that were known as 'the coming down time'. Selling up 'was a quite unbearably public affair. The ruined man stood metaphorically naked before the parish, all his chattels and machinery, his beloved working horses and stock paraded in the yard, whilst his creditors totted up the lots . . . Such ruined farmers often drowned or shot themselves.' I went to a farm sale like this once, in France. Whether the owner had died or was forced to sell I don't know, but I remember the feeling of prying, of something distasteful about rummaging around in the sediments and decorations of someone else's home. The ghost of a person who had worked that land, whose family had maybe worked it for generations, and who knew it intimately, now exiled from their place. A life spilled out onto a dusty yard, disembowelled entrails laid across wonky trestle tables and heaped on the ground. The shame that seeps out of every brick.

When my parents separated, I was told we had to move because the bank was repossessing the house. From that point on, I could not look at that bank's logo without feeling a knot in my stomach. I later learned that, like many childhood stories, the truth was not quite as straightforward; but the narrative I carried for many years was that our home had been taken from us. In my late teens, money was tight again for my family, and at one point I was told not to open the front door because bailiffs were coming and they would take things away if I let them in. Once more, my home felt under threat.

*

15 April 2007. We returned from our pilgrimage to the Holy Land to hot weather – 24 degrees today and no rain for weeks. Ceanothus, early clematis, lilac out, daffodils over, tulips good. Most veg sown. Contemplating cutting down forsythia & lilac.

*

The concept of 'home' – whether we ever really inhabited it, or just yearned for such a place – can be a potent and enduring thing. What does home feel like to me? Today, it is the feeling of pushing my fingers into warm, friable earth; of brushing past a prickly raspberry cane that will soon be sagging with ruby fruit; of plunging my face into a peony flower and inhaling sunlight and desire and sweetness; of standing on dewy grass at dawn, feet strung with pearly cobwebs; and the sound of pans clattering in the kitchen as my husband washes up and I plant food for the table. That, for me – for now – is home. Fixing my body to the soil, working to earth myself.

Gardeners know they can root themselves in a place, old or new. There is an opportunity for regeneration and renewal. They dig up beloved plants to take with them to their next home, or take cuttings that will always connect them to a past garden. What will I take from my garden if we are evicted? Cuttings from the blowsy rose; my mother's hollyhocks, definitely. Dried sweet-pea pods and a few raspberry canes, maybe. I am surprised to realize that I would leave everything else.

We decide to stop waiting for the eviction letter to arrive and instead take matters into our own hands. I telephone the estate agent and tell them we will take the house we viewed before. I fill out forms and pay fees, negotiating a reduction because a friend showed us around instead of the agent. The children seem excited, discussing who will get which bedroom; and I try to imagine our furniture filling up this new space. Good friends live next door, and that fills me with joy, as we have been strangely disconnected from our neighbours here, despite being in the middle of town. I love the idea of leaning over the garden fence and having a neighbourly chat again. I can imagine us living there – passing meals through the dining-room hatch, playing football in the garden, ducking our heads to miss the ceiling beams.

And yet. Something doesn't feel right. The possibility of staying in this house is a strong tether. I am still holding onto that hope. I call the agent again and tell her we have changed our minds. I choose uncertainty here over certainty somewhere else.

*

April continues hot and dry. We don't bury the chocolate eggs for our usual Easter egg hunt in the garden in case they melt. My sweet peas are now about three inches tall, and the tulips have all opened out, gasping at their own brilliance. In the side vegetable patch I plant out the beans and peas, hoping they survive the slugs and snails, and dig up endless tangles of ground elder. The dog has hidden the hose attachment, so I have to do all the watering with a watering can. It takes a long time and I have been lazy about it. My cosmos seedlings have dried out. But I think they are salvageable with a good soak.

The courgette seeds have sprouted, the original husk clinging limpet-like to the new leaves, so I carry them out into the shed to harden them off before I plant them out. Despite the relentless heat, April must be approached with caution. It is hard to plan for, and requires attentiveness. The potato bed needs weeding, and as I uproot the bindweed and stray raspberry canes, I turn up a beautiful piece of flint, a quartz formed from layers of dissolved

silicon atoms compacted in the chalky ground. I imagine a pre-
historic woman turning soil that was warmed after the ice
retreated and is now revealing its elements. She sees the glint and
gleam of the rock, lifting the flint and bringing it cracking down
onto another, sending splinters and sparks flying, and in that
moment she understands that the earth has transferred some of
its power to her hands. Later, one of her descendants will place
a charm around his neck for protection and secure a flint to a
spear that will lodge in the smooth flank of a startled aurochs.
He will slice skin and flesh from bones with another flint. This
man's successors will settle in the folds of the hills, catching fish
from boats made with flint axes. One of this group's descendants,
a Saxon woman, tips a basket of rubbish onto a pile and kicks over
a knobble of flint, which settles on the ground and sinks slowly
into the soil. It lies there waiting for some other hand to feel its
cold, hard surface and lift it into the air. Sussex has some of the
oldest flint mines in Britain. These white moon craters in the hills
represent ancient elemental engagements with the landscape that
brought the beginnings of agriculture and cultivation – of what I
am doing now. My mind floats, free-falling through time, and then
back to now as a wren darts into my peripheral vision.

I watch it bathe in the makeshift bird bath – an old cutlery tray I
put on the side wall next to the telecoms building, where I can see
the birds splash and shimmy from the kitchen window. The tray
has three sections, and I imagine the robins, sparrows and pair of
beautiful goldfinches bathing in separate lanes, like swimmers in a
pool who mark their territory in ripples and breath.

According to the Ancient Greek poet Hesiod, when fig leaves are
the size of a crow's footprint winter is truly over, and I notice the
branches on our fig tree have unfolded into tens of clamouring

hands raised to the sky, demanding – what? Rain? They look like fingers preparing for a chef's kiss. The leaves are about the size of a crow's footprint. As I move through the garden, drinking in all this burgeoning growth, the chickens puff and ruffle themselves into a dust-bath dent in the ground, puddling like pancake batter into a sunny spot. They have made several dips and crevices in their run like this, which they visit in rotation as the sun moves across the garden.

It seems to me that almost every part of a garden is underplanted or overlaid with memories. Many of these are sensory: the smells of geraniums on a grandmother's table, or the tastes of past lives. But it is also filled with physical resonances. The Hanging Gardens of Babylon are said to have been created by Nebuchadnezzar to soothe his wife's homesickness for her childhood landscape (though their exact location and origins are disputed). The opulent gardens were thought to be terraced, with stone steps and colonnades and fountains. Planted with a range of different trees and exotic plants tumbling over the tiers, the impression was of a living mountain, echoing the green hills of Queen Amytis's homeland. Even if the definitive story of these gardens eludes us, the reason they capture our imagination is because they tap into the seemingly instinctive understanding of a connection between a landscape and belonging.

I think back to the times when I was gardening and my mother patiently pushed my daughter around the grass on her shiny new bike. I remember my father teaching my brother to ride his bike by running alongside him holding a scarf around my brother's waist, secretly whipping the scarf away so my brother didn't realize he was balancing on his own. Gardens are the scenes of these small personal triumphs, these moments that help us grow ourselves.

They can be a healing portal, allowing us to spiral through time to a remembered past, and yet also grounding us in the here and now, through the mundane tasks or daily labours of digging or weeding. Jorge Luis Borges wrote of a 'dizzying web of diverging and converging and parallel times', and we too are part of this web, just passing through, a temporary collision of time and place. Like the wind and sunlight, we have only a small time to stay.

When I cut flowers for the house, it feels like I'm recognizing this – making the most of the beauty and abundance my garden throws out. I take armfuls of rhubarb and chard along with the customary bottle of wine for a shared dinner, and leave jam jars crammed with sweet peas, cow parsley, cosmos and roses on the doorsteps of grieving friends. I take flowers from my mother's garden to her grave. Evolutionary anthropologists believe we are attracted to flowers because they indicated sources of fruit, and were therefore important for our survival. But the connection between nature and well-being goes far further.

We've always been able to sense the physical effects of gardening, but increasingly science is revealing the chemical reactions behind the mental benefits too. Gardens work on our minds, releasing essential oils that lift our mood and lowering fight-or-flight cortisol levels with their greenness. *Mycobacterium vaccae* compounds in soil trigger a serotonin release in the brain, creating feelings of well-being and boosting our immune systems as we dig or tend window boxes and indoor plants. Studies show that hospital gardens help people heal, and patients with a view of a green space recover more quickly from operations. Just hearing birdsong or running water can reduce anxiety and relieve depression. Being in natural places actually alters the physiology of the brain. It has been shown that greenery and natural landscapes increase feelings of well-being, and this is enhanced when we have some control over, or part in, the creation of that space. If we can make our own way around an outside space, to allow it to seep in and to be changed by it, then our sense of belonging increases.

The psychiatrist and writer Sue Stuart-Smith points out the hopefulness of gardening, and describes the phenomena of 'urgent biophilia', which is 'an almost instinctive urge to sow seeds and tend plants' in response to extreme stress or trauma. There are also lessons to be learned in the way that plants themselves adapt to their circumstances, making use of all available means to survive and thrive. Plants need roots, of course, but, being unable to move, they have developed other ways of creating a secure home and finding nutrients. They create underground rhizome systems, they use the wind or passing animals to propagate their seeds and grow a new generation of scatterlings. They understand connection and how to co-operate.

Tending a patch of land extends that care beyond our own physical borders. My garden nurtures a whole community of creatures that share the space with us. From our domesticated hens to the hedgehogs, woodlice, dragonflies and sparrows, they all make their homes here. Our common Sussex species have seemingly simple nests and burrows, yet the labour involved is astonishing. For the past few weeks, I've been watching a pair of magpies take sticks from my garden and construct a nest in a tree on the other side of the car park. Like the pole a tightrope walker uses to balance, they clutch the sticks in their beaks and wrestle them into place. A wren fetches leaves and fragments to line a neat little nest inside our shed, hopping first onto the door and then darting inside. The nest has been there for years, but the wrens have never chosen it as a birthplace for their brood. Until now it has been a second home, an alternative. I hope this year is different.

Further afield, animals build homes in ways that seem hard to imagine. The natural world is full of incredible acts of ingenuity and resilience: some birds create their nests purely from their own spittle; the underground nests of *Atta* leafcutter ants contain hundreds of fungus gardens that provide essential nutrients, which the ants tend and weed to remove waste material and pests; tailorbirds spend two days sewing a leaf-bag home, securing it with up to 200 stitches; weaverbirds weave grasses into beautiful hanging nests that dangle from branches and have their own unique weaving pattern; and termites use their faeces to create waterproof nests. As I peg out another load of washing on the line and collect warm eggs from the chickens' nest box, I feel I am part of the whole extraordinary community of nest-makers. The garden is full of mothers. Like these creatures, I want a safe place to live and raise my young, and I have to accept that, like their hard-won homes, mine is also impermanent.

Creating a home requires us to let go of some things and live alongside others. It has been difficult to let go of my fears about the impact of eviction on my children. My daughter tells me that when the house was first put up for sale, she often cried herself to sleep with worry, but the boys seemed less upset than I had anticipated. And an article by the screenwriter and actor Michaela Coel challenges my fears about how my children will respond to a move. Like them, she grew up in rented homes, but without the privilege of an outside space, and this precarity, rather than eroding her sense of self, propelled her: 'My family has rented our whole lives. You're always on fragile ground because it's not yours. It gives you drive, an ambition, because nothing is certain.

That is a resilience no person with stability can replicate. You can't forget it. There's blessings to the struggle ...' Moving and adapting to new places makes us more able to see and experience things differently; we become more sponge-like, porous, agile. Children are generally better at this, less rigid and stuck. Perhaps my worries are unfounded.

One evening, after clearing away the day, I track down a film about the sculptor and photographer Andy Goldsworthy. The dancing patterns of light reflected on my kitchen wall at a still point earlier that morning had reminded me of a beautiful column of light he filmed, and I wanted to see it again. Goldsworthy uses natural materials to create ephemeral artworks that are often sucked back into the sea or blown apart by the wind. He understands that even the rocks he works with are not stable or permanent, but instead are liquid mirages of steadfastness. The next day I go for a walk in some nearby woods with my two younger children, and we try creating our own Goldsworthy-inspired artworks. We collect different coloured leaves to make mandalas in the mud, and my son sets a spiralling trail of stones inside a cracked tree trunk. I tell them not to be upset if they are gone next time we come – like sandcastles, they are not supposed to last. The joy is in the creation.

I am aware of the same fluidity even within the curated space of my garden. Each experience of this space is different, depending on who is witnessing it, what the weather is like, what season it is. My relationship to it is different from my husband's, and different again from each of my children's. And the same is true of the house too. Every experience of 'home' is just part of a story that is still unspooling.

It is not that we don't need a sense of rootedness, but that we must find different ways to create it. Going back, giving in to *hiraeth* – our longing for a lost place – will not do this. We must resist the backward-looking urge to return to a previous home and the idealization of place that finds expression in nationalism and exclusionary narratives. I am beginning to understand that I must tend my garden not to recreate a lost Eden, but to tune in to its capacity for growth and change.

*

The lilacs my daughter and I picked have been sitting in a vase waiting for us to attend to them. I wash out some jars and set a saucepan on the stove. She joins me at the table, and I show her how to pick the flower heads off the lilac. Carefully, mindfully, with the particular kind of focus that makes a small triangle of tongue protrude from the corner of her mouth, she drops purple petals into a sieve. I chop rhubarb stalks into chunks and put them in a pan along with the rinsed lilac and some sugar, water and lemon rind. My daughter stirs it with my mother's old wooden spoon, moving back as she feels the heat lifting from the pan. We let it bubble away, releasing a heady floral-tangy scent into the air. When it has reduced and the rhubarb has softened, I strain off the juices – a delicious, runny syrup the colour of freshly kissed lips. I pour it into the jars and seal them. One for us, two for friends. They sit like apothecaries' potions on the counter, reverberating with the molten life force of spring.

The jars have me thinking about my step-grandmother's store cupboard, filled with jams and preserves and pickles. A farmer's wife, she spent her days feeding a stream of hungry men and children, and was clever with her cooking. She could produce a roast lunch for a huge group without seeming the least bit flustered, and would usually put us children to work podding broad beans or beating eggs. She passed on her wisdom to my stepmother, who is a skilled cook and makes the best marmalade I've ever tasted. And, although to date my jam and marmalade-making have not been huge successes, maybe my daughter, when she's finding her way in the world, will remember how to make rhubarb-and-lilac syrup one day and she will be back here in this small, noisy kitchen picking tiny luminous blooms from their stem.

*

I work on the garden in snatched hours and peaceful moments of escape. I sling a rickety net across one vegetable bed, ready for the tendrils of climbing beans in a few weeks' time. Pea shoots, frilly-headed, look for the sun, while pear blossoms, like children's freckled faces, turn skywards. The screenwriter Dennis Potter describes looking at blossom from his window as he lay dying from pancreatic cancer: 'it is the whitest, frothiest, blossomiest blossom that there ever could be, and I can see it'. Those words, 'I can see it', swim around my head – how lucky I am to witness all this life.

The alliums are poised to burst like fireworks, their tight buds enclosing myriad spheres biding their time to explode. Dainty fingers of sweet rocket wear delicate white-green rings, some crusted with four-petalled stars. The extravagant nepeta has replenished its spring coat, bushy and frilled. The rose I pruned too hard stands naked, ashamed of its bareness amidst the swelling greenery around it. A single self-seeded wallflower, a remnant of the previous inhabitants of the house, grows stubbornly amongst the rest of the plants. The plum tree is a chaotic tangle of rangy limbs, but thankfully there is no sign of the fungus or leaf mould that coated it in a sticky syrup which intoxicated numerous flying insects last year. Three broad bean plants rise like clapping hands from the soil.

Alongside the shed, I notice some pink geranium flowers on the sprawling clump dotted with ground elder. There are irises in a new place – perhaps I planted them there? I don't remember. Plump leaves on the columbines look like fancy ballgowns. Saucer-like hollyhocks have emerged under the honeysuckle and everywhere things are stirring, shaking off the winter and settling into their places.

8

BOUNDARIES

THE LONG WALL DOWN THE SIDE OF OUR GARDEN USED TO BELONG to the old naval prison. When my husband was fixing the front gate a few years ago, a passing stranger stopped and told him to be careful of the wall to the right because it's a listed 'Napoleonic' wall. As the house was only built in 1924, I imagine it was part of the Lewes House of Correction, which opened in 1793, and then became the County Jail, before being sold to the Admiralty in 1854 as a naval prison after a new, larger prison was built to the west of the town. This explains the stone embedded in our front garden wall with the words 'Number 1' and a picture of an anchor carved into it, and another similar stone with an anchor and 'Number 3' on the wall diagonally opposite, on the other side of the car park.

The history of the land on which I garden predates this Napoleonic wall. Excavations to the old prison site in 2008 revealed medieval rubbish pits, strewn with pottery, bones and metalwork slag, lying beneath layers of chalk, clay and sandy gravel. These pits extend under the walls, so I presume they continue beneath the earth I dig today. Sometimes the chickens scratch up oyster shells, a common staple in the Middle Ages. After its early insalubrious life as a medieval dumping ground, the land here seems to have enjoyed several centuries of wild abandon. And then the prison was built, and the wall came to mark the boundary line between incarceration and freedom.

The excavation in 2008 also uncovered the footings of some of the seventy cells in which inmates worked, ate and slept alone. It also revealed two wells. Pictures show the prison was an imposing, austere building, with high, dark flint walls and a large, forbidding entrance. It had three storeys, a chapel, infirmary, keeper's house, baths, four yards and, by 1833, a washhouse and laundry. I have been told that an old corn treadmill was built against our current garden wall. It was one of three treadmills installed to keep men exercised and occupied, and also as a brutal punishment.

I find a record of the Lewes prison's treadmill being worked by prisoners from other towns too. Uprooted, sent to an unfamiliar town to serve their sentence, these men also faced the prospect of being 'transported' to the new colony of Australia. The chaplain's report for 1838–9 lists the occupations of the Lewes prison population, and includes cordwainers, carpenters, fishermen and gardeners. The majority were locked up for the crime of 'vagrancy' – for being homeless. Many were children, described in the report as 'neglected, and often deserted, from childhood; left to prowl about in idleness, ignorance and want; to subsist, as they can, by casual labour, alms and plunder'.

When the prison became solely the home of naval prisoners, it was inhabited by another transitory population. Even the ships the naval prisoners had worked on were placeless. Conditions in naval prisons were notoriously bad, with harsh discipline, poor sanitation, predominantly solitary cells, and beds made from just bare boards for the first two weeks of a sentence, until prisoners earned a bed. The people who occupied these cells were sailors who had deserted, or were disobedient or violent.

The navy used the prison site as a jail, a marine barracks, and later an infirmary; after 1910, it was used as a drill hall by the Territorial Army and, in wartime, for housing prisoners of war. A man evacuated to Lewes as a young boy during the Second World War describes how he would watch soldiers practising their drills and firing an artillery gun there. Our house was built between the wars, right up alongside the ex-prison and incorporating the old wall into its boundary. It stood alongside this strange place for decades, until the building was demolished in 1963, and the garden area would have witnessed a whole century of imprisonment and confinement. If gardens are spaces where, in writer and artist Renee Gladman's words, 'the boundary between places has broken', then prisons are the opposite: heavily structured spaces made of walls, fences, bars and walkways. These two contrasting landscapes strangely coexist in the history of my house.

*

A box of plants arrives: the flowers for my cutting patch, which I hope will give me a steady bounty of cut flowers right up to autumn. I plant them out, anticipating the bouquets I can take to friends. The rambling rose on the shed needs tying in. As I catch my arm on a barb, I suddenly remember sticking the smooth side of rose thorns to my nose as a child and pretending to be a rhinoceros. I pull up bindweed stems that look like deep-water sea creatures, those anaemic translucent beings that exist in an entirely *other* realm.

My son's pond is a coagulated green sick. I scoop out some of the duckweed using an old fishing net. I fear the pond is too near the hedge, and consequently keeps filling with fallen leaves, and is too much in the shade to be a real source of biodiversity. When the pond was finished and filled, I bought water lilies and oxygenating plants, keen to encourage insects and other small creatures. But the dog lifted most of them out and scattered them around the garden each time I replaced them, so I stopped bothering. Now she is older and a little wiser, perhaps I will try again. Even this small area of water could support dragonflies, water snails, larvae, water boatmen and possibly, excitingly, frogs.

There is a sudden chill in the silken air. The light is pearled, like the apple blossom. Trees in the northern hemisphere are coming into leaf earlier, as global warming changes the seasonal cycles of energy and water, which in turn accelerate warming. Spring itself is shifting. I make a mental note to record the time our trees start to show leaves next year. The pear blossoms have turned into tiny starfish with multiple eyes on stalks, sitting atop green buds that hold the promise of fruit – of pear and ginger crumble, or cold and crisp slices with Manchego cheese, or stewed pears and ice cream.

I spy a red campion in the prairie area that must have self-seeded from somewhere. Perhaps it has lain dormant since one of my earlier experiments with planting a wildflower meadow. However it arrived, I am glad it did. I think I hear a nuthatch. Two surprise visitors today. Then rain, at last. How will it change the garden? The shapes, textures and colours will all shift. Nudged off their stems by the raindrops, the apple blossoms float-fall like confetti. Slugs and snails, previously lurking in the shady edges, will feel the moisture, sliding greedily towards my purple sprouting broccoli and peas. The light becomes muted in the rain, making the greens everywhere sing and the carpet of pink-white apple blossom gleam. I prick out the largest hollyhock seedlings into bigger pots, leaving the rest in clumps to let Darwinism do its thing. A few foamy elderflower heads have appeared in the hedge. This year I will make cordial, bottling up the spring light to keep for darker times.

*

7 April 2010. Very cold, long winter, snow killed ceanothus & broad beans. Then v. wet late March. Daffodils are now lovely & hyacinths & other bulbs. Grass not yet mown. Potatoes in last week on Good Friday. Pam and I have put edging all round the veg plots. Ceanothus replaced. Lots of seedlings on windowsills.

*

I wonder if the inmates of the prison next door ever wondered what lay on the other side of their wall. What would they have been able to see? The top branches of some trees in the field or a swaying hedge maybe. This partial view would have been the closest they got to any green space during their time in the prison. But today, gardening often plays an unexpected part in prisoners' incarceration. Over one hundred prisons across the UK have prison gardens that not only provide fresh food, but also offer a sense of purpose, shared community, improved self-esteem and the chance for prisoners to reflect on and process their individual struggles and rehabilitation. Studies show that people with problems of substance misuse are less likely to go back to drug-using behaviour if they are involved with a prison garden, and many projects embrace organic methods as prisoners try to exclude chemicals from their own bodies. Giving prisoners the chance to nurture something and exert some control over their environment has been shown to have a positive impact on prisoner behaviour and staff morale.

This need for a sense of control is a common thread in the experiences of people who are forced to live in places they wouldn't have chosen – whether that is a jail, an unfamiliar country, or a refugee camp. I discover a remarkable story of British men held at Ruhleben internment camp, in Germany, during the First World War. Crammed into small stables (the camp was previously a racecourse), starving and hundreds of miles from home, some of the 5,000 internees began creating a garden. They formed a horticultural society and sent a letter to the Royal Horticultural Society in England requesting seeds so they could improve their miserable surroundings. A desire to create beauty amidst grimness and desolation was the initial aim; before long their plots were flourishing, with marigolds, asters, brachycome, begonias, antirrhinum, dahlias and roses – all bright splashes of colour amidst the dour camp compound. They planted climbing plants to cover the barbed wire, and soon began to grow food for the internees. They tended figs and oranges, and filled vegetable beds with tomatoes, lettuces and leeks. They awarded prizes for produce, and there is a lovely photograph of some of the men posing proudly with their pumpkins outside a hut.

There are similarities between this camp garden and the projects run by the Lemon Tree Trust, a present-day non-profit group which helps Syrian refugees living in Kurdistan's camps to create their own gardens. Again, the aim is both aesthetic and practical, and, as with the prison gardens, there are health benefits for those involved. The same plants are grown in these refugee gardens as in Ruhleben. While the camps are not prisons, for the inhabitants there is little freedom to choose whether to stay or go. Aveen Ismail, one of the garden project organizers at Domiz, a camp that is home to around 26,000 refugees, explains that 'creating a garden was a way for us to heal and remind us of home'. Another man said: 'I couldn't believe my ears when I heard I could have a garden here . . . We've all been displaced and are suddenly living in a desert without trees . . . I see life in this garden. It cleans the air and gives people hope.'

A woman who works with refugees tells me the most popular things she gives out are atlases. Displaced people need to plot their journeys, to find their home place on the map and register the space in between. While there is no roadmap for making a home somewhere that may always feel foreign, refugee gardens can help people feel more connected to their present place. Like the prisoners treading the mill next to my house, or the British men trapped in a German camp, these people have been uprooted. Working new soil, watering fledgling plants and growing fresh food is a chance to build self-respect, independence and community.

*

In which a moon, a prison and a love story collide.

Ours is not the only garden with a naval prison in its past. About thirty-five miles away is Sissinghurst, a mecca for garden enthusiasts, renowned for Vita Sackville-West's beautiful planting and her husband Harold Nicolson's clever structural landscaping.

A dive into the history of Sissinghurst reveals that it, too, was once a naval prison. Originally a Saxon pig farm, the moated medieval settlement later became a significant Tudor estate. Years of neglect saw the farm and castle buildings fall into disrepair, and during the Seven Years War of 1756–63 it was taken over as a camp for naval prisoners of war. The prisoners were kept in cramped, draughty rooms, sleeping in hammocks with little access to light or fresh air. The Middle Court area had shops, and prisoners were able to obtain permission to work beyond the enclosed and guarded garden boundaries, but daily life was mostly grim.

The guards were violent and even shot some prisoners without cause. There is a story about a guard spotting a light in one of the Tower rooms, and, when his request to extinguish the candle was ignored, he opened fire with his musket. At least one prisoner died from injuries resulting from the shooting. The guard was found to have been mistaken: he'd seen either a reflection of a lamp in the window, or the light of the moon, which was said to shine brightly on that particular spot at a certain time each night. Why am I struck by this story? Because the later occupant of the Tower, Vita Sackville-West, created her White Garden so that it would look luminescent in moonlight.

The moon and gardens have myriad connections. There is a long tradition of biodynamic gardening, which follows the moon's cycle. There are those who prefer to garden at night, such as the poet Emily Dickinson, whose problems with her vision meant she often gardened by moonlight. Folk wisdom tells us to sow and transplant under a waxing moon, and this has been borne out by scientific research showing that lunar rhythms impact plant growth, in part due to the tidal movement of the water all living things contain. Along with the fact that it's more likely to rain just after a full or new moon, which will give your seedlings a healthy watering, the patterns of the moon directly affect how plants grow. Sackville-West herself wrote a poem entitled 'Full Moon', in which she describes her lover skipping 'in the pool of the moon as she ran . . . / But she climbed on a Kentish stile in the moonlight, and laughed at the sky through the sticks of her fan'; and one of her lovers, Virginia Woolf, compared her to the moon after Sackville-West's long poem *The Land* was published to some success: 'Yes, that yellow moon is rising on the horizon – Everyone admiring Vita, talking of Vita.'

In a piece for her garden column, Sackville-West describes how she 'cannot help hoping that the great, ghostly barn owl will sweep silently across the pale garden next summer in the twilight, the pale garden that I am now planting under the first flakes of snow'. Barn owls, with their white-pigmented feathers are more successful at hunting when the glare of the moon on their white bodies paralyses their prey with terror. In an exhibition I saw at the Turner Contemporary gallery in Margate the artist Katie Paterson created a piece of music in collaboration with the moon, turning the notes of the *Moonlight Sonata* into Morse code and bouncing them into space. She translated the rebounding soundwaves back into musical notes. The resulting music was an eerie rendition of a familiar tune, with pauses and gaps where sound had been absorbed. Night and its moon-haunted shadows offer a space for mysteries and hauntings, for impossible passions and the blurring of the clear edges of identity. The marriage between Harold Nicolson and Vita Sackville-West contained dark corners in which each pursued other love affairs. Sackville-West also experienced a sense of rift and dislocation within herself, feeling as if she were split into two sides: masculine and feminine. She seized her chances at love and embraced her fluid identity, all against the backdrop of the incredible, rich, overflowing garden she tended. I want to stand in her White Garden at night, under a cool, clear moon and see how it shines.

Whatever the truth about the shooting in the Tower, Sissinghurst was in an indisputably sorry state by the middle of the eighteenth century. Furious prisoners destroyed much of the remaining buildings and furniture, and the dead were buried in an area where visitors now picnic. The ruins and surrounding estate passed from one family to another, and by the time Sackville-West saw the house in 1930, it was a working farm with decrepit ruins and an 'arrowy tower'. She 'fell flat in love'. Having created a beautiful garden at their previous house, she and Nicolson were undaunted by the prospect of tackling the grounds at Sissinghurst; in fact, she relished the challenge of waking the garden from its slumber, writing, 'It was Sleeping Beauty's garden; but a garden crying out for rescue.' What they created was to become one of the most visited and imitated gardens in the country, a place that would influence garden design across the world.

*

My first visit to Sissinghurst was with a friend on a quintessentially dreamy summer's day. Everywhere I looked I saw exquisite beauty and aliveness: the daisy-smattered prairie grass near the entrance, the rose garden casting dappled shadows in the blue-hot day, the shady Nuttery, the blazing oranges and reds, the gently drooping apple trees, the ancient battle-scarred barn. It is hard to imagine the squalor of the naval prison, the horror of its rank, dirty infirmary, the deliberate demolition of a place now so carefully and lovingly restored. The area that made me catch my breath was the White

Garden. Small beds stuffed with silver, green and white planting
are separated by narrow paths, with a rose-covered arbour in the
centre. I didn't have a sense of there being edges or shapes, just an
overwhelming, luminous fullness. It was disorienting, like being in
a blizzard. Turn one way: as lamb's ears stroke your legs, spears of
Veronicastrum virginicum 'Album' and white delphiniums first grab
your attention, giving way to puffs of phlox, campanula, mallow,
and then smears of white rosebay willowherb rise out of a carpet
of creeping forget-me-not, geraniums and violas. Turn again:
now you see only silver – sea holly, *Eryngium giganteum* 'Miss
Willmott's Ghost', and artemisia. Then again: a froth of cosmos,
Crambe cordifolia, *Rosa* 'Madame Alfred Carrière', ox-eye daisy,
white campion and the striking weeping pear nodding humbly at
the splendour of it all.

The layout of the grounds is based on the idea of 'garden rooms',
and the bones of the design are credited to Nicolson's geometrical
plans. The first space is a large enclosed lawn with beds around
the edges and the house along one side; facing you as you step
inside is the Tower, slightly off-kilter and not in a direct line with
the entrance. As you pass under the Tower's archway, you find a
subtle grid of separate gardens, bounded by walls and hedges but
each offering a tantalizing glimpse of the next. There is an *Alice in
Wonderland* quality to it, making you feel like you are falling deeper
and deeper into its beauty. Behind the walled gardens is a large,
wild-feeling orchard with a lake at the end. It all has the perfect
balance of untamed and curated, structure and flow. Sackville-
West's planting was based on the principle that one should 'Cram,
cram, every chink and cranny'; it is an informal garden overflowing
with abundance and tumbling from one beautiful view to another.
She was not concerned with traditional wisdom about colour or
texture, instead creating a space that looks like it is just about to

tip into chaos. She wanted a 'release of spirit from the jail of shape'. It is alive and exuberant and utterly wonderful. Every cranny, crammed with love.

Like her approach to love, Sackville-West's vision for Sissinghurst was romantic, free and loose. Her intense affairs with women had caused great damage to her marriage – more so than Nicolson's relationships with other men (she ran away with one lover for whom she seriously considered leaving him). Creating the garden helped heal these wounds. She approached marital troubles in the same way she created her garden: 'Let us cram with flowers every threatened rift.' Despite these tensions, their marriage remained loving and strong, and after her death Nicolson was bereft, wandering the garden (*her* garden), weeping. Sackville-West is best known for Sissinghurst, but also as the muse for Virginia Woolf's *Orlando*. It is no surprise that her garden contains a queer energy, a sensuous, seductive slipperiness, with the different 'rooms' almost like different identities we can try on: bold and vibrant, cool and alluring. Linear and circular. Masculine and feminine. She wrote that the place 'fills me with a mindless deep repose, / wherein I find in chain / the castle, and the pasture, and the rose', interconnected and deeply rooted in its history.

Much of Sackville-West's vision was fuelled by the loss of her beloved family home, Knole. As a woman, under the archaic inheritance system of her class, she had no rights to the property following her parents' death, and she found herself disinherited. She returned there at night, alone (by moonlight, I picture) to walk in the garden. She wrote afterwards, 'I may be looney but there is some kind of umbilical cord that ties me to Knole.' She is another exile, and she uses her garden at Sissinghurst as a cure for this sorrow. There is an echo of this heart-strong connection in the writing of her grandson Adam Nicolson. He describes how many of his thoughts and significant events are 'strung out across my life, like the lights marking a channel . . . tied to and founded on Sissinghurst. It is the shape of what I am. I do not own it but it is *my place* . . . My nutrients came from this soil.'

When Harold Nicolson died, his son Nigel felt unable to finance the upkeep of Sissinghurst along with paying enormous death duties, and he donated the house, garden and farm to the National Trust. Nigel's son Adam and his family lived there for a time and drove much of the current emphasis on having a working farm producing hops and food to sell in the restaurant, bringing livestock and smaller-scale farming back to the land. Yet Adam felt he was not truly at home, his claim on the place simply his heritage and life there rather than any legal documents of ownership. Like us, he was living in a house he did not own. Sissinghurst, he writes, remains a place 'drenched both in belonging and in the longing to belong'.

*

24 April 2013. We planted the potatoes with Grace & Evie. Winter very cold & long & hard. I mowed the grass for the first time on Sunday & the plant pots went out yesterday.

4 April 2015. I mowed the grass for the first time this week. Chilly, rainy time but spring flowers are wonderful. Peony is just showing & lilies of the valley. Mike & Mary manured the roses & attacked the weeds around the raspberries. Tom planted the potatoes today – tomorrow's Easter & his birthday.

*

I am pegging out the washing on a breezy April morning. White sheets billowing on the line. A memory of a garden – luminous, bathed in creamy light – floats into my head. Sissinghurst stays with you long after you first see it. I think of the French prisoners stranded there in 'the garden of England', smashing furniture in the outbuildings; of the newly incarcerated sailors unfurling their blankets to go to sleep on the floor in the naval prison beyond my garden wall; of the hungry men picking lettuce under a barbed-wire fence in Germany; of the refugees whose homes in lush, green Damascus have been ground into rubble and who find themselves in a tent in a dusty land with endless horizons; of the man I met in the café outside the British Library who told me how his home was originally Palestine, then the camp at Gaza where he knew by heart the roads and routes so intimately that it became home, then London, where he felt homesick not for Palestine but for Gaza, destined – as are all those who have moved overseas – to always miss *somewhere*. And I think about all the layers of different 'homes' we inhabit at any one time, how resilient people are, how strong that urge to create beauty out of uncertainty.

*

It is hard now to think back to what my hopes for the garden were when we first moved here. In our previous home, the garden was much smaller, a narrow strip of lawn with a flower bed and path on one side, and an apple tree at the end. My husband built a shed on stilts for the children to play in, and there was a sandpit under the apple tree. It was an extension of the house rather than a distinct or determined place – simply another space to play in. But moving here, I saw the chance to create something new and beautiful. The garden evolved as my knowledge and curiosity grew, rather than being planned. The last two families who lived here before us had marshalled the borders along the right-hand wall into some kind of order, with wallflowers and geraniums and lilies, a patch of wild red clover and herbs dotted about. I decided to tackle it one area at a time, working my way round – and round again.

There is something about gardening that taps into a desire for order. Perhaps it's connected to Puritan Christian teachings about conquering the deviant wilderness and being a 'civilizing' force, shaping landscapes into neat, clearly separated areas. In many Western cultures, we have come to regard the 'wild' as pagan, heathen, dangerous and corrupting. Take, for example, the regimented rows of vegetables marked out by string (which you will find in my garden too – I have not shaken off the love of clean lines) that characterize so many allotments and gardens. To avoid feeling overwhelmed, we construct hedges and boundaries, keeping the chaos beyond at bay. But to think a garden can be truly defined or confined within a rigid scheme belies the messy fluidity of nature. Being a gardener, for me, is to allow space for change, to question proffered ideas of natural purity and nostalgia, and instead to make our home within a mutable world. We can imagine our own roots not simply as tendrils delving into the earth, but as seeds that get blown across borders and boundaries, as pollen that feeds other creatures, as leaves that shelter birds whilst turning sunlight into life force. We can look up as well as down.

The first area I worked on after we moved in was the north-facing bed directly opposite the kitchen window, because that was most in my sightline from the sink or sitting at the table, looking out to the edge of the garden. Next, I dug over the longer bed running parallel to the back wall, where a few sunflowers and poppies grew. Once that area was clear, I realized I needed a means of getting around – to drift, dawdle, ebb and meander – and a way to break up the planted areas. I dug up some old bricks from the chickens' area and began laying a path. I bought gravel (not enough) and liner, and started carving out some new boundaries. There was no real plan, I simply followed the existing 'desire paths' – the routes that felt instinctively right. I paid a friend to lay concrete slabs for another path, and joined it to the brick path behind the main border with gravel. There are too many different materials and not enough continuity, but I don't notice that any more. The brick path is wonky and purely functional, yet it sits in just the right place, separating the flower beds and the wilder hedge-side area. These boundaries create paths for the feet but also routes for the eyes, drawing your gaze in a desired direction, creating a visual flow around the space. But I wasn't thinking about that: I just wanted to get to the chicken run without walking through nettles and mud. Recently, I have mown paths through the long grass area, to give more softness and movement to the lawn.

These paths are meaningless for the plants, of course. Seed heads float wherever the breeze takes them, disregarding borders or boundaries. For many plants, birds are essential conveyors of next year's crop or blooms, carrying seeds in their faeces. Some seeds attach themselves to the fur of passing animals as a means of transportation, while others, like the hellebores in my shady bed near the pond, burst forth in an explosion of life. Things sprout where I least expect them.

Nothing seems more surprising to me than the changes I witness in my own children. The smudged pencil-marked heights on the kitchen wall demonstrate their vertical growth, but I was not fully prepared for the storms and emotional turmoil of the teenage years. My children's limbs are growing faster than their self-awareness, making them seem clumsy and out of synch with themselves. They struggle with anxiety, fearing change or exposure; they have pains in their legs from the sheer pace with which they are growing. I try to hold onto my youngest child's innocence and playfulness, but simultaneously feel impatient with school runs and playground chat. I am straddling the world of young children and young adults, and not managing either particularly well. They do not feel ready to fly the nest, yet they long to be free. They need to be prepared for the journey ahead. But I can't face that next stage of growing up and growing away, not quite yet. I still want to hold on to this moment in our lives, amongst the flying and flowering of spring.

As a mother, my own boundaries have been constantly blurred for years, my body merging with other beings. At first my relationship with each baby was a secret, hidden, mine and mine alone. Then the swollen belly on which strangers pressed their hands, my body suddenly a public space, it seemed. Then the tumbling kicks and swivels felt also by siblings and father. Then a turning inside out; a tearing wave that pushes them into the world. During childbirth women shapeshift. We don't feel our edges, just the fire at the core and the waves – those tumbling, engulfing waves. At one point during each birth, I have been sure I am about to die. Utterly certain of it, knowing it more clearly than I have ever known anything. And then a breath, a bearing down and all the roars of all the mothers who have gone before, and it is done.

Life with a newborn has no boundaries either. Days and nights blended into a constant tangle of feeds, snatched sleeps, laundry cycles and intense love. When I was away from the baby, I jolted as if electrocuted, my body unable to process the separation. Slowly they grow, and they grow away, teetering further into the world, but the invisible cord still pulses. I am left wondering who I am and what my purpose is, now they can keep themselves alive. This time in my life is all about separation. It is about adapting to a new role and finding a shape for this constellation. A motherless mother.

MAY

9

BLOSSOMING

A NEW MANAGING AGENT IS OVERSEEING OUR DECEASED LANDLORD'S properties. She arranges to visit our house to ascertain what essential work needs doing. Every time I see the agent's number on my phone or get an official-looking letter I feel as if a cold, smooth pebble is sinking into my stomach. There is a collection of them there now. Dread-stones, rattling around; my ballast.

On the day of the inspection, I tidy and clean, but the agent still looks taken aback at the state of the place – the peeling paint, the tired woodchip wallpaper that holds the house together like a wrinkled old skin, the kitchen with no drawers, and the bulging paper on the sitting-room ceiling where water has leaked through from the bathroom. She is immaculately dressed in expensive-looking clothes, with designer lips and handbag. I feel a sharp stab of shame and embarrassment, suddenly seeing our home through her eyes. I notice the things we have just got used to, and feel her pity prickling like a nettle rash across my face. She has no reassurances about whether the house will be sold or not, but does resolve to fit a new bathroom and rewire the electrics. She marches from room to room with her clipboard, noting down inadequacies, faults and unpleasantnesses. 'At least you've got that lovely big garden,' she says with a brief, immaculate smile. Yes. Yes, the garden. Always the compensation. Always my saving grace.

The first iris is unfurling. I catch a glimpse of it as I walk past one morning and stop to look at it properly. Bright and exquisitely painted against the slick green leaves, it is like a fragile jungle creature emerging from cover. The sunlight illuminates each thin vein of its papery petals, revealing a furry yellow landing strip for the bees, and translucent leaves where the stem connects to the flower. These leaves feel hard and crinkly, making me think of the Amoretti biscuit papers my father sometimes set fire to after dinner. There is such a contrast between the delicate flower and the strong daggers of its leaves, and again with the gnarly roots sitting like clenched knuckles on the surface of the soil. Next to the iris, a clump of columbines nod their bonnets at the fat woodpigeon swaying in the elder tree. The astrantia nearby is nearly blooming: one central, folded star orbited by five satellite stars, a never-ending galaxy.

The peach tree has fallen sideways again – I decide to admit defeat and dig it up. Cow parsley dots the edges of the garden like an explosion of lace doilies. The first delicate elderflowers are forming in the hedge. As a girl, I used to stick sprigs of these flower heads through my pony's bridle to keep the flies away (though elderflower is usually used as a mosquito repellent, so this may have been more fanciful decoration than practical help). I think of a horse's flanks flecked with sweat, the warm, sweet smell of its neck, the metronomic rhythm of pounding hooves . . . Traffic mumbles in the wings. A car horn blares. I am back. Surveying my vegetable patch, I notice the chard has bolted, making a run for the sky, and the row of broad beans are fattening up. The garden is in motion, rising, opening, thrusting towards the light. Predicting some unwanted late-summer gaps in my back flower bed, I plant two *Aster amellus* 'Veilchenkönigin', *Penstemon* 'Apple Blossom' and more gaura. I have never been good at successional gardening, and this year especially I want to keep some of the beauty for as long as I can, to resist the inevitable dwindling.

In the town where we live, 1 May – May Day, or Beltane – is usually marked by celebrations. Morris dancers gather across the town, all clogs and bells and ribbons. There is a garland parade, with children wearing examples of their parents' gardening prowess or foraging skills around their heads. I love how exuberant the day feels, full of flowers and noise. The garlands drip with blossom and hedgerow plants – things I can find in my own garden but am always resistant to weaving into a garland, preferring to watch from the sidelines. This year I could have gathered apple blossom, cow parsley, roses, wild rocket and columbines – although the columbines are past their best, their purple and pink heads drying into upright green, seed-filled goblets; they are in various stages of undress – blooms fading, seeds setting, just the central part of the flower remaining, petal-less. The wild rocket has blown over, splayed like a drunkard across the back of the border. And the lilac, once so bold, is now crinkled and clove-brown, the petals flaking as I search for seed. Its purple spikes look as if they have been singed in a candle flame. I am always sad when the lilac goes over, but I remind myself that a flower is merely a prelude, a stage before the life-perpetuating seeds can develop. Flowers are not ends in themselves; they are simply a perfect moment of being.

*

My daughter has become fascinated by worms. I find her in the garden one morning, wearing some safety goggles and my gardening gloves, her plaits dangling down like puppet strings as she examines a worm with a magnifying glass. Everything looks too big – the gloves, the goggles. She shows me what she's found and gently puts the worm back down on the ground. We talk about how worms need moisture and darkness, how it's not kind to keep them out in broad daylight. She carries it over to the edge of the grass and puts it down. There is a tricky balance to be struck between encouraging my children's interest in tiny creatures, and ensuring the safety of the woodlice and spiders they house in ice-cream-tub homes. This feels like an important lesson: that the natural world is not there for our benefit, to teach us or be exploited by us. At mealtimes I find myself sharing some of the astonishing facts I've discovered with them, to show them the magic that's there if we only stop and look:

> The hummingbird's heart beats ten times a second.
> There is a moth that drinks the tears of birds.
> Blood, sap, fluid flows in every living thing, uniting us in an
> infinite liquid tide.
> Suriname toads give birth through their backs, the babies
> clambering out of their mother's skin.
> When a young swift leaves its nest it won't touch any surface
> for two to three years, living entirely and unimaginably in
> the air.
> The caterpillars of the common blue butterfly sing.

I hope some of this stays with them. Years from now they might come across a moth trapped on the wrong side of a window and wonder if it had once landed softly on a sleeping bird's neck and slipped its proboscis into the corner of its eye. They may experience panic and, as their pulse races, remember that the tiny body of a hummingbird can hold its fluttering heart safe. When my children have flown this nest, they may take years to finally land.

It seems to me that encouraging children to see the natural world with awe and respect is our only chance of survival. I discover that 41 per cent of the world's insects are currently facing extinction. That would be the biggest extinction event since the dinosaurs disappeared. Destruction of their habitat and the increasing use of insecticides are killing these tiny creatures eight times faster than larger animals at risk of extinction are dying. As insect populations decline, there is less food for their predators, impacting the entire food chain. In parts of China, people send their children into apple trees to hand-pollinate the blossoms because there are no bees left. Scientists and engineers are developing prototype robot bees for what feels a truly dystopian vision of the future. Without insects there is no life.

My response to the damage humans are causing is often hopeless despair and anger. But that is not generative or useful. What do we do when we feel overwhelmed by the ravages of the Anthropocene and can't see a solution? Tend our micro-communities. Spread love for the natural world amongst our children. Think how to respond to Terry Tempest Williams's question, 'How do we put our love into action?' In this garden, I can begin by supporting and making homes for the small creatures and insects.

*

16 May 2004. Hot sunny day & first 'Mary Rose' & crimson clematis came out. I drastically cut back the lilac, creating

*lovely new space. Pruned forsythia. All veg now sown &
we've just dug up the spinach – chard still going strong.
Garden giving me huge pleasure.*

*29 May 2006. After dry winter, cold wet May with a few
lovely days. Water butt never full – leaking?? New wooden
swing seat where bower was, bower becoming living
willow structure down the garden. Ceanothus current star,
columbines & irises good. Only one 'Mary Rose' bud out &
eaten by something. Lush tall growth, only veg we can eat
is rocket.*

10

FLIGHT

I AM WATCHING AND WAITING FOR THE FIRST SWIFTS TO ARRIVE. Every May they return to breed, screeching and circling above my garden. They are temporary residents, staying as long as they need to rear their young, and then lifting off as airborne creatures once again. By late summer they will all be gone.

Migratory birds (which make up around half of all bird species) undergo extreme physical hardship and some lose a significant portion of their bodyweight over the course of their journeys. A swift weighs only around 75 g to begin with; when they arrive here they may weigh no more than a lightbulb. The migrating instinct is so strong that it overrides the perils of the journey. Each year they come, driven by genetic programming and an irresistible itch for home that rises from their tiny bones and charges their feathers. Albatross spend up to ten years at sea before returning to their birthplace to mate and breed. They may travel for up to 1,500 km to make this return, their huge wingspan devouring distance as they glide towards their home place. For smaller birds, like swifts, these epic odysseys are even more remarkable.

Since as far back as Roman times, swifts have made the journey to Britain from Central and Western Africa to breed, yet, despite our long relationship with them, there is still much we do not know. Their speed and constant movement make them difficult to study, but we can get closest to them when they nest in buildings. Sadly, modern construction methods do not provide enough access for swifts, who need older structures with eaves in which to nest. As buildings are demolished and replaced, many nesting places are being destroyed, and this – combined with pesticides affecting their food supply – is severely reducing swift numbers. Swifts are not designed to land; their feet are too small and their wings too long to allow them to balance and give them enough propulsion to take off again from a flat surface. They are built entirely for constant movement. For a bird that lands only to create a home, it seems even more important that we ensure there are safe places for them to breed.

Studies have shown that swifts are not only supremely agile at low levels, skimming rivers to drink or hoover up swarms of insects, they can also climb to great heights. In fact, twice each day swifts fly right up to the edge of the cloud layer in order to feel the winds from large weather systems. This allows them to sense what is coming and plan their flight accordingly. What a lesson for us: to observe our surroundings and absorb those messages; to constantly have a 'weather eye' on what is coming, and learn to adapt to what the wind may bring.

*

Early evening. I sit at the table under the lilac, doing nothing except listening to a blackbird singing loudly. The sun is a vanishing red mouse. There is a faint smell of manure in the air, seeping down from the hills and blending with the lingering scent of lilac. An ash cloud of midges squalls in the dusky light, rising as if from an invisible fire. Suddenly, a steely grey shape catches my eye. A swift! Three! The first sighting this year. They slide across the sky, flutter, glide, high above the town, then over our street, then one catches a thermal above my head, resting on the wing before dipping out of view, calling, 'Peep, peep, peep.' Life, rippling and reeling all around my quiet core.

I look forward to this moment every spring. This year the swifts' return feels even more welcome than usual. They embody a sense of timelessness, of continuation and resilience that resonates as loudly as their calls. The sky is alive with small triumphs. It is always moving.

*

By mid-May, the dawn chorus is so loud it spills its notes into the sky and holds the whole landscape in its reverberations. The birdsong will stop once the birds go into moult in the summer, so I push my bedroom window open and drink it in. Alongside the swifts' unmistakable screams, there is a quieter call from a regular visitor, a collared dove, who has been tapping at my daughter's bedroom window with its beak.

When I was a teenager, an elderly woman rang our doorbell, and as I opened the door she pushed past me and into the house. She walked straight through the hallway to the kitchen, looking confused and asking what had happened to her furniture. Not long after, there was another ring at the door, and a flustered younger woman explained that her mother had lived in the house a long time ago and was now suffering from dementia. How shocking and terrifying it must have been to stand in a place she was sure was her home, only to find it completely changed and full of strangers. It seemed so sad to me, watching her get bustled out again, expelled from a place of safety where the world had once made sense.

Years later, soon after we had moved here, my husband found the previous tenant's boyfriend standing in the garden, staring at the borders. When my husband asked what the man was doing, he replied, 'Just checking up on my plants.' He had let himself in through the garden gate to pay homage to his hoped-for garden. Another lost soul, wandering into a space where he did not officially belong yet over which he felt he still had some ownership. He was a herbalist, and over the year his girlfriend lived here he had planted pulmonaria, tansy, a witch hazel, rosemary, thyme, borage and fennel. The plants were not in one particular patch but scattered around the garden, as if he had found the perfect position for each one, with no concern for curation. These were plants that needed to survive in order for him to work. And he had come to see whether they were thriving. If we have to move house, I imagine doing exactly this: climbing up the back wall to peer over to see what has become of my mother's hollyhocks, my honeysuckle and my rambling rose. For now, though, there are potatoes to attend to.

I bank up armfuls of straw and grass clippings around the potato plants to keep out the light that will turn the tubers green. Bindweed coils up through the soil, spreading in curly puddles across the ground. Such entanglements. As I pull out a clump, I uncover a red ants' nest, and the tiny creatures rush to repair the fissure I have just created. I move on, guiltily leaving them to their work. In the back vegetable patch, I sow a row of beetroot and take out the rangy chard that has gone to seed. We use that phrase to describe a person who is past their prime, yet for a plant this is a time of survival and reproduction. The seeds are a sign of ongoingness and hope. As I uproot the chard, its seeds rain down onto the soil. Some of them will appear next year. They will survive the frosts, rains, snails and birds, pushing upwards as if this is what they have always done.

We have not had much rain for the past few weeks, so I lug a watering can around, refilling it several times in an effort to keep the vulnerable new plants alive. I find watering tedious and am often lazy about it, resulting in needless losses and drought-stricken plants. It just feels too much like housework somehow, and I come out here to escape all that.

Inspired by Charleston, I pot up some dianthus to bring colour to a rather overlooked area by the back door. I tie in the broad beans that have been battered by recent winds. To my annoyance, I realize that I have absent-mindedly thrown away the small pots of sunflowers I had planted with my friend's seeds, so I sow another batch and resolve to get better at labelling things. The last of the sweet-pea seedlings go into an old tin bath by the French window, and I press down on either side of their stems to push them deep into the soil, like the hearty two-handed shoulder clap you might give someone in congratulation.

I plant echinacea and *Verbena bonariensis* in the prairie area, searching hopefully for signs of the pony tails and bunny's tail grasses. There is a lot of grass, but I am not sure if it is the right kind. The sweet rocket nearby smells intoxicating – like Parma violets and liquorice brewed into an elixir. The roses are dotted with buds and all over the back border alliums are ready to burst. As I tie back the honeysuckle again, I remember reading that it always twines clockwise (as seen from below) whilst bindweed twines anti-clockwise. The Gaelic words for this are wonderful: the honeysuckle grows *deasilwise* and bindweed *widdershins*. We may have language to describe this phenomenon, but we can only wonder at *why* it happens – 'wonder' in both senses: to consider, and to be struck with awe. However much we try to understand her many movements and patterns, nature always holds something back.

*

5 May 2008. Today our garden was one of twenty-eight open for Christian Aid. Around 150 people came round & it was very happy, though a relief when they left. Tulips mostly over & ceanothus not quite out, but bluebells, forget-me-nots, lilacs, veg quite good.

*

The swifts make regular evening fly-bys and I wonder how many of them have swooped and shrieked over this garden before, in previous years. Do they recognize it? Do they notice what has changed? In the animal world the creatures who migrate each year, who leave and return, live in a ceaseless dance with impermanence. While human nomadic cultures have always moved according to the season and followed the source of their food, most contemporary mass movements of humans are one-way. They are often the result of problems caused by global systems and climate disasters. In other words, we flee *from* rather than travel *to*. And, unlike the swift, there is little prospect of return. Even voluntary relocations such as moving house tend to be one-way journeys: when we say goodbye to a place, there is usually no going back. But our homing instinct is still strong within us. And like animals, we have the desire to 'nest', to make a home where we have landed, no matter for how short a time.

The memory of the temporary homes I have left behind allows me to navigate my past, like signposts to each segment of my life. I do not remember events according to the years they happened, but instead they are connected to the place I was living in at the time. I imagine that for the birds returning to their far-flung nesting sites, some kind of placeholding memory exists that stretches back in time beyond their own lives as part of a kind of collective memory. Perhaps the ancestors of the tenacious robin in my garden who guards his territory so fiercely also perched here, watching humans go about their baffling days. Or past generations of swifts navigated to the same patch of sky but looked down on the medieval dumping grounds, or the field beside the naval prison, or the greenhouse in the garden. This invisible pull to ancient nesting sites is fascinating.

Consider rooks. They will roost in 'ghost' rookeries, places where their ancestors once nested but that haven't been used for decades in between. In Derbyshire, a raven roosting site had been unused for 170 years, but once the birds returned to that area, they chose exactly the same spot. Carbon dating of gyrfalcon nests shows that some have been used continuously for 2,500 years. Place, it seems, can become part of the inherited psyche. Perched precariously in our garden hedge among the branches that tussle and bend in the wind, there is long-abandoned twiggy nest. It feels like a privilege that a woodpigeon or sparrow decided that this place was home and toiled back and forth with sticks, feathers and bits of moss to raise a family. Each spring I wonder if a new bird will move in, gather its own leaves and twigs, and transform it into a home.

How do they find their way here, these creatures that populate the skies and earth? A complicated invisible forcefield of magnetic energy, patterns of light, polarization, the position of the stars and sun – all creating a map by which they navigate. They voyage mysteriously through the world in a manner that makes our reliance on our multi-voiced satnavs all the more pitiful. A honeybee communicates a source of pollen through a dance that shows where the flower is in relation to the sun. The Clark's nutcracker, native to North America, hides food supplies at various points over 100 square miles and imprints the geometrical patterns created by landmarks around each site to find them again. Ants create a walking map, some counting the steps from their nest, others travelling in ever increasing circles and memorizing the landmarks around their home. Mullet, seals and salmon smell and *feel* their way back home or to breeding sites, creating an olfactory map on their outward journey that is so deeply imprinted in their memories they can tap into it on their way back.

Take the story of a sheepdog who escaped from his new home in Cumbria and over two weeks navigated the 240 miles back to his original home in Wales. Was he using the same patterns of smell to track his journey back to the familiar air of his old farm? I imagine how it might be to move through the world, separating locations according to scents. Would the air here smell of grass, hops, salt and petrol? As well as their own combination of smells, different places even have individual *sounds*, imperceptible to the human ear. An infrasonic hum deep in the belly of the earth emanates from vibrations on the ocean floor, creating a frequency and sound that pigeons are thought to use as a means of navigation. Aboriginal peoples in Australia create songlines that reflect the spirits of a place and connect them with the cardinal compass points; and the first sailors used the stars and rudimentary navigational instruments to read their way home.

Most of us have forgotten how to tune our senses in to the earth, to use these reactions as signposts and prompts. Many indigenous peoples have no concept of being 'lost', no words for 'left' and 'right', because their bodies are not separate entities existing on a certain plane, but part of the land through which they pass. From detailed oral descriptions of landmarks handed down through generations, to carved wooden 'maps' with notches for every inlet and peninsula along the coastline, humans have created their own memory routes. Using invisible aural maps, the Inuit people of Greenland navigated their coastal waters by learning birdsong, distinguishing the different calls of nesting birds along the shore and heading homeward when they reached the call of their place.

In my years of watching the swifts above the garden, I have only just discovered where they nest nearby. A road around the corner has several nesting boxes. As the birds approach, they gather building materials, ready to breed. I wonder how it must feel to finally be still; whether they experience the strange motion sickness that lingers after you get off a boat, when the ground still buckles as if it is liquid. What would my life be like if I knew I could stop moving? I sometimes feel like the cartoon character who keeps going even though they have run off the edge of a canyon, and only falls when they realize they have run out of ground. If I do not look down, I can keep going. This house is where I have raised my children and come back to from holidays with a sigh of relief. It has become the pause in my flight, but perhaps it suits me that it is only a pause? There is a muscle memory, a twinge that is readying itself to fly. Occasionally, I think about what it would be like to walk out of the front door and just keeping going, my legs not touching the ground again, the rest of my life lived on the wing. Answerable to nothing except the hum of the earth and the patterns of the stars.

*

15 May 2009. We worked very hard again for the Open Garden – about ninety people came. Since then Tom has sawn down most of the lilac, I've put in a delphinium & lupin as the old ones have disappeared. We're planning what to put in the ex-holly ex-lilac corner & clearing around it. Carrots, lettuces, chard, onions, garlic, broad beans doing well. Pear and French beans less so.

*

A pigeon appears at our back door. It walks inside, and my husband shoos it out. It comes back, walks determinedly across the room and hops onto the stairs. Pausing, it looks around and then continues up, going into my bedroom as if it had just got home from a busy day at the office and needed a lie-down. There is a ring on its leg, which I presume means it is a homing pigeon. After some flapping about, it allows my husband to shoo it out again – through the bedroom window this time. I was out when this visitor came, but when he tells me about the pigeon, I feel strangely moved by its sureness, its confidence that it knew exactly where it needed to go. I think again of the old woman walking into our house, certain that it was hers. A memory of hearing about a previous tenant keeping pigeons in the shed sparks a romantic idea that this pigeon has been lost for over a decade and has finally found its way home. But it was probably just curious. I still look out for it now, though, hoping that one day it will hop up to my desk and find me thinking about migration and homing, and tell me its secrets.

In the village of Ditchling, just eight miles from here, a woman called Len Howard lived in a cottage filled with birds. Howard was a naturalist and amateur ornithologist, and she opened up her house – known locally as Bird Cottage – to the wild birds. She kept the windows ajar all year round and drew pictures of the sparrows, blackbirds, robins and tits that visited. She discouraged human visitors, as they scared the birds, living as a recluse with just her avian companions. Howard got to know the birds so well she said she could distinguish facial expressions – including when they were in love. Imagine that: being able to read a robin's desire in its face, to discern happiness in a tiny winged god.

One afternoon, a jackdaw slams into the bedroom window, in front of my face, and the sound echoes across the glass. A clamour in the apple tree reveals a group of other jackdaws, alerted by the bang. What did this visitation bring? A warm, slow wind from the hills; a warning; a plot; an opportunity; wet, black rain; an oil slick; a peppercorn eye. I look for a mark on the windowpane, a shadow of splayed feathers and bone, but there is no trace.

*

Builders and decorators are suddenly everywhere, with half-drunk cups of tea and strange flattened pencils. The house is being patched up, painted and plastered. The papering over and sealing up of its crumbling, tired old bones sparks fears in me that the rent will go up or the house will again go on the market, with a facelift this time. These changes are surely not for our benefit. I remember Vanessa Bell's approach to tenanthood and try to enjoy the improvements and accept the not-knowing.

The garden is the perfect place to practise this noticing and embracing of change. There are so many transformations taking place at any one time. The morning dew disappears without trace, fleeting and silent. Silver beads hang on the hazel branches waiting to unfold. A painted lady butterfly lingers briefly on my chard: its journey – from egg to caterpillar, then wrapped in its silky sarcophagus and finally, brilliantly, emerging as colour manifest as wings of dust, as lightness and thirst – is full of potential dangers. And yet, there it sits, its wings pulsing softly in the sunshine.

I find increasing peace in this thought: the garden will continue if we leave – *when* we leave – even if it takes on a new shape. The next tenant might turf over the flower beds or build new raised beds where our trampoline once stood like a flapping monument to past childish joy. They may hate gardening and instead leave the place to 'rewild' itself, giving it over to the brambles and dock. New chickens will rootle around for worms and grass. Weeds I have tried to supress will lie dormant, biding their time. The land might be sold and built over, but something of my time in the garden will remain beneath the soil. I will carry the things I have learned out here with me to my next house, making a fresh start if I am lucky enough to move somewhere with a garden, and planting traces of this unlikely paradise in pots or window boxes if not.

*

The natural world, of course, is in perpetual motion, adapting constantly to changes in climate or habitat, until those changes are impossible to live with. Often, these alterations are driven by human behaviour, forcing animals to learn new survival techniques or develop different strengths. Long-tailed macaques in Thailand have learned to apply their dexterous use of rocks for cracking mollusc shells to opening the palm nuts that grow on palm oil plantations. Chimpanzees in Guinea and Uganda have adapted their feeding habits to forage for cultivated crops as well as wild food sources. Urban great tits have been shown to use a higher pitch in their calls than their rural counterparts, in order to be heard above the traffic noise. Nothing is static and nothing remains the same.

Yet there are deeper, ongoing cycles beneath these changes that offer reassurance to the rootless or uncertain. The turning of the seasons – from the abundance of summer to the shedding of autumn and the bareness of winter to the burst of fresh life in spring – and the setting and rising of the sun are certainties that give me solace. I am drawn to my garden for the incantations of infinite repetitions – the same small tasks to complete every year, like washing out the seed trays at the end of winter, or cutting back dead growth; the same plants recurring over and over, yet never exactly the same, even from one moment to the next as the light changes or their colours shift or a bee lightens their nectar load; the swifts repeating their migratory journeys, summer after summer, spring after spring. Then there are the repetitions of grief, the incessant echoes of absence and the dull reverberation of loss. Living with change and uncertainty is challenging. I am not good at it. But it is the marrow of life, learning to manage transitions and flux. Like Larkin's trees we must 'Begin afresh, afresh, afresh.'

11

WORDS

A SWIFT DIVES LOW OVER THE GARDEN, SHOWING ITS DOLPHIN-SLEEK underbelly. Tonight is the Flower Moon, calling to mind the poet Mary Ruefle's observation, 'Nothing, it seems, makes the living as happy as a flower. Flowers are among the most anticipated things on earth.' This sense of anticipation is what is so intoxicating – and distracting – about gardening. Out here, I can forget the latest wrangling between the agent and the builders. Instead, I wander amongst the beetles and weeds, with meringue-peaked clouds melting into a sky made from layers of cigarette ash, washing into pink and then the palest eggshell blue that contains just a whisper of the heat of the day, the clearness and brilliance of it.

A soft dusk. I can hear the chickens taking themselves off to bed, hopping onto their wooden steps with a plump thud, shaking their feathers and chirruping before taking up their positions inside the coop. I sit at the back of the garden. Perhaps if I stay here still and long enough, the ground elder will slowly engulf me, making me part of the garden itself. I think of the jobs that need doing tomorrow: potting on the cosmos seedlings, weeding, planting out the courgettes. I like catching glimpses of people working in their gardens – a flash of secateurs as you stop at traffic lights, a man kneeling in service to his petunias, a woman in a hat briskly plucking something from the ground as your train creeps past. There is an unspoken, private purposefulness; we busy ourselves with only we know what.

The sparrows are squabbling in the plum tree, thrumming up into the air all at once and then clattering across the garden. I notice that the broad beans are flowering, their delicate pink and black petals adding an unusual darkness to the garden. Soon these will stretch into velvet-lined pods – the 'blankety beds' my children sang about every year at their school's harvest-festival assembly. Behind the beans the fig tree branches are bushing out, sheltering the puckered fruits underneath. From here the house looks smaller than it is. I think back to how unloved it was when we first arrived; how, for all our cursing its cold and damp, we have brought it to life.

The previous tenant told me it was freezing here in winter, so I bought everyone woollen thermals to protect them from the draughts. Back then, our four young children were growing as fast as our debts. We expanded into the space, loving the high ceilings, but most of all the garden. The children bundled noisily about, making a playroom of the garden. This was before the magnetic pull of computer and phone screens anchored them inside. There were endless days when they wrestled on the trampoline, flinging each other around, often wearing capes or costumes, my daughter delighting in the joy of having three older brothers bouncing her into the air with their jumps. As they landed, the energy was exchanged and sent her flying up, then she tumbled back down as they launched into the air again. The garden was the backdrop for outdoor science experiments, water-pistol wars, pizzas round a fire, camping out in the tent.

I loved having a kitchen full of children, making pastry stars and painting with potatoes, reading the same reassuring bedtime stories, folding four little dressing gowns, and hearing the sound of bare feet padding along the landing. I had chosen to surround myself with people, had put myself at the centre of their world, blurring my edges. With this happy melee came plenty of moments of fury and utter, bone-deep exhaustion. There is a short story by Helen Simpson in which she describes how a mother 'had broken herself into little pieces like a biscuit and now was scattered all over the place'. Sometimes I felt like a tiny pile of crumbs. When I needed help, my mother would come and stay, bringing old margarine tubs filled with redcurrants or gooseberries, and shopping bags containing muddy, snail-nibbled lettuce from her garden. Together we would tackle the garden here, working quietly side by side, pulling weeds or dividing clumps of snowdrops. As our hands busied themselves, I would wonder if she saw God in this place, in these snowdrops. I wondered what it must be like to see Heaven where I see only light and amniotic clouds. We divided plants like cells. It was at the outside table that we talked about her terminal illness, my daughter wriggling on my lap as my mother gave me a small piece of yellow paper on which she had written a prayer. *I will leave, and you will be OK*, she seemed to be saying with each fold of the paper. Around us the garden – nature, life – carried on relentlessly.

*

30 May 2011. We were away for three weeks. April was v. hot & dry, May dry & warm. Many new plants (annuals, beans) died for lack of water while we were away. Mowed grass & daffodils, huge weeds to pull out all over veg

*garden. Irises just about over, roses, peony, weigela all
lovely.*

*18 May 2012. March warm & sunny, April cold & wet.
Mike has finished the new seating area & grass is growing
patchily where two veg beds were. I mowed down the
daffodils this week. Still eating chard, rest of veg a bit slow
& disappointing. Abutilon & citrus pots out now, but still
v. cold nights.*

*

I cannot separate these memories or my sense of who I am and
have been from the house, the garden. As humans, all our stories
are inextricably interconnected with nature and the landscape.
We don't need to 'get back into nature', because we are *part* of it.
We have always known this, but often forget it. Ancient myths and
folk tales are full of transmutations – a forest hag with lion's claws,
a man with skin mottled like a magpie, Daphne transforming
into a tree to escape Apollo, or melting ice vapour that turns
into men. Myths tell of lands made from the flesh of slain giants,
whose bones became mountains; of underground hill-folk and
cave-dwelling giantesses; of the queen who lived inside a duck's
egg; of the garden of Eden and mankind's Fall. Our ancestors
looked to the landscape for explanations. They wove the world
around them into narratives of birth and conquest and creation:
the forests, corn stalks, holy trees, rimy ice-cold streams, hawks,
witches, the moon, ice, honeydew, bone ladders, milk-white mares
and gloom. The earth has given us stories for as long as we have
communicated.

The garden has its own particular vocabulary – its litany of Latin and traditional folk names casts a kind of spell even before you understand how the words relate to what you see growing. I try to learn the names of wildflowers, birds and new plants: devil downhead, moonpenny, *Papaver orientale*, fairy lace. These words contain the unfolding story of my garden: the food to come; the sudden visitors to the bird bath; the bunches of flowers standing on mantelpieces and tables; the histories of past triumphs and failures written into each patch of soil.

As Emily Dickinson gardened while everyone else slept, she tended plants and flowers that would find their way into her poetry, as motifs and metaphors. She described herself as 'a Lunatic on Bulbs', and often represented herself as a daisy or clover in her work. A keen botanist, Dickinson collected plants and stored them in a herbarium that contained over 400 specimens. Despite rarely leaving her home in Massachusetts, she had a conservatory where she grew exotic plants so she could travel 'virtually'. It was pulled down after her death, but recent excavations as part of a restoration project have revealed its foundations. The project will recreate the garden as Dickinson knew it, including typical cottage-garden plants like hollyhocks, iris and phlox, as well as more exotic species. We know that around the house were orchards, long flower beds and vegetable beds. There was a summerhouse covered in roses, which also feature frequently in her work. Dickinson's garden and her imagination and her poetry spring from the same creative soil.

Another poet, Elizabeth Bishop, was also a keen gardener. She saw the messiness and danger of nature, and seemed stifled by its relentless recurrent patterns. But she also drew comfort and inspiration from the plants and landscape around her. In 'Vague Poem', she uses roses to describe a lover's body, likening the folds of the vulva to the petals on a rose. Desire here, for Bishop, is crystalline, buried like geological layers, difficult to extract, but blazing and luminous when held up to the light. Bishop's reflections on nature are imbued with darkness and a strong sense of physicality. With her troubled past and battles with alcohol addiction, she was not always in control of her body or her mind, aware of the hidden forces and the power of the unseen. In her poetry, she explores the boundaries between self and surroundings, depicting nature as the mother that threatens to engulf and destroy her, but also as a source of inspiration and intimacy.

Dickinson and Bishop both wrote from a point of immediate physical connection to the places they loved and lived in. But places can exert just as powerful an influence if they exist only in memory or the imagination. Daphne du Maurier often dreamed of her house, Menabilly, in Cornwall (the inspiration for Manderley), and was filled with sadness and grief when she woke up to find she was not there. Out of this burning absence came her greatest novel: *Rebecca*. Similarly, Katherine Mansfield, despite never entirely shaking off the pull of her birthplace, Wellington, New Zealand, describes a house called 'Isola Bella', near the French-Italian border, as 'the first real home of my own I've ever loved'. She fell heavily for the south of France – the sea, the mimosa and tangerine trees – but did not stay there long. She left for Switzerland in 1921, suffering from the tuberculosis that would eventually kill her. Just before her death in 1923, aged thirty-four, she wrote, 'I simply pine for the S. of France.' Forever nursing a sense of rootlessness, Mansfield's writing became a way to inhabit these places she longed for but was unable to reach.

When Voltaire was exiled from France, he set up home in Genoa, with a fervent desire to create a magnificent garden. He wrote to his agent asking for 'artichoke bulbs and as much as possible of lavender, thyme, rosemary, mint, basil, strawberry bushes, pinks, thadicee, balm, tarragon, sariette, burnet, sage and hyssop to clean our sins'. He was enacting a vision of simplicity and oneness, where the borders between indoors and outside were blurred, and as he cultivated his garden, he became more compassionate towards the fates of others. He understood what it meant for people to be forcibly removed from their homes, imagining how it might feel if he were wrenched from his garden. His well-known phrase, '*Il faut cultiver notre jardin*' ('We must cultivate our garden') has been translated to mean 'We must work our fields,' and, 'We must build a better place by love.'

*

7 May 2013. Everything v. late after long, cold winter. Mike & Mary weeded the path and the edges today & things look tidy. Daffs just about over, plum & pear blossom beautiful. I planted Pam's osmanthus under Anne's tree.

16 May 2014. First rose out before first peony.

*

I have begun dreaming of a writing shed, a space in the garden that is wholly and indisputably mine. On a holiday in Wales a few years back, we visited Laugharne, in Carmarthenshire, and I spent a long time looking at Dylan Thomas's writing studio, imagining what I could create if only I had the physical and mental space. The image of this place stayed with me, and I began hunting down other writers' garden rooms or outside places. Whilst the art studio and rooms of Charleston are evocative places, still humming with the energy of those who lived there before, it is sheds – liminal, less clearly defined spaces – that really capture my interest. George Bernard Shaw had his built on a rotating podium so he could track the sun. Roald Dahl's writing hut, which he described as 'a place for dreaming and floating and whistling in the wind, as soft and silent and murky as a womb', was inspired by his own visit to Laugharne, and has been meticulously recreated at the Roald Dahl Museum in Great Missenden, complete with his removed hip bone and other writing talismans.

One of the most well-known writing sheds is Virginia Woolf's 'lodge' in the garden at Monk's House, East Sussex. The first time I went to look round I was dismayed to find the house and gardens were closed to visitors. Making do with a peripheral view, I walked through the churchyard and looked over the wall into the garden. You can get right up close to the writing shed without crossing any boundaries, and I sat under the horse-chestnut tree that spills over the wall, thinking about her work and imagining her sitting at the desk that she describes as 'full of character, trusty, discreet, very reserved'. I wondered if these are the key components required of a place to write. For Woolf, the view, the garden and her lodge provided the right balance of peace and creative inspiration.

It was in a garden as a young girl that she had an epiphany. Gazing at a flower, she had a forceful and glorious realization, recounted in *Moments of Being*: '"That is the whole," I said. I was looking at a plant with a spread of leaves; and it seemed suddenly plain that the flower itself was a part of the earth; that a ring enclosed what was the flower; and that was the real flower; part earth; part flower.' It was a moment of clarity and reason, a sensation that she would return to as she examined the urge to explain and illuminate the world around her. And later it was to a garden that her husband, Leonard Woolf, would turn in his efforts to keep her alive.

The Woolfs bought Monk's House, in the village of Rodmell, near Lewes, in 1919. It was a weekend and holiday home, a bolthole from London. With its white weatherboard front, oak gate and white rose spilling over the garden wall, it is a modest but beautiful house. The previous owner, Jacob Verrall, was a keen gardener who grew vegetables in tidy rows and looked after the 200-year-old orchard. He kept the rest of the garden more wild, with fruit bushes, cabbages and flowers running into each other. Verrall was left heartbroken and depressed after his wife died in 1915, and it is said that he slowly starved himself to death, despite the abundance around him. A strange foreshadowing, perhaps, of what this garden and house would later see.

When Leonard and Virginia Woolf arrived, the garden contained several old walls – ruined piggeries, a granary, a laundry and an earth closet. Virginia initially set up her writing desk in the old tool shed but later they built her lodge at the back of the orchard. From her bedroom, she looked out through curls of climbing rose onto asparagus beds, a cutting patch and Leonard's espaliered fruit trees.

There he is, in a tweed waistcoat and wide-legged trousers, his gangly body stretching up to puff toxic clouds of insecticide into the apple trees. His head turns in the direction of the church beyond the garden, where a bell is tolling at the funeral of a local man. He sees a great owl flap out of the ivy on the church tower. This feathered ghost silently skims above the orchard and lifts over the house, clasping the dead man's soul in its talons. Each morning Virginia 'surges' across the garden to write, cigarette in hand, settling into her shed, where she will create some of her most brilliant works, amongst the apples, long grass and cackling rooks. A tobacco tang lingers in the air behind her, her footsteps darkening the damp grass.

*

More than any other I have visited, the garden at Monk's House feels full of ghosts. I am not sure if this is connected to Virginia's death by suicide in the River Ouse nearby, or whether there is something particular about the place that retains its past so close to the surface. When I return, having checked the opening times, I'm ushered first into the house. A knowledgeable guide tells me about the green-painted sitting room and Leonard Woolf's 'fish hospital', in which poorly fish were brought from the pond to recuperate. Walking through the quiet house, there is none of the ebullience of Charleston, but a more measured feeling – partly due to the more straightforward decoration and furniture, but also, I think, because it still holds something of the sadnesses it has witnessed. In Virginia's bedroom, accessed by its own door, which gives it a separateness and even greater sense of being a private space, I feel like an interloper, and am eager to leave. Bedrooms are intimate places – we are born, make love, dream, die in them. It feels wrong to be in here. Besides, the garden is calling.

As I step outside the bedroom, I am struck by the scent of what smells like jasmine but is in fact a lilac. The garden at Monk's House is laid out in a similar way, if on a smaller scale, to Vita Sackville-West's garden at Sissinghurst. Leonard Woolf used the same idea of garden 'rooms' to create areas with different atmospheres and emphases. These sections are linked by brick paths and landscaped areas, often using relics of the garden's history, like the mill stones set into the corners of a terrace, or the flint walls that create more formal boundaries. I want to see the writing shed first, so I head along wobbly brick paths between low walls covered with ivy and clematis, past the contemplative busts of the Woolfs beneath a magnolia tree, and out into the orchard. The twenty-four apple trees produced plenty of fruit, which Leonard stored in a loft above Virginia's wooden writing hut. He also donated apples to the village children to stop them scrumping over the garden walls. The wind is always blowing here, adding its insistent susurration to the soundscape. I follow a curving path cut in the grass, moving past beehives, buttercups and bluebells through longer grass dotted with white daffodils.

At the far corner, under the chestnut tree, and buffeted by clouds of cow parsley, is Virginia Woolf's lodge. The large desk in the middle of the room faces the doors, looking out on the garden and hills beyond. She was untidy (she wrote in her diary that 'The litter in this room is so appalling it takes me five minutes to find my pen') and, although the lodge is neat and orderly now, I imagine it strewn with cigarette butts, books, paper clips and pots filled with purple ink. There is a low chair on which she would sit to write, resting a notebook she had bound and covered herself on a sheet of plywood on her lap. Stacked up against one wall are a set of deckchairs, ready to set out on the paved area in front when friends came to visit. It is as if she has just left the room, scraping her glasses off her nose, rubbing her eyes and lighting a cigarette before flinging open the doors and glancing across to Firle Beacon and the valley below, where her sister exploded paint onto canvas.

Beyond the writing shed is the bowling lawn, a large grass area with a dew pond and flower beds. Two elm trees, named 'the Woolfs', are long gone, but would have stood like keepers of the garden. Through a small hedge lies the kitchen garden, now allotments for the villagers. It is neatly divided into segments, each looking well cared-for and productive. I feel Leonard Woolf would approve. His garden journal, begun in 1919, reveals just how bountiful the garden was in their time at Monk's House, until the entries stop in 1956. In this tatty brown notebook, now with a faded red spine, bare and spilling its fibres, he lists the amount of produce and how much the surplus was sold for. There are lists of irises and fruit trees. He meticulously notes the expenditure on garden books, seeds, plants and the wages of Percy Bartholomew, the gardener who helped him for almost twenty years.

Alongside the garden journal, we can also read Leonard Woolf's diary – a pale green, less battered notebook in which he notes his observations of the garden and life at Monk's House, beginning in 1920. We see him planting potatoes, digging up the grass around the fruit trees to plant bulbs, sowing lupins and nasturtiums, rejoicing in his zinnias and gladioli, and observing the first swallow of the year sitting on the clothes line. He also records the failures: potato blight, drought, gales, incessant rain. The entries in this diary become sparser as the years pass, ending with a paragraph per year, mostly recording the weather and significant events. It ends with a garden wish list:

Dazla rose
Crimson King clematis
Cardinal poppies
Carnations

While her husband very much controlled the planning and overall layout, Virginia also enjoyed working in the garden. She describes 'weeding all day to finish the beds in a queer sort of enthusiasm which made me say this is happiness' and was inspired by what she called 'the shape and fertility and wildness of the garden'. Her works feature ninety-three different types of flower – the garden finding its way into her prose. Leonard saw the countryside and their garden as a place of healing for his wife. He would bring her to Monk's House for respite from the hurly-burly of London or when she suffered episodes of depression or mental ill health.

Amongst the bees, asparagus, apples and tulips, her mind slowly came back into balance and her torments receded. She bottled fruit, wrote letters and lay in the garden until the storms passed. But she also missed the excitement and social life of London, sometimes feeling smothered by the quiet. There was a tension between what she describes as 'enjoying this immortal rhythm in which both soul and eye are at rest', and feeding off the creativity and vitality of the city. As wartime approached, the Woolfs spent more time in Rodmell, watching warplanes skim low with a 'cadaverous twanging' as they passed over on the way to bomb London. When Hitler was about to give a speech on the radio, Virginia called Leonard in from the garden to listen. But he refused, saying, 'I shan't come. I'm planting iris and they will be flowering long after he is dead.' He knew that garden time transcends worldly time.

The garden was also a great source of comfort for him. Out here he would escape fears about the war, work through his worries about Virginia's health, and relax a little from the state of high alert he constantly maintained for signs that she might try to kill herself.

This is part of the appeal of gardens for me: as I try to help my children navigate their own struggles and pain – whilst also knowing that I am completely unable to control the outcomes – the garden often feels like a space where I can, for a time, lower my emotional vigilance. I find myself furiously pruning or pulling up weeds, seeking solace and reassurance in the new growth my trimming will stimulate, or in the seedlings that will come. At other times, the garden is a haven for the rest of the family. Whether they are easing a sense of panic by sitting and listening to the birds, or thwacking the punchbag hanging in the shed, it contains our emotions and provides a space to work things out. Thanks to the walls and hedge, it has always felt like a safe place, where the worst that could happen was a scuffed knee or nettle sting. I realize how much I have looked to the garden as a place of comfort. I can understand Leonard Woolf's urge to cosset Virginia, to hide her away from harm in a garden filled with life. In her last diary entry before she jumped into the River Ouse, pockets filled with stones, she wrote, 'L is doing the rhododendrons.' Her ashes were buried under one of the elm trees in the garden.

After his wife's death, Leonard remained at Monk's House. He fell in love with the (complicatedly married) artist Trekkie Parsons, wooing her by leaving boxes of fruit, flowers and letters on her doorstep. Parsons was also a keen gardener, and their relationship, though platonic, flourished. Botany and gardening was their connection, and when Leonard died in 1969 he left her the house. He believed that 'What has the deepest and most permanent effect upon oneself and one's way of living is the house in which one lives. The house determines the day-to-day, minute-by-minute quality, colour, atmosphere, pace of one's life.' It is clear that Monk's House – and its garden – was not only a touchstone in his life, but it shaped who he was. His ramshackle greenhouse, full of huge, glossy tropical plants bursting through the windows, and the beds stuffed with flowers ensure his spirit lives on in the garden.

Before I head back to my car, I stand on the terrace, close my eyes and imagine Virginia Woolf walking through the walled garden, across the dew-spangled orchard, grabbing an apple from a tree where Leonard is planting crocus and narcissi, and striding into her cabin. A loud song thrush in the trees beside the lane sings me home.

*

Five cirrus clouds daub the sky, as if a painter had dipped her brush in water and cleaned it on the cerulean blue background. A magpie *ack-acks* in the elder, hopping to the top, turning its head to follow the calls of a nearby crow. He glides off into the car park next door. They seem so purposeful, all these birds, as if they always know exactly where they are going and why. I sit in indolence, working my pen, turning my face to the sun to bleach my vision. Slowly, evening folds itself over the garden. Inside, my family are having baths, staring at screens, drinking coffee, petting the dog, clearing away the supper. This house has become a strange but precious receptacle for all the stuff of our small lives. It is as if simply by living in this place we have become like smooth, worn grooves in the floorboards. I remember being struck by the way a stone step into the local church, where I sometimes go to light a candle for my mother, has been dented and polished by the feet of generations of worshippers. Our routines, our repetitions, our patterns; I cannot see how they will fit anywhere else.

I cut some youngish nettles to make soup, sink hedge cuttings into the ground next to a row of pea seedlings as supports, and wind netting between two poles for my climbing beans. I am creating structure, form and scaffolds for my young plants, a backbone for the garden. It gets too dark to work so I put down my tools and look skywards. Venus hangs high behind the wall, crisp and stark and glacier-like, despite its extraordinary heat. It is the brightest thing in the sky after the sun and moon, and it will throw its light into the garden nightly until it is gradually swallowed up by the sun's glare. A day on Venus is the same as a year on earth. The moon is at its furthest point from our planet. Time, once again, feels plastic. Before I go indoors, I pause a moment outside to absorb the sky. There is a strange quality to the air, as if the borders between worlds, time zones, past, future and present have thinned. I wish I could slip away, just for a short while.

*

20 May 2016. Mowed down daffodils. First rose (yellow 'Evelyn') peony & weigela. Bluebells over. Both much enjoying conservatory makeover, sitting & looking at garden. Carrots, lettuce, beetroot sown. Potatoes & beans coming up well. Mike & Mary cut forsythia down to improve view. Irises big & good.

*

Many writers bring gardens into their work. But there is a poet who made a poem out of his. The place is called Little Sparta. Set in the Scottish Pentland Hills amid gorse-filled moors with huge skies,

Little Sparta was created by Ian Hamilton Finlay in 1966. The six-acre garden is the result of his attempt to place language directly into the landscape, making a garden that could be read. Merging quotations from poems with over 200 artworks, architectural forms and sculptures, Little Sparta is a playful manifestation of words made into place. As the present head gardener, George Gilliland, says, 'It's not so much an arrangement of *plants* as it is a placement of *ideas*.' Hamilton Finlay was known as a 'concrete poet', fascinated by the physical shapes of language and words, and by their arrangement on the physical page. Landscape, for him, became simply a page on which to unspool his words.

Little Sparta is based around what seems an eclectic mix of themes: a romantic idea of the sea, Classical culture, the French Revolution and the Second World War. Visitors will find the huge golden head of Apollo bursting from the grass, as if his body is still buried beneath the soil (it reminds me of being buried in sand on the beach, when only your head pokes out and you experience that strange claustrophobia that makes you suddenly jump up and scatter sand everywhere). Like much in the garden, this sculpture is not quite what it seems. It has the words *Apollon Terroriste* carved on its forehead, but it has the face of Saint-Just, the revolutionary whose ideas about living a simple, rural life Hamilton Finlay embraced. Elsewhere Saint-Just's words are inscribed over a gatepost. You will also find a stone bird's nest filled with marble eggs, and Hamilton Finlay's unfinished *Hortus Conclusus*, a space based on the medieval enclosed garden, where a 'cloudpool' reflects the ever-changing shapes of clouds and sky on its surface, with the Latin words for types of cloud engraved around it. A place of and for reflection.

The Garden of the Sea contains the names of boats engraved on the stone pathway and is designed so that the sound of the wind in the trees is like the tide lapping on the shore. A box hedge undulates in waves, while sculptures of warships double as bird baths; stone slabs bear the words for 'wave' in different languages: *wave, vague, woge, onda, unda*. Even the swells and dips in the ground in this section of the garden seem liquid-like.

Near the edge of the garden, Hamilton Finlay installed a broken wooden fence and playfully engraved it with the word 'Picturesque', asking us to question the aesthetics of the landscape we inhabit and the values we place on certain aspects. It is also a nod to eighteenth-century garden designers who used ruins or dead trees to keep things looking 'natural' and not overly sanitized. Hamilton Finlay's interest in war can be seen in the two brick gateposts topped with stone hand grenades, and in an installation called 'Camouflaged Flowers': plinths carved with anagrams of flower names not only pose a mental puzzle for the viewer, they are also warships in disguise, following the tradition of naming these boats after flowers as a contrast to their deadly purpose. He uses tank tracks as woodland paths.

This is a garden created by an agoraphobic, an artist who did not leave this plot of land for thirty years, and who created a work of art that amplifies the landscape, revealing itself gradually. I have never visited Little Sparta, so my experience of it is purely through the prism of a screen and books. Instead of the sensory responses I would have had as I walked round, its complicated ecology lingers in my memory in snapshots and images. Although I am intrigued and beguiled by the ideas behind it, it isn't a garden I want to emulate, in the way that Charleston or Sissinghurst are. It feels as if the point of Little Sparta is to invite us to *read* the garden rather than take notes of planting schemes. Poets use white space and words to choreograph a reader's breath. In his garden, Hamilton Finlay orchestrates our journey through the landscape in the same way as if he were setting out a text on the page.

The more I work on my garden, the more words it gives me. At first I had to look up the names of plants and had trouble identifying things, but now – without even noticing, as if I've learned by osmosis – the names jump into my head. I see a plant with soft green-grey foliage: 'Lamb's ears – *Stachys byzantina*' I hear. Tiny purple flowers creep around the edge of a flower bed: 'Speedwell,' I tell myself, surprised. It feels as though knowing some of these names somehow grants me entry into a kind of club. Of course, clubs of any kind can be as much about exclusion as membership, and it is important that I don't stray into smugness just because I know my comfrey from my borage. But language plays a big part in establishing a sense of belonging, and being able to identify and name the plants around me gives me a greater sense of being at home here. I open a seam and pour language in.

The Latin versions of horticultural names can feel stuffy and elitist, but I have become fascinated with folk and traditional names for flowers and plants. There is a lyricism and darkness in these ancient words. Take cow parsley, the foamy umbels that are currently dancing around the edge of my garden. Other names it goes by are: 'cow muddle', 'mother-die', 'keck', 'wild-beaked parsley', 'fairy lace', 'badman's oatmeal', 'rabbit meat'. The local Sussex name for it is 'scabby hands'. Comfrey is known as 'knitbone', and borage as 'starflower' – so much more appealing and visceral than *Symphytum* and *Borago officinalis*. I discover the Sussex dialect words for 'mud':

Gawm
Swank
Stug
Slough
Slab
Pug
Slurry
Gubber
Ike
Stoach
Sleech
Stodge
Clodgy

Each one feels like it applies to my garden at different times of year – the *slurry* of the chicken's pen after days of rainfall; the *slab* of ridges of frosted mud; the *gubber* that sends you sliding sideways; the *stoach* that sucks at your wellies. The words play on the tongue and create a poem of specificity and shared experience. We have heard about the multiple Inuit words for snow, but there are interesting conceptual connections in indigenous languages that shed light on how people place themselves within their surroundings. For example, the Apache Ndee language has a word that means both 'land' and 'mind' – *ni*. Place and thought are inseparable. In Mojave tradition, maps are made of songs. They describe movements across and around a place, using words to transverse memory and time. For the Inuit Anouk people, ideas like 'sleep' and 'weather' are alive.

There is an undoubted pleasure in being able to share the language of landscape and gardens with others in our community, and across history. We learn from mistakes and create stories that tell us about our place. We learn to exist within a garden's inherent transience and incompleteness – its eloquence derives from this very fleetingness. I work from side to side, front to back, repeating and returning. Like alliteration and poetry, the recurrences and replications of the garden create a rhythm of their own. It is quiet work, tending this garden, a creative artistry over which I have little control – the kind of artwork where your materials can transform into other matter or fly away, where plants are creative beings in their own right. Like the swifts splicing a familiar sky, our words track and wheel and circle back. Here, shifting between its constantly changing present, its deep past and the cycles of the future, is my garden.

JUNE

12

HEALING

See. There are elderflowers that need picking. My daughter stands below me as I balance on the log store snipping great foamy white flowers and watching them fall softly, like huge snowflakes, into the colander she is clutching. I feel like I am plucking dollops of scented stars from the sky and passing them down to her. We take our bounty of sunlight and stars into the kitchen and shake off any creatures, trying not to dislodge too many tiny blooms. These flowers have been used for generations – foraged, distilled and steeped into home remedies by women who understood their healing properties. They heated elder and plantain leaves, ground ivy and wormwood and mixed them with oil or wax to rub onto aching arthritic joints. They brewed light, floral teas and spooned the liquid between the lips of loved ones suffering from chest infections. They ladled sweet, sticky syrups into jars to preserve and store. My daughter and I, as thousands of female hands have done before us, stir the flowers with lemons, sugar, citric acid and water. We feel like witches. The pan sits for a day, concentrating the flavour and scents, and then we strain it into two bottles. Later in the year, in the chill, damp gloom of winter, we will pour this sweet cordial onto our tongues and taste the summer.

*

*I June 2004. As we leave for Greece, garden for once is
tidy & splendid. Veg in fairly weed-free loaves [?], roses
beautiful (old musk rose & peony & philadelphus all out
today). Irises have been stunning. New space under lilac
planted up & annuals sown.*

*

I come across a story in which a Romany woman advised the
parents of a wounded soldier, blinded at Dunkirk in 1940, to apply
elder blossom to his eyes. At first the flowers made his eyes hurt
even more, and his parents stopped the treatment. But the woman
persuaded them to continue, and after some time he suddenly
saw a flash of light from his mother's wedding ring. His vision was
eventually completely restored. It is such a comforting idea that
by observing and understanding the plants around us, by learning
what they can do, when is the best time to sow and harvest them,
and how to prepare them, we can improve both our physical and
our mental health.

On one of my regular dog walks, I pass through the ruins of a
medieval priory, destroyed in the sixteenth century during the
dissolution of the monasteries. The stone foundations and some
of the walls remain, an echo of the impressive building that once
looked proudly over the marshes and woodlands. In the 1980s, a
group of local historians and school students recreated the monks'
herb garden, using surviving manuscripts and information from
similar monasteries, which often had physic or medicinal gardens

close to their infirmaries. As well as medicinal plants, the garden includes herbs that would have been used in cooking, for making dyes and in religious ceremonies. When my children were little, we spent a lot of time playing amongst these ruins and running in circles around the raised beds of the herb garden, planted with fennel, chamomile, hyssop, blackthorn, blue iris, wormwood, yarrow, chervil, violets and bay, along with many other species. Small arms brushed past the plants, which would give up their scents as the children looked for a hiding place amongst the foliage.

In the Middle Ages, when the original priory garden was flourishing, the practice of medicine in Britain was changing. Until then, women had worked as healers and midwives for thousands of years, using their knowledge of home remedies to treat their families and communities, grinding up lavender and rosemary to make poultices for wounds and swellings, brewing borage teas to reduce fevers, or infusing raspberry leaves to prepare the body for childbirth. But from the fourteenth century onwards, medicine became more regulated and a formal education was required in order to work as a healer. Apothecaries became the recognized providers of medicine and were required to undergo a seven-year apprenticeship in physic gardens and herbalism, as well as studying for exams. They learned to make powders from dried leaves, stems and flowers; use solvents to create essences; and make syrups and tinctures, just as healers had done for generations. But they were mostly men. Across Europe, women were excluded from the new universities so those interested in medicine – or who needed to make money from selling remedies – were forced to work illegally.

The Royal College of Physicians (founded in 1518 to regulate medical practice) was hostile to the apothecaries, whom they often regarded as charlatans, and they actively prosecuted 'illicit' female healers. Punishments for women found illegally practising medicine included punitive fines, flagellation, excommunication and banishment from their communities. This developed into systematic persecution and witch hunts, which resulted in the torture and killing of an estimated 50,000 women between the 1450s and the middle of the eighteenth century on suspicion of carrying out the work of the Devil. Midwifery became a dangerous job – any stillbirth, or a mother dying in childbirth, could be cited as an example of the midwife's satanic motives. Even arriving early to see a patient could be attributed to travel by broomstick and denounced as witchcraft. The narrative of women being more susceptible to the Devil was reinforced by the Church, but women who joined nunneries or abbeys were able to grow and administer herbs as part of their ministry. Across Europe, during the Middle Ages and the Early Modern period, 'sisters' used herbal remedies to prepare patients for the afterlife and to offer comfort in their illness.

What is this female affinity with herbs and bodies? In part, women may have felt uncomfortable going to men with intimate health issues, particularly in highly religious or segregated societies. Women, not men, would attend other women in labour. Women nursed each other's children – in both senses of the word: giving milk to, and providing care and treatment. As herbs are also used for culinary purposes, it makes sense that the people who did most of the cooking would also have the most extensive knowledge of how to grow and prepare them. It is only a small step from grinding spices to smear over a joint of meat to pounding dried bark and leaves to make a medicinal powder.

Inspired by all these women, and in the hope of healing some of my family's ills, I decide to create a medicinal herb patch. Knowledge of herbs has been passed down the female line in families and through indigenous and nomadic peoples, but I have little experience of herbalism aside from the homeopathic remedies I turned to when my babies were teething or not sleeping. So I buy some books, and every page feels like an induction into an ancient kind of magic that has been right in front of my eyes all this time. I clear a patch of ground next to the chicken run. It is a spot that gets some sun but is also partially shady, so it feels a good place to start. I plant a pulsatilla, bought from a local nurserywoman (which I plan to brew into a tea to relieve anxiety). In trays indoors, I sow meadowsweet (to soothe nausea), wormwood (which I discover was used in ink to prevent mice eating documents and letters – a preserver of words), feverfew (for my migraines), chamomile (for skin rashes, and to help everyone relax) and fennel (to ease heartburn). I buy a pole to fix across the space under the stairs, where the dog sleeps, to hang and dry the herbs.

In the garden, I will also harvest the herbalist's established plants and make sure they flourish. Armed with more knowledge, I go to find them: rosemary at the front of the house (for headaches and muscle pain), pulmonaria next to the pond (for coughs and bronchitis), a witch hazel (astringent leaves used for wounds and swellings), borage near the back wall (supports the adrenals and can reduce fever), cranesbill in the side bed (another astringent, good for treating diarrhoea), yarrow (for fevers), daisies (for coughs and catarrh), marigold (for wounds and sprains), and peppermint (relieves anxiety and soothes the digestive system). These plants have been here all this time, and I am only just learning about their powers. It feels good to be doing something that might help ease some of my family's pains and problems.

As well as healing properties, herbs have a strong spiritual significance in many cultures. For example, rue was chosen as a blessing by the prophet Muhammad and is grown by some Muslims to provide protection for their homes. Bay was regarded as sacred by the Ancient Greeks, and the Romans saw it as a symbol of peace and victory. Rosemary has traditionally been seen as the herb of remembrance and love. Both rosemary and bay grow at the front of our house; I once spoke to a neighbour who confessed to picking bay leaves as she passed by, and it made me happy to think of this wildly overgrown tree bringing flavour and peace and triumph to her dishes. Since the fifteenth century, people have given 'tussie mussies' – small bouquets of herbs, foliage and flowers – to loved ones or the sick, and in Victorian Britain the 'language of flowers' became a craze, with symbolic blooms used to convey secret love messages.

There are also many dangerous and toxic plants that the novice herb-dabbler must be wary of. I remember scouring the paddock next to our farmhouse as a child, to check for ragwort that might poison my new pony; and the time when my son, aged about three, put some yew berries in his mouth – a quick-thinking older child immediately told him to spit them out, but we took him to hospital just in case he had swallowed some. He spent a few hours running up and down the corridors and eating jam sandwiches, until they finally let us go. It was a frightening lesson in human vulnerability.

*

I have noticed as I reach middle age that I want to be alone more – not just the familiar yearning for some peace that comes with living in a large family, but a deep need for solitude. Unlike the limpet melding itself to its home, my body is developing a new shape, curving away from the familiar rock. And yet I am striving with all my being to stay, to keep my home. What *is* this home I am fighting for? I am only now seeing that this is part of my work – to reimagine a future and grow it. My place as a woman in the world is in flux, and my garden is becoming a refuge from all that. It gives me space without demanding anything in return. It lets me nurture it with no expectations, and it will carry on if I stop tending it. I go into it tired and overwhelmed, and come out of it replenished. There is a simplicity of indifference out here that is missing in my relationships with my family. I can exist in my contradictory states of fight and flight.

13

LIGHT

NEARLY SUMMER SOLSTICE. FULLNESS. ABUNDANCE. RIPENESS.

The gooseberries are ready for picking. Plump and purple, oozing flesh, some have impaled themselves on the thorns of the drooping branches. It is dangerous work this, trying to avoid the spikes as I pick. Next: the strawberries. But as I reach down to each ruby jewel, they disintegrate in my hands, melting into nothingness. Too much rain. Too many hungry woodlice. My fingers go right through their soft bodies. The prairie area is looking more successful: tall grasses ripple and dance, dotted with the starry umbels of the *Ammi majus*, and echoing the sound of the summer wind. I dig up the first early potatoes. But I am a little disappointed: only four potatoes from three plants. There are lots of smaller tubers, so I wonder if I am digging them up too early. Perhaps my no-dig patch needed longer to clear itself of weeds.

The solstice: lilac light on leek flowers. A golden, glowering day; from now on light gives way to darkness. It is the beginning of the dying of the days, the time of Joan Didion's long, blue twilights, 'the gloaming, the glimmer, the glitter, the glisten, the glamour'. It feels too soon. It always feels too soon. There is so much left to do! So many summer days left to enjoy! Just a little longer, let us soak up the sunlight and store it in our veins to warm us through the winter. The sun stands still. I set to a bit of light hoeing, a job that feels like running the hoover round. It gives me a chance to assess the state of the garden. By now the best of the flowers are going over, but the vegetables are giving things a valiant second wind.

A builder lets himself into the garden through the back gate. He has come to take down the scaffolding put up months ago by another builder whose repairs were put on hold by the probate wrangling. Mysteriously this other builder also suddenly appears, and the two men start arguing about who has the right to take down or keep up the scaffolding. They wave their arms at the house and the scuffed scaffold boards before both going away again, leaving the scaffolding in place. Later that same day, a different man rings the doorbell. He has come to inspect the scaffolding on behalf of the landlord. I let him into the garden. My brother's family are visiting and we are having a barbeque. My daughter is teaching my brother to hula hoop. She stands beside us, spinning a hoop on her hips, round and round and round, nonchalantly spiralling her body as the man tells me about his exploits as a sea captain and how this qualifies him to inspect whether the scaffolding is safe or not. The managing agent has condemned it, and it was she who sent the first builder to take it down. The hula hoop turns colourful, hypnotic circles as strangers loop in and out of the garden, deciding its future, while my children clutch plates of salad and burgers and watch, powerless, from the edges.

*

*4 June 2006. At last, some summer sun & today the first
'Mary Rose' came out. And a peony, but the ceanothus is
still the star, along with white irises.*

*

In search of new garden horizons, one afternoon I drive east through
the baking fields of the Weald with a friend to visit Derek Jarman's
garden at Prospect Cottage, Dungeness. On this midsummer day,
tourists troop past the cottage on their way to ride a mini train
around the Dungeness nuclear power station or have a pint under
its towers. The eeriness of this squatting monster gives the whole
place a surreal feeling. A blazing sun blanches the sky and throws
light back off the shingle into my face. I walk around the garden
unsure of where to tread – with no defined boundaries, I feel
suddenly lost and uncontained. A woman stoops to photograph an
orange poppy. There is something sad about this. The poppy itself
is pretty unremarkable, yet she is right up close, as if the fact that
it exists *here* makes it noteworthy. I wonder how Jarman would
have felt about all these strangers poking about in his plants,
pressing sweaty hands against the windows of the cottage to peer
inside. I know he welcomed visitors and encouraged people to take
cuttings, being an unashamed cutting-stealer himself. In spite of
the unease I feel as another ogler of this intimate garden, I think
Jarman would have been pleased to see his creation enjoyed and
celebrated by all these people. As an artist, writer, activist and film-
maker, his adult life was lived in collaboration, with generosity.
The garden is another act of kindness and interaction.

Next door there is an ordinary bungalow, with old cars ricocheting
up the front garden and a washing line strung with flapping

bedlinen. What do the occupants make of the beauty and strangeness across the way? Walking through Jarman's garden, I notice how the gravel eddies and swirls, rather than leading us along formal paths past defined beds. It feels like I am standing in a rock pool with water moving around my feet. There is a seductive flow, a lack of edges and constrictions that feels perfectly fitting, given how Jarman lived his life.

Set in this unlikely pebbly desert in the shadow of a nuclear power station, Jarman's garden became an expression not only of his art but of his childhood memories and his journey with illness. In his beautiful, powerful memoir, *Modern Nature*, he recalls an early enchanting, where gardens implant themselves in his memory: 'Flowers spring up and entwine themselves like bindweed along the footpaths of my childhood.' Jarman grew up in a peripatetic RAF family, often living behind barbed wire, separate and segregated. At the age of four, he began gardening, at the family's house near Lake Maggiore in Italy. When he was five or six he was given a book called *Beautiful Flowers and How to Grow Them*, and from this early start he grew pelargoniums, pumpkins, camellias and mulberries. For him, 'flowers sparkled in my childhood as they do in a medieval manuscript'. These were rare joys in what was an unhappy and repressed early life. He kept all his boyhood gardening tools, and I imagine the wooden handles worn smooth by his hands, the rim of the spade where his boot rested as he levered the earth, the trowel marked by hidden stones as it slapped the ground.

Jarman experienced his first sexual awakenings in the garden too: 'Day after day I returned from the dull regimental existence of my English boarding school to my secret garden . . . here our hands first touched; then I pulled down my trousers and lay beside him.' Unfortunately, his explorations with another boy were discovered and he found himself in exile from not only this secret place but from his own body. These early experiences may have implanted an erotic connection with outdoor spaces, an association between wildness and the expression of desire. Parks, woodlands and gardens have long offered privacy and anonymity for members of the queer community, and, for Jarman, cruising in Epping Forest became a way of disappearing into pleasure. As a young closeted gay man, like thousands of others, he lived a life separated from his true sexuality, hiding a vital part of himself from a hostile world.

In contrast to his fenced-off early years, when Jarman joined the Slade School of Fine Art he came out as gay, and then in 1986 as HIV positive, at a time when this was still seen as a social stigma. He was one of the few public figures who acknowledged their diagnosis. He was not just 'out' but vocally campaigned for gay rights, demanding better HIV research and creating art about sexuality and queerness. Jarman's films fuse myth and history with contemporary storytelling, blurring the lines between past and present in the same way a garden contains echoes and vibrations from across time. This blending of art, politics and his affinity for natural spaces found living form first in the pots and containers he planted with exuberant flowers on the fire escapes and walkways outside his London flat (where he also raised two chestnut trees grown from chestnuts picked at Chekhov's grave), and later in the garden at Prospect Cottage in Dungeness.

He initially came to the beach next to the power station as part of a recce for a film location. When he saw the small fisherman's cottage, with its tar-black cladding and bright yellow woodwork, Jarman impulsively spent his inheritance on it, imagining it as a kind of living backdrop for his films. Captivated by the idea of creating beauty in this strange shingle wilderness that tracks the path of the sun, where salty winds scorch your skin, he decided to make a garden that would thrive in the harshest of places. A garden that would contain the plants he loved as a child but that was also forward-looking. A garden that would reflect his curiosity, courage and openness, that celebrates life and colour and boundless hope. There are no fences here; as Jarman writes, 'My garden's boundaries are the horizon.'

To start creating his garden, he removed two brick-bordered beds at the front of the cottage. He dug manure into the shingle and staked a dog rose to a piece of driftwood he adorned with a pebble necklace. During his walks along the beach, he collected toothlike flints to create informal edging and foraged for strange industrial debris like radar reflectors, anchors, chains and groyne debris. The garden began to emerge, with circles of plants stuck hopefully into the shingle amongst geometric shapes created by standing stones and flints. Circles of gorse and trails of yellow-dusted broom grew alongside irises, poppies, santolina, helichrysum, rue, lavender and marigolds; he planted silvery sea kale at right angles to the shore rather than along it, as the plants would naturally grow; driftwood reached upwards instead of lying horizontal on the shingle as it was when it washed up. Jarman subverted expectations in his garden as much as in his work, and the essential queerness of nature, its plurality and shifting, is the perfect mirror for his art. It is forbidden to import soil into the area, so he filled vegetable and herb beds with straw and surrounded them with sun-bleached sleepers. His activities caused some consternation among his neighbours: 'At first people thought I was building a garden for magical purposes – a white witch out to get the nuclear power station. It did have magic – the magic of surprise, the treasure hunt. A garden is a treasure hunt, the plants the paperchase.'

Reflecting these childhood games in the spirit of the garden, Jarman understood how gardening connects us in spirals of time: 'one is entering into another time . . . it turns and returns in cycles. Those are the resurrection cycles in my life.' This sense of evolution and rebirth grew more significant when he became ill. As HIV took its slow, terrifying toll on his body, Jarman continued to tend his plants. The place acted as 'a therapy and pharmacopoeia' to which he would return on release from hospital with a portable oxygen cylinder, in the care of his devoted friend Keith Collins. When he was ill, instead of wearing his trademark boilersuit, he gardened in a djellaba, his hospital ID band flashing on his wrist as he tended his herbs.

As Jarman's health deteriorated, his garden became more important to him. It stubbornly countered the fragility of life with its riotous abundance. Tending it was an act of faith – a purpose, and a creative impulse as his strength seeped away like the tide. His last film, *Blue*, charts the awful progression of AIDS through the body. It speaks of the 'slow blue light of delphinium day' – the light he saw as his vision waned; he captures colour and light in a film completely devoid of actual images. From this visual void, Jarman poured his last reserves of energy into the garden at Prospect Cottage until he was too ill to continue. Collins looked after the house and garden following Jarman's death in 1994, allowing it to continue to evolve, despite its growing status as a shrine to its incandescent, joyous creator. In a seemingly inhospitable place, Jarman conjured up colour, form and a shaggy, constantly changing landscape: a vision of how to find beauty in any surroundings. 'Paradise haunts gardens, and some gardens are paradises. Mine is one of them,' he writes.

Puffs and clumps of plants resemble sea urchins amidst the shingle; spears and spikes draw my eyes suddenly upwards and I see the ocean liner of the power station looming on the horizon. Rare lichens, reindeer moss and creeping dodder create soft pillows on the pebbles across the road from the cottage, where we sit and eat drooping sandwiches. I snap off a dried seedpod from an everlasting sweet pea that has self-seeded nearby. The air around us is still and luminous but somehow humming. It is an extraordinary place. I slip the sweet-pea pod into my pocket and feel it thrumming all the way home.

*

My garden, and the chalk on which it is built, is permeable. Like the desert at Dungeness, this part of Sussex has also been shaped by the marine. Millions of years ago, tiny sea creatures floated down to the bottom of the silky warm ocean. As time passed, their fragile shells bound together to become 'ooze', sedimenting into soft chalky rock. The seas receded and land masses reared up towards the skies, creating the nearby Seven Sisters, the white cliffs of the South Downs. The bones of Saxon warriors and slain Britons were added to these ancient layers of skeletons; farmstead families buried their dead beneath the glowing chalk. The bright white paths beloved of the artist Eric Ravilious cut through the hills around my hometown, tramped by fishwives walking from the sea to market with juggs of mackerel and oysters on their backs, leather boots pressing unseen Roman coins deeper into the earth. When they returned with empty baskets, they descended the chalk hills to wait for their men at the edge of the black water that lapped and churned at their feet.

In 1799, a clever young shepherd named John Dudeney carved a hole in the chalk on the Downs and used it to store books. This library provided him with entertainment and education while he tended his flocks. He covered the opening with a flintstone and added to his collection, paying for the books by catching and selling wheatears and moles. His chalk-dusted books taught him to identify the stars that he saw each night from the hill; he learned to speak languages he had only previously imagined; and he taught himself algebra and geometry. But it is said he paid a price for all this learning. His curiosity led him to stare at the sun during the transit of Mercury and badly injure his eye. Nonetheless, he went on to become a well-respected schoolmaster and astronomer, and set up the Philospher's Society in Lewes. I imagine this stargazing, sun-pierced boy curled up against the chalk ridge, plucking a book from his library to read while his huddled sheep doze quietly, their white bellies rising and falling, their breath huffing steam into a warm cloud.

The shepherds and fishwives are gone, but the paths remain, and still the ground keeps moving – cliffs crumble with great groans into the sea; the chalk fills with water and expands with frost; droughts reveal ancient pathways and sites previously hidden from view. Each movement releases more light from beneath the soil, unearthing the shining grave of countless tiny creatures. When I dig my soil, I turn up chalk and flint from their earthwise bindings, imagining seams of light and porous rock below.

Sometimes I feel my life here is just a trick of the light. When I was young, I used to dissociate, telling myself that if something went wrong (a bad haircut or an unkind word at school), it didn't really matter because none of it was real. I still feel this sense of unreality sometimes, as if I'm living inside a story I have created. Have I dreamed the lines and curves of the Downs, shifting in their emeralds and ochres and whites as the sun works the sky? Did I create a ghost garden, a make-believe home from imagined shapes and movements? When I look out of my bedroom window, maybe I don't really see the rusty shed doors and gnarly apple tree; maybe I've just been blinking in the glare of the sun somewhere else, the outline imprinted in negative on my eyelid. The light here can play with your thoughts. I watch as the sun crawls below the horizon and the garden settles into a deep blue. Gardening is like carving, working with something that is already there, honing and refining, taking bits away. And in this place I am carving light from chalk.

The hot, dry days of June also feel permeable, as if life pours through them without sticking. There is no word from our landlord or the executor about whether they have settled the probate. There are fraught telephone calls and arguments between estate agents and executors, but still we are in limbo. It is easier somehow to stop fighting and just let time run through my fingers. As I work in the garden, I remember the writer Michael Pollan's advice: to try to think like sunlight, like wind, like water – where will I go and how long will I spend there? My mind floats. New ideas drift in. Thoughts sink and settle. My mind floats on.

Author Ann Wroe writes that 'all the light by which we see is ancient, having journeyed from the first crack of time, it surely carries with it all manner of memories, disturbances and ghosts'. Just look: here, in this shaft of sunshine on the path, is the builder digging foundations for our house; there, greying the wall with leafy shadows, is the shepherd boy sitting with his book; rippling the pond is the reflection of a woman hoisting her tunic out of the mud with one hand and carrying a pot of fish bones and eggshells to throw on the rubbish tip in the other; and in a tiny puddle of sunshine there is the ghost of a minuscule coccolith giving up its bones to the ooze.

14

BODIES

After an impromptu trip to a tat-filled garden centre, I plant out my haul of plug plants: cabbages, more broccoli and beetroots. Reds and greens to keep my family nourished. The dog keeps digging in the vegetable bed, so I construct a flimsy net fence with old sticks and string to deter her. She steps haughtily through a hole at the bottom and carries on burying my husband's shoe amongst the brassicas. A fair amount of our time out here together is spent with me cursing her and asking why she can't be more like Nigel, Monty Don's obedient, steady golden retriever on *Gardener's World*. I embroider ideas and images of an ideal garden and try to coax its creatures into cooperation. A dog who sits quietly, gnawing on a tennis ball as I work. Slugs that don't destroy my flowers. Pigeons that don't peck at my kale. Butterflies whose eggs don't turn into caterpillars that work my cabbages into a braille text that can be read only by touch. The garden does what it will. Attempts to control it are usually futile.

I discover two secrets: a sea holly I had forgotten about, lurking under the lilac, and two bunny's tail grasses I had abandoned hope of, now defiantly swaying their furry heads beneath the taller stalks in the prairie area. One of the roses has buckled under its own beauty, the weight of its blooms snapping a stem and leaving the flowers face down on the grass, bowing for an encore that never comes. I feel guilty for not tying it up, but I never really liked this rose – too bubblegummy and brash – and now the garden has made the decision for me. It has to go. My spade cuts a square around its base, nudging the roots, tearing the plant from the earth. I carry it to the compost heap with a flash of guilt and hurl it onto the pile of waste.

The peony next to the shed has just two huge, frothy flowers, and these are also drooping. They smell divine and I lose myself in their undulating frills for a moment, face nuzzling the petals. Then I snip. One juicy flower remains. There is something sensual about the particular pink of this flower, about the folds and heady scent. For such a delicate being, it has a strangely meaty, fleshy look to it. Pink is a conundrum. My daughter has gone through various phases of demanding everything be some shade of plastic pink. I resisted where I could. It can be a cloying colour, gendered and sexualized when it comes to toys and children's clothing. But the soft, dusky pink of the peony is something else. It is a lover's flush, a pale dawn cloud, a cat's paw pad; a drop of blood in a swirling bath.

I suddenly recall an evening, years ago, in our old house. At six weeks' pregnant and with three small children, I was exhausted, sinking into the liquid relief of my ritual evening bath. I sponged my body, and saw a small pink clot floating beside me. There was no mistaking this pinkness. I was bleeding. In my heart I knew what was happening, but I could not move. I wanted to spend these last few moments drifting with my tiny baby before my body let it go. Later there was bright red blood, bigger clots. I went to the loo and felt the embryo slip between my legs and plop softly into the toilet bowl. I did not want to look. I flushed it away – unseen, untouched, but not unloved.

The same warning pinkness came once more, a few months later. Again, I was pregnant, this time with twins. Two identical beings, the size of grains of rice, had appeared on an early ultrasound screen, recommended after my previous miscarriage. Two miniscule hearts. Two more pulses vibrating through my body. We joked about how we were 'going to need a bigger boat'. And then we didn't. This time the pink appeared in my knickers. It grew faster, redder and thicker until once again, with a stab of pain across my stomach and a slippery shudder, two tiny embryos fell from my warm belly.

In Irish folklore the souls of dead babies are said to return as sedge warblers, singing consolation to their mothers in the earthly world. I am glad I didn't know this at the time – birdsong would have taken on too heavy a significance.

It took me some time to get pregnant again. The miscarriages had rocked me. For the previous five years, my identity had been purely *mother*. I had given birth at home three times, with no medical interventions or drugs, after uncomplicated pregnancies. I had trusted my body and fallen in love with each baby as soon as I felt their fluttering presence. I had produced milk that sustained, nurtured and comforted three healthy, pink-cheeked boys. With each pregnancy and breast-feeding baby, I ate the right foods, did yoga, used natural hair dyes and face creams, stopped drinking, smothered my desire with exhaustion. I gave my body over to motherhood. But now I couldn't keep a baby alive. *What good was I?* After I saw the two stripes on yet another pregnancy test, it felt like I didn't exhale until that beautiful, pink, perfect baby girl tore out of me in the early hours of an April morning beside the hearth. As I gathered her slippery body to my chest, I let go of those other small, slippery creatures who came before her and whom she would never know.

Motherhood is a condition of perpetual uncertainty. I know this feeling, have made a home of it. I have practised letting go of things I can't control and of accepting an unknowable future. So why am I finding it so hard to cope with uncertainty now we might have to move? Unlike the fears that foreshadow every birth, thankfully a potential eviction is not, for us, a matter of life or death. Yet it feels like a very real threat to my family. *What good am I* if I can't provide a stable home for my children? That feeling knows its way around my body. It knows how to seep into every knot in my shoulders, how to throb across my head, how to thicken every breath. But we have survived worse than this, and others have endured far greater hardships.

I am beginning to understand that the loss of my childhood home – the place that has haunted me throughout my life – is at the core of why I am struggling so much with the possibility of moving from this house. That move had such resonance because it was bound up with losing my family unit. The house represented a life before divorce, a feeling of contentment and security. A few years ago, I decided I had to go back and somehow exorcise it from my heart. The owners let me walk through the house; I touched the walls and breathed in its air. I felt like I had no claim on it, that it was clearly, definitely, someone else's. Although I have mostly let that place go, the idea that I might be inflicting a similar experience on my children feels devastating. My anxiety about losing our current home is inextricably entangled with the fear of losing my family. I am not sure how our family – and my marriage – will weather an upheaval like this.

*

25 June 2006. Because we leave tomorrow (Montenegro & Albania), we've harvested all the early potatoes & broad beans, giving lots away. Potatoes less delicious than other years, beans good as ever. Mangetouts partially harvested, raspberries, redcurrants, blackcurrants, lots of gooseberries. Spinach & rocket bolted.

*

June is when the garden looks its best. There is a wild extravagance everywhere, from the blushing *Rosa* 'Wedding Day' dripping over the back wall, to the flopping spears of nepeta, pocked with hairy bees. The bigger, showier alliums are nearly over, but the pompoms of the smaller *Allium sphaerocephalon* have started to unfurl, ready to reveal their blackcurrant faces. Some trusty stalwarts like the hardy geraniums need a trim to reinvigorate them and encourage flowers for the next few months. I cut handfuls of their leaves, releasing the pungent, citrusy, verdant scent. Oil from the rose-scented geranium has been used as a glow-enhancing skin and hair product since Egyptian times. Studies have shown it is also anti-inflammatory and anti-bacterial, and could even help treat people suffering from neurodegenerative diseases like Alzheimer's. Inhaling its aroma is said to reduce stress and anxiety. I tear off a leaf and rub it between my fingers, the smell instantly intense.

The day lilies are flowering nearby. Orange-yellow egg-yolk petals peel back on themselves, baring their throats to the sun. Each flower will only last a day, but more will come from every plant in a cascade of fleeting brightness. These flowers were here when we moved in and I have never really liked them, but their rhizomes are so interwoven with the iris tubers around them that I am too afraid to try digging them up. Besides, who can object to such a low-maintenance flash of fire?

My climbing French beans are developing tentative pods, the size of a small child's finger. I leave them to fatten in the sunshine and feel a thrill of anticipation about picking them soon. I will steam them; sauté them in garlic and butter; toss them with French dressing in a salad; and maybe leave some to turn into haricot beans that I will dry and store for winter. There is something incomprehensibly magical about how these small beans can hold all the information and potential needed to shapeshift into a stalk that will bear many more pods, each containing yet more beans. I think about how my ovaries were filled with eggs that carried cells from my grandmother's body. We women contain each other. Looking at the beans, it is impossible not to think of 'Jack and the Beanstalk', with its message of aspiration and ambition. Every time I plant a seed into the soil, there is an echo of this magic – *What next?*

Last year I moved a salvia from the main flower bed purely because it was the wrong colour. It felt a superficial reason to uproot a plant that was thriving where it was, but the red of *Salvia* 'Hot Lips' was jarring with the pinks and purples around it. It died shortly after I transplanted it. My mother had one in her garden and I loved it for the daily reminder of her. Now there is just a gap where it was. And everywhere in my life, there is a gap where she was. Since she died, I have had a permanent feeling that something is amiss with the world – a peripheral lack, an out-of-kilter wrongness. I plant a different salvia in this space, a dark-purpled flowered variety called 'Love and Wishes'. It is small now but will spread its delicate spires into the blankness. I want to fill all the gaps, stuffing life and growth wherever I turn; filling, filling, filling.

*

Since moving here, we have filled the gaps inside the house – not just with the ever-increasing stuff of life, my children are filling it with their bodies. Doorways now require ducking under, gaps under beds that used to provide hiding places can only just accommodate one outstretched arm and the tangle of legs under our small kitchen table causes arguments as we jostle for our own space. I discover that you can fix a bottle around a pear bud and the fruit will grow within the glass. I think about how we fit our homes, and how we outgrow them. I feel like I fit here perfectly. As I go about my daily routine in the house, I am aware of moving through a space that I inhabit with all my senses. I know instinctively where to put my hand in the dark to find the light switch, and how to anticipate the drop of the stairs without needing to see where I'm walking. The house has mapped itself into my sensory memory.

And my family has also imprinted itself on the house. In our kitchen, there is a wall with scribbled pencil marks noting the names, dates and heights of my children. It is a map of their growth, and in every accumulating inch I remember the shaky first bike rides, the clutched fist around a crayon, the first day at 'big school', and the moment when they overtook me in height. Watching the marks grow higher and higher reminds me of the shocking speed of growth in the garden in spring and summer. It seems unfathomable that the tiny shoots can have sprung so fully and quickly skywards. The long, deep time of winter when their seeds lay dormant seems to have passed at a different speed. My children's full, busy lives make their growing seem all the faster compared to the slower early years, when we were all at home and our daily rhythms revolved around simpler things.

The garden, though, is where I feel this connection with the passage of time most keenly, most physically. The eternal cycles of life are all around us as we sit or work out here. Like our bodies, the garden ages, decays and replenishes. Gardening is a bodily activity – it's not just the physical work, but the way we interact with the soil, plants and creatures around us. We create medicine from herbs and flowers, we make salves from plants to heal wounds, we are nourished by vegetables and fruit – gardens keep us alive. Sometimes, when I step outside the house, I feel the effect immediately: the sense that the garden is changing the rhythm and course of my thoughts. As I settle into planting or plucking weeds, there is room to think – a kind of thinking by osmosis as I am absorbed in the work of transformation and creation. I find a flow state, my mind loosening as my hands move, out of habit, performing these everyday tasks. A form of muscle memory takes over.

*

Parts of my body, and of my children's, lie buried in the soil of three different gardens. When our first child was born, we decided that we would bury the afterbirth rather than simply discard what is in effect the body's only separate organ. Until then the only placenta I had seen was a cow's, an alien horror scene that I unwittingly witnessed after jumping over a fence as a child. Now, seeing the strange bloody sac that had joined my body to my baby's, which had kept him alive and contained cells from his body, was a viscerally animal experience. I remembered the cow's placenta and felt the shared mammalian work of birthing. Examining the veins blossoming like tree branches and the thick umbilical trunk, I felt immediately connected to all the women before me who had grown and birthed babies, whose cells laid down these secret passageways and canals where life pumped gently between their bodies. It seemed wrong to just throw it in the bin.

The word for 'placenta' in German is *Mutterkuchen*, or 'mothering-cake', which I find pleasing – back to the biscuit analogy. It comes from the Roman cake called a *placenta*, after which the round, flat organ was named. In many cultures, the placenta is seen as a baby's older sibling or twin, and therefore is given a ritual burying. The Maori word for 'placenta', *whenua*, is the same as the word for 'land'. Indigenous Navajo, Maori and Indonesian peoples believe burying the afterbirth reinforces the baby's connection to the place of their birth. Some believe this will also keep the child close to home. In Bali, placentas were traditionally hung from trees in coconut shells, and in some areas of Africa they are swathed in blankets and buried beneath trees. The Hmong people buried their babies' placentas in their homes (the placenta of a girl child was buried under her parents' bed and a boy's under a central wooden pillar) so that when they died their soul could return and await rebirth. In Islamic cultures, placentas are buried to return part of the baby to the earth from which it was created. This association with trees, roots and the earth is significant. It recognizes the importance of place in a baby's, and its mother's, life, and reflects a connection across time from past to present to future. What sustained a life in the past will give nourishment to the soil and nurture the trees or plants where it is buried. What grew with us – or grew us – will bring us home and allow our soul another life. Giving birth is wild; leaving the placenta in a wild place feels apt. Burying this part of myself and my baby felt like a way of marking (and mourning) the end of the pregnancy and the shift into parenthood, of restoring some equilibrium between the woman I was before the birth and the changed mother I became.

My first son was born in Melbourne, and his placenta is buried under a rose bush in the midwife's garden. Although it felt slightly woo-woo to be carrying a bloody sac in an old ice-cream tub across town to bury it in someone else's garden, it became a tradition for us to give this part of me and the baby to the soil. Just after my second son's birth, we had had to move from a rented flat and were not sure how permanent our next home would be, so my father kindly (and not without some horror) let us keep the placenta in his freezer until we decided what to do with it. My mother agreed we could bury it under a plum tree at the back of her vegetable patch. We held a short ceremony around the compost bin as I shovelled earth over this meaty miracle that had kept my son alive. Two other placentas were later placed in the ground of the house we lived in before this one, fertilizing the Sussex soil for other living organisms. Leaving these pieces of myself in various gardens now feels a foreshadowing of the scattering that comes with motherhood.

I have become porous, soaking up the needs of others until my roots feel unstable. What cuttings have I taken from myself to make this life? What grafting and hybridizing have I undertaken to make my body and mind into the right shape for motherhood and wifehood? When my children grow up and leave, what will remain? The home I have made for them – or will make for them in the next place. This garden – or another, in the next place. But in between their visits, who will remain? I am no longer sure who I will be, as a mother, or as a wife. My marriage needs tending, but I feel I have little left to offer. Over the years, the hurts, neglects and stresses have fallen like frail shells to settle in layers of sediment, obscuring all the good things buried beneath. I keep waiting for one of us to sink to our knees and start frantically digging with our hands to rescue it.

For all its fluidity, the garden is at least a physical, tangible space that I can, to some extent, manipulate and create; a family is much more amorphous and slippery. The roles change over time, often without you noticing. Teenagers do not want you, yet they need you. The ambivalence is painful and hard to navigate. One night they come to you, trembling, saying they are too scared and exhausted to go on. You smother your terror and offer comfort and reassurance, then lie awake thinking of all the catastrophes that might befall them. Another time they can barely contain their contempt as you embarrass yourself yet again in some innocuous way. I have to embody *mother*, yet also disappear entirely. I wonder if anyone else in the family is fighting for the same thing. I remember Maya Angelou's words that we 'carry around home between our teeth'. Like a knife, perhaps, ready to be drawn in defence. Or a tongue, waiting to articulate belonging. Or a mouth full of desire and craving. It seems to me that in a garden we carry home between our hands, moving it, shaping it, encouraging it to grow; and sometimes destroying it.

✳

Animals and birds make homes with their bodies. They know these physical connections to place. The swifts know them. The worms know them. But, unlike humans, they do not leave much in their wake. Another trip to my mother's house, this time with my brother and sister, to pack away the last of her things. We arrive with boxes and empty cars to remove furniture, books, childhood mugs, favourite tea towels and family papers. Piece by piece, dismantling the life she and my stepfather built there. He doesn't want any of these things around him, confined as he is to one room and with no sentimental attachment to worldly possessions. But for us, each of these objects is a receptacle of memories, just as people contain our memories, stored like seeds waiting to come back to life. It is a privilege to hold my mother's memories in my head and in my hands as I riffle the pages of her girlhood books and fold the woolly jumpers she had put away ready for a winter that she never saw.

The heart has gone from the house. We gravitate to the garden, escaping the echoing quiet, and I notice the changes since she stopped tending it. Despite my stepfather enlisting some help, it hasn't been enough to maintain the place as it was – weeds have overrun the vegetable patch, and there are gaps in the borders where my mother would have planted more Michaelmas daisies or roses. The pot of plants I gave her after her terminal diagnosis (rosemary for remembrance, lavender for calm, snowdrops for hope, chamomile for 'energy in adversity') stands alone next to the old swing chair; most of the plants in it have now also gone. Eventually we go back indoors. The house seems frozen in time, like the Pompeiian families mummified by ash and lava. It is not a home any more but an interruption. Stasis has settled everywhere, apart from the sitting room, now a bedroom, where my stepfather lies ghostbound.

These traces seem so utterly inadequate as markers of her life. They do not capture her laughter or her voice, nor her secrets or dreams. Scientists have recently discovered a new race of human ancestors through traces left in our DNA, but no one has unearthed any physical evidence of them. They are ghosts that have left their inscription in our chromosomes, but their bones, songs and homes have vanished. These two states of being can coexist: the total lack of physical evidence, and the material remnants of everyday objects with which we build a life. My mother's bones lie not far from the house, covered by her wedding dress, in which she chose to be buried; a corpse bride waiting for her love, who will join her in the plot soon. The bones of those ancient ancestors lie unseen. They have simply vanished, and the only trace is a marker on the strange laddering double helix that plots our DNA. My mother has simply vanished, and yet her house and garden contain traces of her. I go back outside and fill some pots with earth, then snip cuttings from her peony and a climbing rose. Lots of the cuttings I have taken home from here have died, but I keep trying. Every visit ends with this ritual of taking and transplanting, hoping the plants will put down roots in my soil. Her garden continues in its own way. Life continues.

*

There has been an argument. I retreat to the garden, heart-bruised, while the boy nurses his hurt indoors. I water the pots I took from my mother's garden – two of the rose cuttings look promising, and the peony stems haven't wilted. Hope. Digging clears my head, so I decide to tackle the weeds in what will be my cutting patch. It is carpeted with sinuous clumps of bindweed that seem to have no beginning or end. My spade jars and scrapes on the hard earth, but eventually the patch is ready for planting. I carry a tray of fire: *Dahlia* 'Ambition', 'Zingaro', 'Gallery Art Fair', 'Totally Tangerine', 'Purple Flame' and 'Melody Harmony'; blood-red *Rudbeckia* 'Cherry Brandy' and yellow 'Goldsturm'; and chocolate cosmos. I set the plants in their places, flanked by two hollyhocks and a *Euphorbia oblongata*, which I love to cut and put in vases of flowers for its zingy green foliage. The cutting patch looks orderly and hopeful. It has helped.

The chicken coop is full of sparrows. They disappear like magic, melting into the air when I click open the gate. Listen: the hens are *broack*-ing; a collared dove calls, *My toe hurts*; traffic thrums; my son thuds and twangs a basketball against the hoop at the side of the house. Smell: the rambling rose, hot grass, cat shit somewhere, a waft of strawberries. I busy myself with planting foxgloves. When I was young, I spent a night in a Welsh cottage sleeping with a foxglove bell on each finger to make my wish (for a pony) come true. This was the first time I really understood the power of folklore and magic. Spells were not purely the realm of fairies and magicians; thanks to nature, I could conjure them myself, with just a few flimsy purple flowers and a wish. I grow foxgloves now for the bees and their tall spires, but their magic lingers. The soil is so dry it is hard to dig a hole; it just keeps filling up again, the crumbly earth falling in on itself. Fat bees nuzzle the powdery comfrey heads, which dip as they disappear inside the narrow pink trumpets in an endless cycle of work, joy, work, search, joy, work. The air turns suddenly summer-soft: rain is coming. After parched, hot weeks the breeze brings the promise of a drenching.

I pull a plump snail from the rim of my sweet-pea pot, and automatically snap off a few deadheads from the pinks as I pass. The garden is awash with pale pink – the creamy froth of the rambling rose has been scorched to a blush. Its unsightly rash reminds me of measles, spotted pebbles, a moth's wing, a blackbird's egg – ripples and images from elsewhere reflected along the back wall of the garden. The squash are starting to flower, their flaccid green-orange trumpets snaking across the new vegetable bed. One of my mother's hollyhocks is in bloom. It is painted in a wash of dusky apricot, with delicate veins leading to a ring of deep pink with a six-pointed star that holds the fuzzy stamen. Inside, feather-like quills radiate out to lighter shades that blend into a pale greeny-creamy-pink across the frills of the five petals. The light seems to be sucked inwards. I have passed these flowers so many times but never stopped to really look. It is like falling into a kaleidoscope.

The privet hedge sends its white flowers up to the sky, dropping tiny flakes along the edge of the garden like a seasoning of salt. I pull up limp handfuls of ground elder in the flower bed and they collapse in the heat. A cutting I took from my daughter's rose has taken root and is now over half a metre tall, hidden behind some columbines; I haven't noticed it until now. I cut off the shoots around the base of the apple tree and use one as a prop for a sagging gaura in a pot. As I press the twig into the soil, I discover a gold foil-covered chocolate coin, hidden in some long-ago treasure hunt and never discovered. Wild strawberries sidle along the wooden sleeper separating the lawn and beds. The garden gives up its treasures when it is ready. It invites me to find joy in small, everyday things: in the swag of the plum tree, the light playing on a petal, the crisping husks of the lilac blooms. By paying attention – and attending – to these plants and this place, I can quiet the unsettledness that courses through me. I press, tidy, snip, pull, prune, water, stake, pick and dig until my heart beats in garden time.

JULY

15

FAMILY

I HAVE HARDLY HAD ANY TIME TO WORK IN THE GARDEN RECENTLY. Life has seeped into every corner, leaving little space for anything else. On 14 July, the anniversary of my mother's death, I finally get out into the garden and do some weeding. I am surrounded by the same flowers that last year I cut to put on her grave. Some were grown from seeds from her garden, creating a strange feeling of circling back. On my first visit to the cemetery after her death, I sat clutching my flowers and enviously watching a worm slip effortlessly between my world and hers. I wanted to climb in beside her and pull the turf over my head like a blanket.

Now the garden is beginning to fade. The dahlias have been ravaged by snails; there are far fewer potatoes than I had hoped for; the prairie area is browning and desiccated, making a different noise now when the wind whips through it – less swish, more rattle; the wild meadow patch is populated by more weeds than wild grasses; my sweet peas are friable, disappointed ghosts of their former heady-scented, bright incarnations. The wise gardener knows that if things don't work out there's always next year, but I can't be sure there will be a next year here.

Yet, despite these disappointments, I find much to celebrate around the garden. And what feels more important is the fact that we are still here to see it, in all its glorious failures and beauty. I pick great bowlfuls of delicious raspberries, tart yet sweet, leaving bare green nipples on the canes. I remember taking a yoghurt pot filled with raspberries from my mother's garden to her in the hospice, and the sheer joy she got from eating them. They were among the last proper food she ever ate, as the tumour pressing on her throat made swallowing increasingly difficult. It is a comfort that she felt so happy as she ate her raspberries, that her body was getting its final nourishment from fruit she had grown with her own hands on her home soil. Her kitchen cupboard is still full of washed-out yoghurt pots and margarine tubs, awaiting bounties that never arrive, for journeys they will never take.

A self-seeded honesty, alone on the grass, is drying out. I much prefer its dying form to the blooms – the pods like flattened dice, like paper moons, like communion wafers, like finely sliced potatoes, like a woman in a veil, like the pages of an ancient book. Each disc is a translucent time capsule. Around the honesty, in the failed wild meadow, I find clover, plantain, buttercup and dock – all habitats for diverse species. By creating and tending a garden without over-perfecting, leaving some areas rough and wild, I have inadvertently made space for countless creatures. Instead of swatting at flies in the house I now usher them back outside, seeing them as part of the interconnected ecosystem that holds us all. Paying attention to the lives teeming on and beneath the surface and in the air has helped me consider people more wholeheartedly too. As I tease my climbing beans up their poles or train a clematis against a fence, I am learning to let go of perfection and to see the value in showing care and being in service to this place.

I pick rainbows of chard and harvest the last of the furry broad bean pods. Fat, curled climbing beans keep up their steady profusion, and I fill my hands with as many as I can gather. Shoring up my sense of things coming to an end, I buy a flowering quince to train along the side wall and some wallflowers to bring winter colour to the flower beds.

It is 9 p.m. on a warm evening. A moment of stillness by the back door. Three swifts wheel and swoop low over the garden. A magpie cackles. I wander through the garden collecting seeds and dropping them into envelopes, and hear the whistle of a pigeon's wings as it sails clumsily out of the hedge. The garden exhales and settles down for the night. The seeds in my hands pulse with the potential for life. But they will wait their time. A pause.

*

The roses are bells pealing, *Summer!*, giddy in the wind. A small moth, white with a dark-brown border around its wings. It might be a box moth (bad news for neighbours with box hedges), or a magpie moth. Instead of simply watching it dance from leaf to leaf, I am preoccupied with trying to identify it.

As I google images of garden moths, I am struck by how the act of trying to name this creature is taking me away from enjoying it. This is one of the things I am learning to love about gardening: alongside the satisfaction of being able to identify plants and creatures, it is in the blurred edges – unidentified weeds, self-seeded flowers in the 'wrong' place, a fruit tree that never fruits – that real wonder lies. I put my phone away and watch instead for a few seconds before the unidentified moth is lost to the sky. It is a creature made of dust, its whole life lived in stages of transition until this moment when it has matured and is free. Soon there will be a brush of dust on a surface somewhere, a soft brown smudge the only trace of its extraordinary, fleeting existence.

When it has gone, I decide to do some radical pruning of the plum tree. I don't like slicing into trees; I hate the tearing noise the saw makes and am wracked with guilt knowing that my plum tree will respond to these wounds by sending messages across a hidden underground network to nearby trees warning them of potential attack. As I cut, I mumble embarrassed apologies to the branches. I have become a mutilator, a threat, in this place that I love. There is a violence to gardening – we dent, cut, stack, chop, pick, dig, snip. The tree looks forlorn and misaligned. A brutality enacted for the sake of aesthetics and the convenience of not having to duck every time I go into the chicken run. But the tree will send sap to heal the gashes.

I harvest more beans and shiny-skinned courgettes. Each one feels like a tiny triumph for my faith that we would be here to enjoy the garden's bounty. Yet I can see that this is also a skewed way of thinking. Yes, some of the buds and blooms and berries and vegetables have come from a chain of energy I set in motion that produces things I and my family will be lucky enough to enjoy. But I haven't *won*. We are still living from month to month, my stomach lurching every time an official-looking envelope flops through the letterbox. This growing season is not about the *ta-da!* moment when I carry armfuls of garden produce into the house. It is not an *I told you so*, stick two fingers up to the estate agent kind of victory. Instead, as the year unfolds, I see that this whole time I have really been learning to live with uncertainty and impermanence, rather than defeat them.

I realize this precarity also feels particularly complex because it strikes at the heart of my role as a mother. It threatens my identity as the maker and keeper of a safe home. It is not easy for me to make peace with what is happening, to be at home in not-knowing. I am someone who makes lists, who plans ahead, who anticipates problems before they arise, and devises complicated strategies to solve and sort and mend when things go wrong. Like the little white moth, my children are learning about the pain and vulnerability of growing into the world. They need help and I cannot fix them. So what can I do? Approaching adulthood can feel terrifying, yet these acute anxieties pass; they may circle back, snapping at our heels again later, but we know by then that they will not stay long. I hold my children and reassure them, and this calms their fluttering hearts a little. Maybe that is what home is, really, just some loving arms to hold you when you feel you cannot go on. I think about my mother's silent house and how it is not the walls and doors that made it homely, but her energy, spirit and love. If I can't control my family's future, I can at least create a place that always feels like home, whether that is here or somewhere else.

The trick is to hold lightly. As my children grow, part of me wants to cling on to the earlier versions of them that I have loved – the milk-soft babies I held close every night, the warm pudgy fingers gripping my hands as we walked, the bright faces freshly scrubbed from their bubble-filled baths. It is hard work this continuous leaving behind. The fact that as they are growing up, my body – their first home – is simultaneously decaying sometimes feels too much. Yet it also makes me part of this change. I am holding too tight to everything. It is time to begin to let go, to pour my love for my children into the soil that holds them and hope that their roots are strong.

*

*20 July 2004. Last potatoes harvested today, nearly end
of masses of raspberries – 20-30 lb? Transplanted sprouts,
not leeks yet. Ate broad beans & mangetouts every day
for a month, now carrots too. Lifted some onions. New
buddleia by little shed – annuals under lilac disappointing
– not enough rain, though not much sun either. Too
many redcurrants. Plan to cut down damson.*

*

As I flick back through the past two years' notes in my gardening journals, comparing the initial plans with the way the garden unfolded in reality, it occurs to me that I spend too long looking backwards and not enough time thinking about the shape of my future. It is not just the futility of thinking about the imagined gardens and the failed aspirations, but a sense that now might be the time for looking forward. I suppose the situation with the house makes this harder, but I wonder about what the stories of the past are giving me that any vision of the time to come is not – at least, not now.

Once upon a time . . .

So many of the stories we read to our children, and our parents read to us, begin like this. These stories are rooted in a time and therefore a place.

On a time there lived . . .

But not a specific time, more an existence as part of all time. A time that could be a distant speck on the horizon or breathing warmly onto our neck. Garden time is like this. A garden is a physical space but it is also a space that exists across time, full of layers and vertices that are evidence of movement and change, but in different ways. As we pass through a garden it changes, and it changes us. It alters time. Take the dandelion clock, that simple game played by children who create time with their breath. One o'clock – *huff*. Two o'clock – *huff*. Each breath sends seeds into the air, where they will float or drop according to the wind and humidity and landscape. Some will take root and wind themselves tightly into the ground before unfolding their golden faces to the sky. When their time comes, they will shed their skin back into the air and start again. *Once upon a garden.*

I realize I am marking time in the slow changes of my body and the rapid growing of my children. There is a space opening up in the near future. What shape do I want it to be? What do I want my life to look like? I can plot a vegetable patch or herb garden, but can I design the last phase of my life to be a place of abundance, love and freedom?

The French have the same word, *temps*, for 'weather' and for 'time'. Both are always moving, changing; both are beyond our control. At least, this is partly true of the weather. Human behaviour and exploitation of the planet is causing changes to the climate and weather patterns. Extreme weather 'events' are more common, and, even in our little corner of Sussex, I have noticed drier springs and wetter winters. Hard frosts are infrequent. Snow a rarity. If we do not try harder to stop these changes, our gardens will have to adapt in order to survive. We will need to grow drought-resistant varieties, or plants suited to warmer weather. Their future is uncertain. Our future is uncertain. Three o'clock – *huff*. We are running out of things to blow.

Weathering – the collision of weather and time – constantly changes the garden. The wooden fence around the chicken run has grown soft and moss-wrapped with years of rain and not enough sunlight. Our outdoor table and chairs are slowly rotting, stripped of their essential weatherproofing coats through neglect. My improvised brick path has become slippery and uneven, buckling as the soil swells with moisture and rises again. Rust rinses down the side of the shed's ugly corrugated skin. The structures of the garden are slowly evolving, just as the life inside, above and beneath it bursts onwards, worked on by time and weather.

In pregnancy, time is marked in weeks, trimesters, developmental milestones. Your body is taken over with another person's tides. I remember vividly the weather on the night my third son was born: a wild storm, the sky splitting over the hills as I paced the sitting room, bellowing animal groans into the thunder. There were tornadoes in the north of England, the roofs of schools and houses ripped off, trees felled, homes flooded. There is an old wives' tale that storms bring on labour, and my son was ten days early. I felt the power of the weather deep within my body, and it felt perfectly possible for the birth to be in the hands of the winds and rain. In fact, evidence shows that low barometric pressure does affect the water in a mother's body and the baby's amniotic fluid, making it more likely for the amniotic sac to rupture and labour to start. The shifting weight of the air and the waxing gibbous moon that night called the seas to rise up and my boy to burst into the world. I also remember the weather on the day my mother died:

hot, humid, cloudy, sullen. We had the window open and flies kept coming in.

*

Another visit to my poorly stepfather, whose cancer is eating away at his spine and coursing in his blood. Until recently, the disease had a modest appetite, remaining contained and controlled by drugs. But, like seeds that receive a sudden burst of rain and a few days' sunshine, it has sprung into life. An abundance of tumours. The house deflates around him as the spiders and moths encase empty rooms in silk and dust. I sit opposite his bed, awkwardly folding my legs underneath me, hands bunched in my lap, taking up as little space as possible. We talk in stilted sentences, unable to reach each other. Until I tell him about my garden. Suddenly, time has opened up and he is back in his allotment, before he met my mother, a widower doing his best to raise his children, slinging bags of muddy potatoes onto the kitchen table and lining up green tomatoes on a sunny windowsill.

We exchange stories of blight and poor harvests, moving on to laugh about how his vegetables were always tiny – perfect miniatures of what they should have been. He tells me how to earth up my potatoes, and even though I know how to do this, I let him tell me, afraid that this portal will suddenly slam shut and we will be plunged back into stiff silence. He has given me, my mother and my siblings so much; and yet the only words I can find are about vegetables. When he is tired of talking and I have to get out of the house, away from the reminders of my mother's absence, I go into the garden and look at his weed-covered beds, at the asters and roses my mother planted that defiantly erupt with blooms. Out of habit, I snap off some seed heads and slip them into my pocket. I cry out, quietly, 'Oh!' I don't know why. I feel my voice being blown away on the wind, disappearing, dissolving into the air, the weather, time.

16

ROOTS

THERE ARE DANDELIONS EVERYWHERE. I HAVE BEEN TRYING TO ignore them, but I can't put off tackling them any more. I prefer the jobs that require a lot of movement and dramatic changes, but I am trying to get better at these unappealing tasks. I take my pocket knife and my phone and sit on the grass at the back of the lawn. With a podcast to listen to and the late afternoon sun on my back, the work of digging around each dandelion and levering its roots from the soil begins to feel almost relaxing. There is something soothing about the repetition, the slowness and deliberateness. I sit and uproot small yellow suns, moving in increments towards the house, a pile of weeds growing in my bucket. I only stop when I notice small pillows of blisters on my palms.

Let me show you the dusk. The moon hangs palely like a shrew's rib. The swifts are hunting in a trio, screaming against the blue-orange sky. They are the ultimate symbols of transience, tiny anchors cast out and plunging continuously through the depths. I look forward to hearing them every evening but am already anticipating the day when they are suddenly gone. The other garden birds are quieter now. The ebullient song of springtime has shifted into a muted conversation as they go into moult. Their bodies are working to refine and recalibrate for the heat. Their mating and breeding is done. There is no energy left for throaty choruses. The garden is a collection of exhausted ephemera, a last-ditch attempt at realizing the vision I had when I set out in March with seeds and trays and hope as the garden rose dripping from winter.

We have two new chickens, and one has feathers like a peregrine falcon. At first they don't understand how the door to the coop works; they have none of the grace and agility of the swifts that swirl above them, so I have to unceremoniously pick them up and post them through the gap every evening. They seem so hopelessly domestic. The falcon-chicken also has not grasped the concept of boundaries, flying noisily out of the pen area and landing on the roof of the old bike shed. She then doesn't know what to do and just stands there crowing. I contemplate clipping her wings, but this seems an unnatural and disproportionate defacement. What right do I have to take away the gift of flight, or tinker with the extraordinary aerodynamics embodied in the hen's secret feathers? Once I have shooed her down and deposited her in the coop, there is a moment of squawking as the bossy older hens muscle the newcomers off their perch space. The whole 'pecking order' display is fascinating. Usually when you introduce new hens, after a couple of days things settle down, but I keep careful watch to make sure that the treatment meted out to new arrivals does not turn brutal.

*

My daughter and I are lost. I have ignored my instinct and allowed my phone's map to lead us in completely the wrong direction, to a house in the middle of nowhere. We should be at Wakehurst, the National Trust garden and seed bank. I swear quietly and turn the car around in the driveway of a house confusingly named 'Wakehurst'. Already a reluctant companion, coming along out of a sense of duty and boredom, my daughter looks increasingly fed up. Half an hour later, we turn into the amply signposted car park at the correct Wakehurst. Picking up a map at the entrance, we decide to walk down to the lake. We have been here before, a long time ago, when my daughter was straining to escape from the confines of a pushchair and would run headlong towards any open water she could find.

This time, we walk together, following the map. The gardens don't make a huge impression on me, but I love the watery bits that feel wilder and more alive. We are really here for the seed bank. I want to learn more about their work recording and cataloguing seeds from around the world. I am intrigued by this repository of suspended life, of all these envelopes and packages just waiting for their time to awaken from their slumber. It reminds me of fairy tales again: Sleeping Beauty, awaiting her prince to release her from her frozen state, or Snow White trapped in a poisoned sleep.

Inside the Millennium Seed Bank, we find display cases showing incredible seeds from every part of the globe: moon-like orbs, long cylindrical husks with perforations like cheese graters, discs with holes like dried orange slices, fuzzy starbursts. All perfectly evolved to create, disperse and contain life. These particular seeds had less poetic journeys than their wind-blown or bird-strewn relations. They were sent to Wakehurst in envelopes, identified by the herbarium at Kew, assigned an ID card, and entered into a database. Half the seeds are left in the place where they were collected, to ensure some natural continuation. The new arrivals are given a voucher to show they are part of the seed library, then dried to increase their longevity, placed in cloth or paper bags and stored in depositories with low moisture levels. If a whole miniature fruit arrives, it is ripened and the seeds collected, processed to remove extra layers, X-rayed to spot possible damage, hand cleaned and sieved, then placed into glass bottles and jars. These time capsules are frozen at −20°. Humans have collected and stored seed for thousands of years, but the scale and scope of Wakehurst's seed bank is extraordinary.

My daughter is mildly interested in all this, but is fast tiring of me pointing out remarkable facts and shapes. She is keen to start our picnic. I tell her that the research carried out here might help find crops that will withstand climate change and disease, that her grandchildren might be planting and eating new varieties of plants that originated in this place. The seed bank also stores seeds from the plants most likely to die out as a result of changes in weather patterns and destructive or exploitative human activities. It is a place of penance for the damage we have caused. By understanding the work here, I want to assuage my guilt about the mess my generation have made of the planet. My daughter wants some crisps.

*

The iniquities of land ownership are connected to the exploitation of other lands and peoples in the name of empire or colonial trade. The British have been very good at talking about respecting borders when it suits them, and destroying ecosystems and communities when there is money to be made and power to be grabbed. Many of the plants we grow and love in our gardens are the result of such exploitation. Many of the places donating seed to Wakehurst are regions that have been plundered by the same system that is now perpetuating climate change and a refugee crisis.

Trudging back to the car, my daughter and I talk about what she most liked about our visit. She says the lake. When we get home, we fill loo rolls with soil and plant some more French beans. These are less remarkable than the exciting, other-worldly seeds we saw earlier in the day. But even a humble bean contains stories of its own – grown since the mid nineteenth century and now a popular choice for home-growers, this variety, 'Blue Lake', doesn't need bees for pollination, which might ensure it continues if the decline of our insect populations continues apace.

*

13 July 2005. Today, after a long time & a lot of money, the well project is finished. It looks & sounds wonderful & I love it. The path today was the final touch. Broad beans over, loads of lettuce & red fruit – blackcurrants over, lots of ice cream & jam made. The 'Paul's Himalayan Musk' looked fantastic in late June, but it & the other roses aren't blooming now. Sprouts & leeks waiting for end of raspberries to be transplanted. Two Christmas trees doing well, but no lupins this year.

*

Although I have found out plenty of information about the prison next door, and fragments of the history of my street, I am still struggling to establish what this garden looked like before the house was built. Why does it matter to me? Perhaps I want to understand the historical roots of this plot of land so I can feel that I have a greater claim to being here? Perhaps it comes back to that sense of belonging. On old Ordnance Survey maps, the area seems to have been a field up until the eighteenth century. In a sketch of the naval prison from 1854, I see that where our front gate is now, there was an arched gateway in a higher wall, with steps leading to what looks like a field or garden. By 1899, a map shows some buildings along our north wall, where the fig tree now stands. These bear the symbols for glass structures, which means they were probably greenhouses. I feel an unaccountable frisson of pleasure at this – the idea that, although our house was not yet built, the garden was already a garden. It looks as if it was part of a communal piece of land running behind the terrace, or possibly the large garden belonging to the end house.

In Victorian times, glasshouses became highly desirable. They were places to experiment with exotic plants brought back from the colonies, a status symbol as transparent as their panes. From the mid nineteenth century, the abolition of the glass tax cut the cost of glass dramatically, and greenhouses became a realistic aspiration for the middle classes, rather than being purely the domain of the wealthy. Along with a feverish fascination with botany, which saw explorers plunder plants from colonial outposts and remote islands, the Victorians were also keen to pioneer scientific developments. A glasshouse was the perfect way to marry these two interests, providing a controlled environment in which to coax exotic plants to life despite the cool, damp climate.

Perhaps the person who tended plants long ago in the glasshouse here grew fleshy apricots, tender pelargoniums, pineapples or tall palms. If so, this land has been gardened for at least one hundred years. A greenhouse still shows up on maps from the 1950s, when our landlord's family moved out. Perhaps it was dismantled by the tenants who moved in. There is no trace of it now, although I have often longed to install one. I love the mellow quality of light filtered through glass, and the way each pane creates a frame for the spaces beyond. But the combination of financial constraints and multiple football-playing children firing balls around the garden has prevented me from indulging.

The National Buildings Record archive shows that the row of houses next to ours (where the telecoms building now stands) was demolished in 1943 following extensive bomb damage. There are numerous photos of the street after this bomb, but none shows our house. An Ordnance Survey map from 1945 shows the house and a slightly wider garden, plus two outbuildings along the north wall. Behind the back wall there is a builder's merchants. Yet the house only exists in these fragments, in snatched corners of photographs and as an absence on old maps. It seems to be constantly eluding me, slipping through the records and my fingers.

I decide the answers might lie at the local records office. Armed with a pencil and my notebook, I order a box of papers. I discover that on 31 March 1924, Basil Brooks, a hardware merchant already living on our street (possibly the owner of the end-of-terrace house and this plot of land) submitted plans for a new three-bedroom residence. At that time of year, the land here would have been stirring, birds arriving from warmer winter homes, trees turning their focus to the light, crocuses and daffodils adding colour to the grass. I can picture Brooks and his builder pacing up and down the garden, measuring and planning; imagining an ideal house.

He takes a letter of application to the planning office. Charts are drawn up, following a traditional Edwardian layout, with airy rooms and plenty of light, wide bay windows, high ceilings, set back from the road, with a small front garden, a modest porch; two storeys, with living rooms off a hallway and a kitchen at the back. A small team of local builders arrive and start digging the foundations. Masons and bricklayers haul hods of red bricks from Warnham brickworks in nearby Horsham, and begin making the bones of the house. Roofers climb scaffolding to hang the slate tiles in overlapping rows, like a game of Patience. Carpenters in flat caps and aprons hammer window frames and fix joists and floorboards carefully into place. A smooth skin of plaster is pressed over the walls and painted in the fashionable pale tones of the time. Passing foundry workers carrying satchels filled with bread, cheese and bottles of cold tea exchange pleasantries with the builders on their way to the ironworks nearby. Electricity and plumbing connect the interior with power and services. Eventually, the work is done. The first inhabitants move in. The garden is hedged off.

The next record I find of the house is a 1934 planning application to extend the bedroom. By now the house is the property of our landlord's family, and they will remain the owners for at least another ninety years. From some point in the 1950s, when they move out, the house is rented to tenants. Its life as a transient home place begins. Some tenants, like us, have stayed for many years, while others simply landed on their way to somewhere else. The road at the front swims with a steady stream of people who are nowhere. I think about all those who dug this patch of earth before me, and wonder about their stories, their dreams for this garden, their attempts to find in it a sense of belonging amongst all the flux.

I keep digging and, at last, I find a picture of the house. The photo was taken from across the street after the 1943 bomb; it shows the windows and gable of our house sitting further forward than the terraced houses, with the same wall at the front. The story is that the German bomb bounced down the street, destroying terraces on both sides and splintering the windows at the front of our house. Glass shards remained in our landlord's grandparents' piano. I wonder if one of the outbuildings in our garden was an Anderson shelter. It must have been terrifying hearing the destruction all around. I am surprised our house even survived.

At the same time that they were dropping the bomb on our street, the Nazi regime was involved in a planting scheme designed to test their theories of genetics and racial superiority. A Soviet botanist, geneticist and researcher named Professor Nikolai Vavilov had been collecting seeds from across the Soviet Union. He died in prison. The Nazis were interested in continuing his research on plants and seeds to discover more about cold endurance – possibly with a view to feeding their population as they expanded into the colder East, but also to pursue their ideas about natural selection and survival of the fittest. In 1943, they planted barley, wheat, oats and rye in an effort to learn about seed manipulation. Food, gardening and farming have always been political. As the Germans were tilling the soil for these seeds and observing their green shoots, the houses on our street were ripped open, fronts flapping off, the domestic suddenly rendered public. Brick by brick, they came down, leaving mountains of debris and dust, and a row of back yards and gardens smothered in rubble.

The photograph is a joyous find. But I am hungry for more details; I want to know what the stone foundations in the chickens' pen used to be, who ate off the broken blue and white crockery I turn up in the soil, who buried the beer bottles along the back wall, whose hands tugged at dock and nettles and picked blackberries for pies. I am getting closer to understanding the life of this place before we moved here, but there are still so many tantalizing gaps.

17

SHARING

THE SWIFTS HAVE GONE. WHAT TRIGGERS THIS MIGRATION? A reduction in insects? An internal magnetic pull? This might be our swifts' first journey to Africa, or they might be regular returnees. Some live for up to twenty years and will know their routes well. They may recognize the chalky hills that melt into a grey sea, then the arable fields and mountains of France before soaring over the dry Spanish sierras and clearing the sands of the Sahara. You have to believe they will return. Underneath a silent sky I am cleaning out the chickens, shaking fresh straw into the coop, and the smell takes me back to looking after childhood pets and horses, carrying spiky slices tugged from between orange binder twine, and watching fields of stubble burn nearby, the blackness rising in clouds out of the gold.

By the end of this month I will be putting the chickens to bed one hour earlier than in June. The days are slowly, almost imperceptibly, shortening. The garden keeps working even in the dark, digesting the sunlight. Sitting out at dusk, the chickens safely in their coop, I watch bats flit under the apple tree and whip away into the gloaming. They might be pipistrelles, but they are so fast I cannot make out their shape or size. They are furry bullets tearing up the air, filling their bellies in readiness for hibernation. They can hear shapes. The hunger of winter is a bass note suspended in the summer air as they hunt. The bats' ability to navigate by sonar reminds me suddenly of a film about the academic John Hull, who lost his sight. He described standing listening to rain fall in his garden and how the sounds of water hitting different surfaces created a sense of depth and space. The garden amplifies and echoes, helping us find our way if we tune in to our senses.

*

On a warm late-summer's day, I visit another local garden: Farleys House. The house is open to visitors, and you can walk around the gardens for a small charge. I am with a friend who has been before, but it is my first time. I have read about the collection of sculptures in the garden, but it is the vegetable and herb gardens that I am most interested in.

Farleys House is near Chiddingly, East Sussex. In 1949, it was bought by the surrealist artist Roland Penrose and the photographer Lee Miller, who restored it and transformed it into a weekend retreat from post-war London. Like Charleston, Farleys became a focal point for some of the most exciting artists working at the time, including Pablo Picasso. They were drawn by the sociable dinners Lee Miller created, the expansive landscape and the sense of artistic freedom. Beyond the garden perimeter to the south, on the horizon, are the Downs, with the Long Man of Wilmington in clear view. When Roland Penrose first saw this giant chalk figure carved into the hill from his garden, he felt it was auspicious – that Farleys was in harmonious alignment 'with the sun, the moon and the stars in the heavens'. In fact, the farm and the chalk man are connected by a ley line that runs north towards the Pole Star.

After viewing an exhibition of Lee Miller's extraordinary photographs, my friend and I wander across the farmyard and into the garden. Stepping through a hedge, we come to the herb garden. The herbs I sowed earlier in the year have failed dismally, and my hopes of setting myself up as a dispenser of healing potions for my friends and family are diminishing. Miller's herb garden is huge and abundant, with billowing waves of parsley, clouds of thyme and fronds of chives. Fennel spires pose at the back, like the sculpture behind them, taking up space in their own piece of art. I want to find out what is flourishing here, and how these plants were used in the course of Miller's time at Farleys. What I discover is a story of dark and light, of old wounds causing new damage, and the power of a garden to ease at least some of this pain for a while.

*

A photograph: a young boy sits on a patch of grass. He is wearing green-grey dungarees and a small smile. Behind him is a vegetable bed with what looks like lettuce, peas and a bushy fennel growing in it. In front of him is a basket of freshly picked vegetables: courgettes, tomatoes, artichokes and a bunch of rosemary. The boy is Antony Penrose, Roland Penrose and Lee Miller's son. His parents are down from London for the weekend and they are gathering food for dinner.

Inside, the house is basic but has filled up with artworks by Penrose and their friends – Picasso, Joan Miró, Paul Éluard, Lynn Chadwick, Max Ernst and Richard Hamilton. When Penrose and Miller first bought the farm, the garden was essentially a field and an orchard, but, with the help of their gardener Fred Baker, they have created a space that provides food and is home to Penrose's sculptures and those by friends like Henry Moore and Heinz Henghes. Penrose's architectural training honed his spatial awareness, which he has applied to the design of the flat lawn, with its soft, scalloped edges. He likes informal lines, installing a wiggly hedge between the lawn and orchard that he has dotted with fruit trees. Like Monk's House and Sissinghurst, the landscaping is designed around the idea of garden rooms, and is intended to display the sculptures to their best effect.

Fred Baker has dug four substantial vegetable beds on the south-facing end of the garden and covered one with a huge fruit cage to keep out badgers and birds; he plants flower borders filled with bright annuals (known as 'Fred's wow'), and has created a herb garden for Miller. This is Miller's greatest treasure. She wanted it near the house (which caused some conflict with Penrose and his vision for the garden), and she has filled it with rosemary, basil, thyme, sage, different types of mint, tarragon and fennel. She loves growing aromatics like basil, chives, parsley and alliums. Chicory and celery don't do well at Farleys, but with Fred's help her herbs are flourishing and are added to all the meals she prepares. Miller has commissioned a local carpenter to make her a herb-drying cabinet, and bunches are hung from ceiling hooks so she can make use of her produce through the winter months.

Self-sufficiency was essential when the family first moved in to Farleys, as rationing severely limited what food was available. It is also second nature to Miller. They grow turnips, peas, spinach, lettuce, cabbages and runner beans, and Miller has introduced more exotic vegetables like artichokes, asparagus and 'Golden

Bantam' sweetcorn, an American variety, to remind her of her childhood home. Beyond the garden are cow barns and farmland where their dairy herd graze.

The orchard already contained a variety of apples – cookers, keepers, 'Cox's Orange Pippin', 'Ellison's Orange' – as well as pears. Penrose has a penchant for ancient fruit varieties and plants medlars, despite their less-than-appetizing taste. He also loves ponds; he has removed some stone steps and created an oval pond, which he has then adapted into a more surreal, *trompe l'oeil* feature with a false perspective. A reminder that things are not always what they seem. He has also made a second pond, in the shape of a fish, playing with perceptions of nature and man-made objects. What unfolds over their time at Farleys is a garden to enjoy as a creative work, a personal expression of aesthetic taste and artistry, a place of regeneration and colour, and a source of abundance amidst post-war restrictions and shortages.

On Friday evenings, a procession of cars arrive at various intervals – Lee Miller with whatever food she can muster with her rations, friends, colleagues of Penrose's from the Institute of Contemporary Arts, and hangers-on arriving for a weekend in the country. They slough off the grime of the city and breathe in the farm's clean air, their shoulders dropping and eyes shining with anticipation. Penrose goes straight out to the garden to pick flowers for the house. The boy we see in the garden, Antony, listens for them. He is pleased to see his parents, but his week-time peace is shattered.

Life at Farleys sounds idyllic, and there are certainly plenty of happy things in this little boy's life: the freedom to roam the farm, and his beloved nanny, with whom he shares the house during the week while his parents are in London. But in this photograph there is a hesitancy in his smile, a wariness that hints at a troubled relationship with the person taking the picture – his mother. At this time Lee Miller is drinking heavily and suffering from bouts of depression. She is volatile, disconnected from her son, and unpredictable. Antony wrote later of their relationship: 'With Lee it was not a mother and son relationship but more like a grudging affection between two battle-scarred warriors.' She is not physically abusive to her son, but her unhappiness and the drink unleash terrifying and damaging verbal assaults. 'She was so deadly with words,' Antony noted. The garden has become a refuge for him, escaping into his treehouse or 'helping' Fred with various tasks. He is on his guard in this photograph, sitting on the grass with the vegetables, enjoying being in his mother's company but waiting for the air to change, for the cloud to snap across her face, for her eyes to flash with fury. He is more comfortable making himself invisible.

Being a parent has always been complicated for Miller, partly because of her difficult relationship with her own mother, Florence. At the age of seven Miller was sent away to stay with family friends when Florence was having a breakdown. Instead of being sheltered from harm, she was raped and went back home traumatized, broken and suffering from gonorrhoea. Her mother insisted that Miller did not speak about her assault and administered agonizingly painful treatments to relieve the infection's symptoms throughout Miller's childhood – a continuous violation, which she abhorred. There are suggestions that Florence also condoned – or at least chose to ignore – her husband Theodore's inappropriate behaviour towards their daughter. He would regularly take photographs of Miller naked. While there is no evidence of abuse, it is likely that Miller was so dissociated as a result of the earlier sexual assault that this unusual attention meant little to her. Due to the gonorrhoea, Miller thought she would not be able to have children, so at the age of forty, in 1947, she had been surprised to find herself pregnant. In an article about her son's impending birth and her feelings about motherhood, she likens the baby's bassinet to the baskets Anne Boleyn and Marie Antoinette took to their executions for their heads to be carried in.

A photograph: a woman is lying on a wooden bench beside the brick wall of a house. A window and doorway occupy the right-hand side of the photograph and the outline of a climbing rose twines skywards. She rests her bare feet on one arm of the bench and her head on the other. One hand sits on her belly and in her right hand she holds a cigarette. She has short, wavy, fair hair and is wearing her usual farm attire: a woolly gilet, slacks and a jersey. It may be that the photographer has caught her in a moment's repose, between plucking the chicken for tonight's dinner and preparing the herby green mayonnaise she is renowned for. But it may also be staged. Is she simply relaxing in her garden, or posing to make a statement about her life? Miller is used to being the subject of photographs and artworks, having been a model for *Vogue* in the 1920s and a muse to Man Ray in Paris in the early 1930s. She knows how to create a picture and build a narrative around it.

Miller's modelling career was ended after an unfortunate association with an advertisement for a sanitary product suddenly rendered her undesirable in the eyes of the big fashion houses. She set up her own successful photographic studios, first in Paris, where she worked alongside her lover and collaborator, Man Ray, and then in New York. In 1934, she married Aziz Eloui Bey, an Egyptian businessman, and moved to Cairo with him. Her life there was a stifling stream of expat parties and mental drift, from which she escaped on travels and adventures, learning about Egyptian history, culture and cuisine. Bored with this lifestyle, she returned to Europe for a holiday and met Roland Penrose in Paris in 1937. Seeing that his wife was deeply unhappy and unfulfilled, Eloui Bey agreed that Miller should leave him and move to London with Penrose. She began working as a fashion photographer for *Vogue* and then became their war correspondent in Europe as conflict raged across the world.

For someone who deals in images, the horrors of war and the sexual assault when she was a child must have imprinted themselves on her memory as a series of terrifying snapshots. When she closed her eyes, perhaps she heard a shutter click and saw a black-and-white picture of women cooking over a makeshift brick stove amidst the bombed-out ruins of Nuremberg. *Click.* Bodies piled up in newly liberated concentration camps, the flapping blue and white feathers of their clothing the only movement. *Click.* A man thrusting and grunting over her tiny body. *Click.* Dead men slumped in freight trucks. *Click.* A crowd of Nazi camp guards wearing prisoners' clothing in an attempt to escape capture. *Click.* The silently screaming faces of starved, mutilated Jewish prisoners. *Click. Click. Click.*

Lying on the bench in her peaceful Sussex garden, perhaps Miller still sees these images, even though her eyes are open. They float like ghosts on the periphery of her vision. The whiskey helps.

A photograph: Miller stands in front of a cream-coloured Aga wearing a pale apron, her sleeves rolled up as she works. Shadows of drying garden herbs stipple the ceiling above her. On one hob puffs a black steamer pan and on the other is a deep frying pan. She holds the handle in her left hand and with her right she stirs a sauce she is preparing for her houseful of guests. The kitchen is her domain, but she encourages visitors to help. They are given tasks like sticking labels on preserves, stringing runner beans, and peeling vegetables. Sometimes Antony helps with the cooking, but working alongside his mother in the kitchen is fraught with potential rages and cruel words. Since her expeditions in Egypt, where she learned to embellish their basic tinned supplies, and her experiences in wartime Europe, improvising dishes by making stews in her helmet or butchering shell-struck cows, Miller has nurtured a love of cooking.

At first Miller tried to replicate dishes she had enjoyed in Parisian restaurants, recreating happier times with old friends. She took a course at Le Cordon Bleu in Paris and devoured cookbooks, learning as much as she could about food and the science of cooking. She has amassed so many reference books (around 2,000 by the end of her life) and notebooks filled with recipes that Penrose has built her a library. She conducts exhaustive research and works on recipes until they are just right, determined to perfect each dish. Still in touch with her good friend and *Vogue* editor Timmie O'Brien, Miller has started working on some features for the magazine (though some remain unpublished), and enters competitions to devise innovative new dishes (which she invariably wins). Magazines have begun to run stories about her cooking, with photo shoots in the garden. Antony Penrose believes cooking was part of her recovery process, that 'without this constantly creative and self-replacing objective it is hard to imagine how she would have survived'. Miller herself wrote, 'Cooking is pure therapy.' Cooking, like photography, requires a symbiosis of science and intuition. It seems she has found something that perfectly fuses her artistic flair, the technical knowledge she gained developing photographs, and her need to quiet the demons in her head.

Miller's playful, surreal side also finds a perfect outlet in the meals she prepares. Her famous dish of 'Pink Cauliflower Breasts' echoes an earlier photograph she took of a severed breast, which she placed on a dish after observing a mastectomy. She conjures dishes like 'Goldfish' (cod covered in strips of carrot), 'Bird's Nest Soup' (consommé topped with carrots shaped like eggs sitting on a handful of hay), 'Tomato Soup Cake', and her prize-winning 'Penroses' (mushrooms stuffed with pink petal-shaped piped ham and veal paté). She adorns the table with brightly coloured flowers from the garden. Each meal is carefully thought out and prepared, but occasionally Miller gets too drunk to complete the cooking and the nanny-cum-housekeeper, Patsy, has to finish off.

Inheriting her engineer-father's inquisitiveness about technology, Miller has always had a fondness for gadgets. In the photograph of her standing at the cooker, her mind is elsewhere – she may be devising ways to wash spinach in her washing machine or stuff silver spoons inside a roasting chicken to reduce the cooking time. On the shelves just out of shot are piles of the equipment and labour-saving devices she collects. She has inherited an understanding of preserving and bottling from her mother's family. Soon she must start pickling, slicing beans and layering them in glass battery jars with salt, storing tarragon in oil to infuse mayonnaise, freezing summer puddings made from the mounds of redcurrants they harvest, and making pesto with the basil from her herb garden.

Every meal is like performance art for Miller. She communicates with her audience through food, each dish asking the questions, *Can I reach you? Can I give you something to think about? Can I make you happy?* She cooks, quite simply, to save her life.

A photograph: a table set for lunch on a bricked terrace: two roast chickens and bowls of vegetables, cooked with care and thought, and enjoyed in the sunny tranquillity of the garden. Three guests, plus Miller and Penrose, smiling up at the photographer, who is leaning out of an upstairs window. The garden is both backdrop to and provider of this meal, and countless others. Hating formality and pristine lawns, Miller asked Fred Baker to mow the grass earlier in the week so that the daisies would reappear in time for the weekend party.

The farm and garden provide chickens – caught, plucked and cleaned; potatoes, beans and peas – freshly picked, podded or peeled by guests with drinks in the kitchen; petals strewn over the dessert; borage flowers bobbing in a jug of Pimms; artichokes trimmed and served on a silver platter that no one notices bears the initials AH and a sinister eagle (pillaged by Miller from the Berghof, Hitler's home in Berchtesgaden, Bavaria, one of the only times her secret wartime experiences spill into her present life); vases of lupins, Turk's cap lilies, campanula and roses to decorate the dining table; rabbits shot on the farmland, skinned and slow-cooked in a casserole. The bounty provides not only beauty but sustenance. This garden is full of life and vigour, its vitality as significant as its aesthetics. It feeds the soul as well as the body.

Miller dives into farm life, learning how to cut up a pig carcass, making cream cheese and butter from their cows' milk, rearing geese and hens for eggs and the table. Although she initially found the house cold, draughty and inhospitable, with a new, specially built fitted kitchen and a working range she has grown to love Farleys. In a letter to her mother, she writes: 'You'd laugh at me as a farmer's wife – drying herbs, pickling things and washing spinach.'

Her recipes incorporate ingredients foraged in the hedgerows or grown in the garden: elderberry and crab-apple jelly, chutney, yellow-tomato preserve, apple chilli sauce, and 'Pink Heaven' (stewed rhubarb with whipped cream set in a mould and topped with candied ginger).

The garden is also a playground for her artistic and surrealist companions. Walking between the hedges, you might find Roland Penrose's first wife, Valentine, charming snakes beside the pond with young Antony watching, enthralled. There may be a lively croquet match in full swing on the lawn. You could stumble across a naked man leaning against a tree, sharpening Miller's kitchen knives, legs open to the sunshine. You may glimpse any one of the most prominent artists of the time chasing geese out of the lettuce bed or picking tomatoes.

Despite her ongoing struggles with alcohol, depression and family, Miller finds a place to reinvent herself at Farleys. Like the artworks she and Penrose so joyfully display on the walls, she has learned to anchor herself in the house and the garden, poring over seed catalogues in January to source the vegetables they would grow for the thirteen meals she was already planning for the next Christmas. She has found happiness in cooking for others, and keeps notes of her friends' likes and dislikes so she can feed them their favourite dishes when they next visit. For Miller, food is about survival and defiance, but also about celebration and artistry.

Food became a 'lingua franca – a bond that connected her with everyone who entered her life', writes Miller's granddaughter, Ami Bouhassane. Miller was constantly reinventing – herself, through her varied professional roles; and the food she shared with friends. She was a shapeshifter who, as a result of what we now would acknowledge as post-traumatic stress disorder, unwittingly harmed much that was caught in her eddying wake, but who was also known for her kindness and generosity to others and who embraced mutability and adaptation.

Whilst the house, the garden and her cooking could not cure her or ameliorate the damage she had endured – and inflicted – they did provide essential respite and a place to pour her creative spirit. After her death from cancer in 1977, her ashes were scattered in the garden, later joined by those of others. The circle closes and rolls on: these people who ate, slept, laughed and cried together share their last resting place amongst sculptures, apple trees and vegetable plots. Their dust sinks beneath the surface to give life to plants that in their turn will feed hungry mouths.

*

My friend and I sit down in the shade and talk about art and love and families. We start walking again, passing through a tall, clipped hedge, cut to form two taller, gatepost-like towers, and then running in a lower belt across the garden. A striking sculpture lies in the grass, like a half-buried giant, fibreglass limbs separated from its torso. Its form reminds me of the sculptures at Little Sparta, and of the Long Man of Wilmington – part human, part landscape. Clumps of pink cosmos flower boldly from dry, crumbling earth.

As we pass the sculptures that dot the lawn and rise up out of the orchard, I conjure a cast of people onto the lawn. I summon a basket of sweetcorn cobs, beans and potatoes. I open my ears to hear Patsy calling guests inside for dinner, the clink of glasses carried to the dining room, and the laughter as one guest takes off her top, sitting bare-breasted at the table. A bumblebee bumps at a window upstairs, where a small boy looks out on the scene below. A puppy yelps in an outhouse as another nips her ear. Opera blasts from the library. From the barn comes a long, lowing call as a cow nuzzles her newborn calf to its feet. It has a very different feel, this garden, to the other Sussex gardens I have visited. It is less dazzling, yet somehow more alive. Rather than feeling like a recreation in homage to past inhabitants, it seems to be a humble continuation of a garden that was created first out of a desire for self-sufficiency and refuge, and then grew into a place of art and profusion that would nourish and sustain the family and their guests. It is a place designed for sharing, for communality and for celebrating together.

We drive home with our heads full of pictures – Miller's photographs, imagined dinner parties, young Antony. In my garden, we drink elderflower cordial at the small table under the back wall, and talk about our lost mothers and their legacies, thinking about the reverberating trauma that Miller passed on to Antony, and how admirable it is that he's devoting his life to making sure his mother's work and life continue to be seen. Miller's sleepy life in Sussex must have been such a contrast to the frenetic socializing of Paris and the adrenalized atmosphere of wartime. I can see why she liked to surround herself with friends at Farleys. I plot a garden gathering of my own, inspired to conjure up a feast to share. We have to make the most of this weather – of the garden while it still has some blooms.

*

The sound of late July is the wet slap of the hose as I set about the task of watering. Another sound: the startled whir and flutter of sparrows in the brambles near my table and chair when I sit down. The chair is spotted with clots of blackberry flesh and purple bird droppings. The figs are ripening – swollen, flaccid, like distended testicles covered with ants. A cabbage white butterfly skims my face and I spot five or six more darting over the vegetable patch, landing on the broccoli and cabbages. They want to lay eggs from which caterpillars will burst and burrow down into the plant, protected from predators by the brassicas' mustard oil. Adult butterflies use ultraviolet reflections from petals to find sources of nectar, navigating by light. That all this magic is going on quietly as I sit and watch is a constant source of wonder. A gull's shriek merges into the sound of a passing siren.

Pears hang from branches that bow under their weight. The grasses underneath the tree are discarded golden feathers. I think about whether to dig this area over and plant a proper wildflower patch, but suddenly do not have the energy for it all. The heat has leeched my sap. A stream of cyclists flies past the front of the house. I spot flashes of coloured shirts and hear their bells tinging, like those childhood wind-up mini organs with metal hammers that rise and fall on the dotted barrel. The sound passes. Occasionally an apple flumps to the ground. I wander back inside to attend to my family. As I cross the threshold, I notice the petty spurge that has appeared in the pots by the back door. I will deal with it. Another day.

*

At this time of year, gardeners often face a glut. Too many courgettes, bagfuls of lettuce, knobbly cucumbers needing a home.

Due partly to the size of my family (and their appetites), and partly due to slug attrition and my inadequacies, this year I don't have a huge surplus. I have given away freezer bags full of bright-pink rhubarb, taken tubs of raspberries along to picnics, and offered everyone a marrow (always declined). My gardening friends are community-minded, sharing seeds, stories, cuttings and plants across borders and generations. I give one friend some parsnip seeds for next year; he gives me tomatoes. Our gardens merge.

Gardeners are sharers. It is in our bones. Though we are disparate in our approaches – some of us try to control our land and the seasons; others work according to the course of the moon, belonging to the seasons – there has always been a tradition of swapping, donating, stealing and foraging. Skilful gardeners learn how to graft limbs of trees to create new ones. One friend packs an envelope with seeds collected from their allotment to send to another. A knowledgeable neighbour cuts his meadow grass and collects armfuls for a novice to spread over her grass.

When we first moved here, I wanted to offer up spaces in the garden as free allotments – I didn't have the time or skills to make proper use of it, and it felt wrong that all that precious growing space was being wasted, when so many people would love a garden like this. I researched garden-sharing schemes and discussed it with my husband. My impulse was to fling open the gate and let others enjoy the garden, but the practicalities of small children running around, and laziness on my part meant it remained a utopian ideal. But in the end, growing our own food and giving away the surplus also feels like a way of stepping out of the financial and social systems that dictate so much of how we live. By swapping seeds with our neighbours, we bypass the big seed companies that control so much of the world's plant growing, and we retain the resilience of locally grown seeds. Networks of local gardeners have been doing this for generations, but somehow we have been persuaded to buy commercially developed seeds that are bred for things we may not desire, like longevity, when what we really want is *taste*. By sharing, we create abundance where it matters. By exchanging bags of surplus broad beans for jars of jam made from homegrown strawberries, we can step out of history for a moment and create a new story for the way we want to live.

The gardens I have visited, my own unruly space, the gardens my friends nurture, my mother's unkempt garden – I see now that they are all connected. It feels like this is how I can establish a sense of rootedness and feel more able to cope with uncertainty – by understanding that our stories are not unique, that we do not live in isolation, that how we attend to the people and landscape around us really does create and change the world. The simple act of planting and growing enables me to feel part of a community, entangled in networks of friends as well as places. Whatever happens, I can try to cultivate a kind of 'biodiversity of the self', in which I acknowledge and embrace the connections I have with different places, and recognize my shared home on this planet.

*

It is that delicious time of evening when visitors have just left and the air is still ringing with conversations and laughter. We had invited two families who live nearby over for an outdoor feast, with herb-filled salads and colourful flowers on the table, inspired by the gatherings at Farleys. We ate next to the privet hedge, the smaller children running in and out of the house, and the older ones skulking off to their bedrooms with their phones and plates of food. Our friends all left at once, prompted by that inner parental clock that tells you it's past bedtime and there will be tears. My husband and I carry in dishes and bottles, hurrying our youngest off to bed. I dismantle the fairy lights I had strung from the apple tree and fold up the blankets I brought out in case the temperature dropped. A cloud of midges squirms above the table. I hear plates clattering in the kitchen, flushings and brushings as people get ready for bed. My husband sends the dog bounding outside for her night-time pee. She disappears into the hedge and I wait for her in the blue-grey light.

In this fading-summer stillness, I decide to take a rogation walk around the garden. Although I don't have a religious faith, I like this old Christian custom of blessing and praying for all the village's growing sites. Traditionally, this was a springtime practice, when villagers travelled along the boundaries of their community, showing the young boys each marker so they could pass on the knowledge through generations. To reinforce their memories of the particular spot, the boys were beaten or 'bumped' (tipped upside down and their heads bumped against the ground or stone). Over time this cruelty was recognized as unacceptable, and people switched to beating the boundary markers instead of the village youth, giving the custom the name 'beating the bounds'. The last recorded example of this happening in my area was 1919. I wonder if it was a way to take stock after the war, to encircle a home place once more and turn the gaze inward a little.

As I make my small pilgrimage along the edges of our enclosed space, I try to see beyond the bounds. I lift my eyes to the small row of modern houses beyond the back wall. One of our neighbours there (the only one I have talked to, in fact) grew up on a farm near where my mother lived, and she loves hearing our chickens because it reminds her of home. The lights are on in her house, creating that irresistible feeling of comfort that a lit window exudes. I remember that I promised to take her some eggs to apologize for the chickens' noisy dawn crowing. Over the long wall on my left, I watch people come and go in the car park next door. Moving across the garden, alongside the telecoms building, my rogation walk has me stopping to figure out how the dog keeps escaping through our fence. There are gaps I hadn't seen. I reach the pond, which I decide to fill in and relocate to a less shady spot, passing the waning rhubarb that I have been giving to friends in bright, tangy bundles. Followed by phantom footsteps, I refill the bird bath from the outside tap and turn towards the house. Like my garden and the birds above it, I am in constant movement. Yet at the same time I am also grounded in this soil that I hoe and rake. Look up and look down. The answers are there.

AUGUST

18

PAUSE

Purple-pawed and bramble-sore, I pick bowlfuls of black-berries and raspberries to make jam. Back in the kitchen, radio on and windows open, I cut up windfall apples and throw the slices into a large pan with the washed and softening blackberries from the garden and a recent hedgerow haul. I stir in a squeeze of lemon juice and inhale the sharp, sweet smell. The fruit turns into a beguiling, unctuous lava, puffing into tiny craters. As usual, I find I don't have entirely the correct equipment for making bramble jelly, but I have improvised, as I have seen my stepmother do, with an upturned stool from which I have suspended a piece of muslin to make a bag. It looks like a strange inverted hot-air balloon waiting to float us from summer into autumnal skies. As I pour the fruit mixture into its pouch, juice begins to drip gently through its petticoat. I go to bed, leaving the fruit to seep through.

In the morning, the table is a grisly crime scene. I strain off the pulp and matter, and pour the remaining liquid over a mountain of sugar, watching the purple stain and engulf the crystals. Once boiling, this mixture fills the room with an irresistible, almost heady, sweetness. The surface is pocked with bubbles, a fury of syrup and distilled sunlight. I drop a teaspoon of the mixture onto a cold saucer, stretching its plastic skin to see if it sets. My son wanders in, bored with shooting hoops, and I ask if he wants to help. I have learned that he is more likely to join in if an activity is already underway and it requires no advance commitment or planning on his part. He is usually game, not yet fully walled off by teenage hormones. He is interested in the alchemy of the jam-making, leaning over the pan to watch it suck and pop. It makes me think of the potions he and the others used to make in a small well in the roots of an old beech tree, near the monks' herb garden. The children would collect berries, leaves and petals, then add water and stir happily for ages. I know I only have his full attention for a few precious minutes now, so I set him to dropping waxed discs onto hot jarfuls of jelly and marking labels in his scratchy handwriting. We lick the spoons when we have finished bottling this day.

Alone again, I turn to the raspberries and begin in another pan, creating a froth of pink-red sugary mixture, the pan lid huffing soft sighs as the jam exhales its summer heat. By the end of the process, with fewer jars filled than I had hoped, the kitchen is coated in a vague stickiness that takes days to completely remove.

In the garden, the cosmos is flourishing. This is a stalwart plant in my garden, giving up its joyous blooms until well into autumn. I grow tall white 'Purity' and pink 'Antiquity'. Originally native to Mexico and the Americas, some seed is thought to have found its way to South Africa in horse feed during the Boer War and germinated in the baking soil there. Named after the Greek word *cosmos*, meaning 'harmony', the neatly arranged petals represent an ordered universe. The philosopher Gaston Bachelard believed we create an imaginary 'cosmos' – a harmonious, dreamed-up realm from which we learn how to live in the material world. These modest, proliferative flowers know nothing of such spiritual burdens. They simply grow, set seed and die. In summer they feature heavily in the jars and vases I fill with cut flowers for the house.

The sky is quiet. I miss seeing the swifts' steely boomerang forms dancing above my head. It is almost unbearably hot. I haven't been sleeping well. A few nights ago, I woke up in the middle of the night; except I didn't, exactly. I was conscious but I couldn't move. A heavy weight pressed down on my chest and my body was paralysed. Terrified, I tried to call out to my husband, asleep next to me. My mouth made hopeless circles like a surfacing fish, but no sound came out. I tried to flap my hand to alert him but nothing was doing what it should. I tried to breathe slowly, quelling the panic. Maybe I was dying, but maybe it would pass. Eventually I fell asleep again, and woke in the morning physically fine. Some quick research revealed I had experienced sleep paralysis – common in people who are grieving, apparently. My body was mirroring my mother's rigid limbs. My sadness was crushing me. The nights feel full of potential horrors.

One evening, I can't stand the stifling suffocation of the heat any longer, and take a duvet, blanket and pillow out into the garden. I clamber onto the trampoline and make myself a bed, squashing elderberries beneath my blanket. The semi-darkness has removed all outlines and shapes, as if I am underwater and can only see the shade and gradations of light above the surface. I *perceive* rather than see the shapes where the hedge meets the sky, and the contours of the flower beds and shed. The garden becomes a negative space, my senses connecting to forms and gaps rather than details. I hear the muffled thump of a car door and the harsh two-note ping of the bathroom light pull. Gradually, my eyes grow accustomed to the dark (though the lights from the car park next door prevent true darkness), and I lie back looking for Perseids. Streaks of chaos that puncture the orderly cosmos, flashing their tails quicker than wishes. These meteor showers radiate from near the Perseus constellation – hence their name – although those stars actually burned out long before we see the flashing clusters of meteors. The sky holds and reveals time across all its dimensions, spattering us with glimpses into the past while we seek the future. I think about the delicate elderflowers I gathered with my daughter from the hedge that now looms over me, and the soft purple berries they have become. I see the stars these flowers were and the dripping explosions they have become.

Either due to my short-sightedness or just bad luck, I do not see any Perseids. After a while, I begin to doze, semi-dreaming but I find it hard to sleep properly. Although I am much cooler – deliciously cold, even – I feel slightly spooked out here on my own. The garden smells different at night; the shapes seem unfamiliar and the shadows hostile. Our cat suddenly bounds onto the trampoline, making me jump, and then continuously visits throughout the night, purring and nudging; her soft footsteps seem menacing as I slip in and out of wakefulness. I feel like an animal myself, experiencing this strange pocket of the earth from a new perspective – exposed, flat against the surface, my senses working harder. Sleep comes eventually and fitfully. Too soon the garden stirs, with the chatter of a few sparrows and a gentle, pink-smeared dawn stretching over the slumbering town. The chickens shuffle out of their coop, opening their wings and shaking themselves so their feathers puff out. The garden rises from the depths, rinsed with droplets of dew. Another morning. I bundle up my bedlinen and notice the berry-fleck stains on my pillowcase, like paint flicked from a brush. I walk softly through the dew, back into the house and my slumbering family. I slip back into bed, trying not to wake my sleeping husband.

*

I know that some people find the approach of autumn depressing – my mother used to 'feel a bit low' as winter hove into view. But she was also able to see that it would pass, and would often say, 'It's not always dark at six.' I am aware of the garden's ceaseless growing and dying, the unpetalling of the flowers and simultaneous dropping of seeds onto the soil and into the wind. A whitening is happening to the grasses and lawn – like my hair, they are fading, pigment leaching out to leave brittle, blanched strands. Every colour is on the edge of another, in motion between different shades, and we see this vividly in the garden as plants grow, mature, age and decay. How do we describe these colours when they are constantly shifting? I think of Monet's endless variations on his garden, and the pond there: capturing its mutability with rapid brushstrokes, his acute feel for the changing light.

With the coming end of summer, all around the plants are busying themselves with procreation. Seed heads develop their own unique architecture within the beds, holding on to life, scattered across the soil or carried within the soft stomach of a bird. My thoughts dare to turn to next year, thinking about what plants I might grow. I know I could start planning, propagating, spreading seed myself. But will it jinx our situation? I decide to continue planting my faith in the future, and start taking cuttings from a rose and some lavender.

I choose a suitable stem (not too soft, not in flower and from a young plant), cut just below a side shoot and immediately push the cutting into a pot, topping it with the grit we add to the chickens' feed. I am just learning about propagation and have yet to try more complex methods like layering or grafting. Like most of my gardening, I have improvised, plunging odd rose prunings or accidentally snapped branches into the ground, forgetting all about them, and then returning a few months later to see with surprise they have taken root and are growing leaves. The simplest and least demanding way I have found to conjure new plants from old is collecting seeds. I put mine in small brown envelopes, like the ones that used to contain my weekly wages as a waitress. They are like tiny portals into the future, waiting to unfurl under the warmth of the sun.

*

On a cooler day, I plant out fifteen wallflower plugs I ordered. They'd arrived, tufty-haired, in thin boxes, like guards awaiting orders. The earth is damp again, deep brown and moist instead of the compacted dust of the past few months; it is so much nicer to work with. It is good to be back out here after a neglectful few weeks. I place the plugs at the front of the rear flower bed, anticipating a ripple of pastel colour next spring, and creating some continuity with the previous tenants' wallflowers, planted when another family slipped their keys into the front door lock and called out as they stepped across the hallway. The grass is awash with dandelions, beaming their sunny faces up to the sky despite my best efforts – a bad year for them, my father says (but good if you're a dandelion, I suppose). I uproot the runner-bean stalks from the vegetable patch and pull up the dried-up sweet peas from the old tin bath, collecting any seed pods I hear rattling. I replace them with a few pinks for some instant brightness, and a nod to Charleston. I pick two pears hanging fat and almost-ripe, hoping I can eat them at just the right moment – finding the optimum ripeness is a matter of patient observation, then seizing the moment as soon as you feel that slight give in the flesh and see the change in skin colour from green to slightly yellow. The rewards for this attentive waiting are heavenly.

*

It is strange taking steps to reproduce plants and to witness the garden so fulsomely demonstrating its fertility at a time when I am going through a transition of my own. Middle age and hormonal changes are shifting my body away from a place of generation, fecundity and cycles to a quieter, fallow state. I watch as my skin thins and sags, as my bones begin to ache and my body's normal rhythms (of sleep, menstruation, desire, mood) are interrupted by unexpected gaps. My body is melting like a wax candle, sliding into a slump of itself. This gradual yet visceral decline feels so different from the 'quickening' of pregnancy, and the frenetic pace of early motherhood. Time seems slower, duller, muffled – as if a soft layer of snow has settled over it. I am inside a pause.

My shift to infertility is not as bad as many women experience, but it does feel like a long, limbo-like state. My body has nearly done with reproduction; my children still need me, but they are all – even the littlest – approaching the point when they can survive by themselves; so now what? Regeneration, perhaps. An autumn, of sorts, is approaching. A time to retreat and restore.

But I still have energy, thankfully, and am strong and healthy. Just as the garden seems suspended before an inevitable decline, I can feel myself on the cusp of a new life stage. Aging for humans seems like a passive act, just as it is for plants. Yet it also provides the space to emerge from one shape or role and choose how we want to live from now on. The menopause can be generative. I look to my garden to see how to tend to my own change. A rose bush doesn't mind that its leaves are curling at the edges; the bolting chard knows that once its seeds are flung out, its next state is wilting back into the earth; the squat geranium will make no more flowers for a while, turning inwards and downwards. The garden slides on through this late season shedding, dropping, shrivelling, with no rage against the dying of the light. Autumn has crested the hill and strolls slowly, meanderingly towards the garden gate, cap swinging in its hand.

In the garden, I am surrounded by circles: the sun, the moon, the centres of daisies, feathery dandelion clocks, fresh green peas, seeds, apples. The repeating spiral patterns on tiny snail shells, and the frothy layers of overlapping rose petals leading ever inwards. For so many years, my physical work as a mother has run in constant quotidian cycles of care. This has been the pattern of my days, but things are changing.

There is no linear end point (aside from death, of course), except, I suppose, when my children have all grown and moved away. That time feels too impossible - and empty - to imagine. These domestic rhythms are the heartbeat of my life. Sometimes I resent them and sometimes I find great comfort in them. They are always a privilege. Circles are strong, impermeable. They contain things within and keep things outside. But they are also endless. Perhaps I will find a freedom in being released from relentless domestic and bodily cycles and in embracing a more dynamic, linear way of existing – a disruption which allows some kind of end point to come into focus.

Our house is detached, circled on three sides by some form of garden area. Inside this domestic space I too have become detached, inching my way out of the obliterating eddy of family life yet also needing the constant flow. As Vanessa Bell said to her sister Virginia Woolf, 'I have spilt myself among too many stools.' I have been detached from the people I love, paying less attention to nurturing essential relationships and needing more time to myself. Reading a passage by the garden designer and writer Mirabel Osler, I am struck by her description of how a garden can perfectly fit into this stage in a woman's life: 'Women who come to gardening only once their children have left home may find their horizons expanding in a way they never dreamt was possible. Having given out to others in one way or another for years until they felt laid waste, they at last find a place of their own.'

I think about the definition of 'grounding' that means running ashore, being stuck, stranded, helpless. I sense *heimweh* lapping at my feet – unlike *hiraeth*, this is the longing to escape and travel, but it also contains a tinge of sadness at leaving. There is a beach along the coast from here where the sea comes in fast, creating deadly quicksand that sucks hold of your legs and fixes you to the spot. You drown with your body planted immovably in the sand, like seaweed rooted in the seabed.

Entrapment.
Entanglement.
Embeddedness.
Obliteration.

I lose myself in the garden, tuning into the symphonic composition of spikes, umbels, earth, branches and bees. The broccoli is ready to eat, potatoes too. I gather abundance around me to keep the circling estate agents and lawyers at bay. Sitting at the back table one hot morning, I hear a rustle in the mass of comfrey leaves next to me. The dog runs over and starts barking madly into the foliage. I take her indoors and sit quietly again, waiting to see what emerges from the undergrowth. Eventually the rustle starts again. I see a black dot and some bristles, but my eyes can't make sense of the shapes. Then I realize it's a hedgehog. I hardly dare breathe in case I frighten her off. She comes into full view, her tiny feet and cumbersome, beprickled body moving faster than I had imagined possible. She scuttles under the rose and brambles, stopping briefly to sniff the air and check for danger. Then, with a sneeze, she is gone. It is a joyous, unexpected encounter. I fetch a tub of water in case she's thirsty and leave it near the comfrey. Aristotle is said to have believed hedgehogs can predict changes in the wind. In Eastern European folklore, they symbolize common sense and steadfastness. Was she bringing me a message? I need to listen for the breath pause, take a beat, then hold fast.

19

GAPS

August is a bad month for gardening. For me at least (and also, it seems, for my mother – there are no August entries in her garden diary for any of the years she kept it). The garden lolls in a pause between the beauteous abundance of the last months and the start of the autumnal decline. In late summer, I surrender to the fact that once again it has not quite turned out as I had imagined at the end of winter, when I crunched across frosty grass picturing its voluptuous future. A kind of lethargy sets in, a mist of inertia settling over the garden as things start to 'go over'. The garden measures its time by a different, slower beat. I can't cope with the heat and feel like I am moving through treacle until the sun drops below the horizon or a breeze whips up. My garden becomes a space for languishing, for retreating from the heat and bustle of the house and pausing to recharge before the coming autumn.

I sit at the small table near the back wall with a cold drink and watch lazily as gulls glide overhead. My neck is in the sun and it prickles with heat. A familiar sense of disappointment and resignation sinks through my body as I look around the garden at the weedy wild areas and absences where plants have failed: the *Stipa tenuissima* that never blazed beneath the fig, the penstemons that lasted one summer and then never reappeared, the repeated plantings of lily of the valley (my grandmother's favourite flower), which remained buried unseen beneath the hedge, the invisible *Crambe cordifolia*, or the many scabious that simply vanished. I realize that I have become too focused on end results – on how the garden will look at certain points in the year; how it compares to other gardens I visit or see online or in magazines; how it might work some kind of magic and keep us here. There is a fine line between seeking inspiration and self-flagellation.

But, as I gather yet another bowl of raspberries, I catch the honey-sweet scent of the luminous roses that throw their glory all around the garden. In the vegetable patch, it has been a good year for broad beans, beetroot and chard. I remind myself to pay attention to what *has* worked. The cutting patch is a success, bejewelled with bright discs of rudbeckia, rich red antirrhinum, and the few fiery dahlias that have survived the slugs. Cosmos – my trusty filler – is bringing colour and life to the flagging borders. And, most importantly, we are still here to witness it all.

At this point in the year, I invariably make an impulsive dash to a local nursery for plants to plug the increasing gaps. This time I return with gaura, cosmos, coreopsis and astilbe. In the evening, I slowly work each one into the ground or a pot, patching up and trying to stretch out the time of abundance. I have also bought more gravel to cover up the grass that is emerging in the path behind the back bed, as I feel too indolent to weed it properly. I paper over the flaws, creating an illusion of neatness. But it is impossible to hide all the imperfections, and the garden fills its own spaces – weeds, grass, moss – writing its own story.

There is a gravestone in a churchyard near here where moss has grown inside the lettering. The words 'loving' and 'memory' are discernible, and the rest is a greening alphabet soup following unseen lines. The effect is a soft, living text that spills out of the boundaries of carved spaces, writing itself into the story of the person whose body it guards. The botanist and writer Robin Wall Kimmerer speaks of an 'ancient conversation going on between moss and rocks', noting the contrasts between softness and hardness, decay and vibrancy. That old cliché, 'nature abhors a vacuum', is borne out by these incredible organisms that find a home in gaps and in-between places. Moss, and the unrelated but similar-looking lichens, turns surfaces into new forms – a tree stump becomes a thing of beauty, a ruined wall is swathed in bright green drapes, an old brick path becomes springy and spongey. These velvet coverings simultaneously emphasize and hide their hosts, creating different outlines and shapes from existing structures, covering them in earthy beauty. I think back to Derek Jarman's Prospect Cottage, where rare lichens and vivid mosses make their homes on shrubs, shingle and structures. They change the way we interact with and experience these objects, as well as providing homes for microorganisms and invertebrates. Lichens are composites of algae, cyanobacteria and fungus, rather than being plants, like mosses. They can only survive in collaboration; but they can thrive in the most inhospitable places and achieve near immortality through this coexistence. A lesson in cooperation, manifest as delicate filaments, frills and tentacles.

I remember making Easter gardens with my granny, covering a plate with moss to represent grass, then building a tomb from pebbles. I loved how you could peel a long carpet of moss away from a surface. The trick was to keep its fragile structure intact long enough to transport it to your 'garden'. Mosses do not have roots – instead of growing vertically, like most other plants, they grow horizontally. They grow at an impossibly slow rate, some increasing by as little as 2.5 centimetres every twenty-five years, stretching time to its furthest reaches and making a mockery of our hectic human lives. They can survive extensive periods of drought and then instantly come back to life on contact with water. Moss has been part of this planet's ecosystem from the beginning. Early mosses were the originators of all plant and animal life, and created the peat bogs that preserved the remains of our Homo sapiens ancestors. As I learn more about its fascinating history, I stop thinking I should remove it from the chickens' gate, where it gathers in brittle brown clouds along the bottom strut. Instead, it feels a privilege to have such an ancient, careful, creeping organism making its home in my garden.

Moss has featured throughout human history too: in indigenous and medieval societies, it was used as a medicine and to staunch bleeding; later people used it to insulate their shoes and homes, and as bedding for animals; and during the First World War, sphagnum moss was applied as an antiseptic wound treatment. Today, scientists and researchers are highlighting the role genetically engineered moss could play in green biotechnology, the pharmaceutical industry and even cosmetics. Evocative common names for moss species are filled with a folkloric lyricism that reflects traditional tales of wood-dwelling, sprite-like 'moss people': silky forklet, haircap, swan's neck thyme, glittering wood, electrified cat's tail, cushion. There are many more – in fact there are 1,000 different species of moss in the UK alone, and around 20,000 across the globe. Moss is an unwelcome visitor in many Western gardens, where an obsession for neat, tidy lawns makes it something of a pariah; but it is celebrated in Japan as an exemplar of tenacity and patience. When I lived in Australia, moss was one of those inexplicable things I pined for, homesick for the damp undergrowth of an ancient woodland, or the plush skin of a moss-covered stone.

In 1804, William and Dorothy Wordsworth built a 'moss hut' in the garden at Dove Cottage in the Lake District, as a space for William to write, away from the hubbub of family life in the noisy house. It was made from wood and lined with moss, like a 'wren's nest . . . the sweetest place on earth,' as Dorothy described it. She knew how to observe her surroundings, how to really look at the ferns and bracken in the garden, at the old stone walls dripping with moss. This hut, like much of Dorothy's life, was an act of devotion to her brother. If she could have cocooned him in it entirely, she would have.

I love how beings as varied as glacially slow-growing mosses and whirling, wheeling swifts can exist within one space – in, around and above even the most ordinary of gardens like mine. In the course of one swift's lifetime, with all its extraordinary flights and migrations, the moss on our chicken coop will have grown barely a few centimetres.

*

I am weeding in the back flower bed, chasing the infinite spaghetti of ground-elder roots. My trowel suddenly slips deep into a negative space. It feels uncanny. I remove the top layer of soil and discover a gap beneath the billowing nepeta. For some reason, the space makes me think of dead bodies and empty eye sockets. I excavate further, making the hole bigger so I can see what has happened. Although I am accidentally uprooting dozens of bulbs, scattered earlier in the year by their allium parents, I am intrigued by this unknown gap and keep digging. I hit a solid object and reach my hands into the void. I touch something that feels immediately familiar yet incongruous: a vacuum cleaner hose. Tugging and releasing more earth from the edges of this strange plastic snake, I eventually manage to pull the whole thing out. Like a severed umbilical cord, it sits limp on the soil.

I plunge my hands into the hole again. This time I feel sharp fragments and pull out a broken mosaic mirror. Next comes a half-rotted section of a bin liner, then an electric plug and cable. This leads me further into the hole, determined to discover what it is attached to. By now my excavations have dislodged several plants and the flower bed looks like an open grave. Unable to loosen the object at the end of the plug, I go inside for reinforcements. My son and husband come out to help, taking it in turns to dig and heave, like in the fairytale *The Enormous Turnip*. Suddenly the prize is birthed: an old Nintendo games console. My son laughs at this technological relic, and we all feel a little perturbed by the discoveries. Who would bury these things in a garden? Surely it would be more work than just slinging them out with the bins on a Thursday morning? My inability to make sense of this treasure trove of detritus manifests itself in a long and pointless online search for the make and model of the console, so I can determine its age and therefore discover who was living here at that time. My family are used to my disappearing down some research rabbit hole, whether it's trying to identify a long-lost ancestor or obsessing over a choice of paint colour. But there is no satisfying resolution here, just more questions.

Perhaps it is simply a wrinkle in time, a throwback to when this land was a Saxon rubbish dump. But it speaks of how humans treat the natural world, extracting the earth's resources and replacing it with garbage. I somehow feel the need to make some amends for all this, in some small way, within this patch of land. As I fill a bin bag with this eerie jumble of everlasting plastic, I am aware that I am simply moving it from one place to another, but at least I can give back some space to whatever might grow or live here. I hope that, when it is our time to move on, we leave fewer traces. I backfill the hole with soil, and push the bulbs and plants back into place as best I can.

*

No matter how well I know the garden, parts of it still feel mysterious. There are the low gaps at the bottom of the hedge, where the hedgehog scuffles for food; the pile of dead wood I leave untouched for fear of dislodging its community of creepy-crawlies; the shady, scrappy space between the chicken run and the telecoms building. These gaps and thickets are liminal spaces, which resist being fully known. Bushes are often seen as places of transgression or potential threat, but such in-between spaces can also offer a chance for safety, self-expression and freedom. In Celtic culture, these 'thin places' were the borders between worlds, where ghosts commonly appeared. Along two sides of my garden, walls create a firm boundary, but the other side, marked by the straggly, towering privet, is more mutable – a fertile, imaginative space. A man goes missing in the town, drunk and lost for days, and I become convinced his body is in this hedge, that he curled up there seeking shelter and died. Of course, when I tell myself to stop being stupid and go and check, I find nothing. But I remain tentative around these scrubby areas until the poor man is discovered drowned in the River Ouse, washing slowly, bloatedly, out to sea. The river is another kind of gap, a break in the crust and solidity of the surface. It swells, recedes, rises and floods onto the banks, crossing the boundary between land and fluidity: a thick, brown slither holding both menace and life within its liquid grip.

The Ouse meanders through marshy farmland that was once under the sea and home to basking sharks. It eventually leads to my favourite swimming spot, at Tide Mills, near Newhaven. There is just one path running down to the beach from the car park there, taking you over a level crossing before opening up onto a concreted area and the pebbly beach. In the gap between the road and the sea lie the remains of Tide Mills village. There is not much left – some walls and footings either side of the path, and the odd piece of industrial debris rising from the creek's mud at low tide. But as I follow the siren call of the sea, scattering skylarks in my wake, the ruins seem to hum with stories. The tide mill was originally built in 1761; designed to harness the force of the sea, the mill powered sixteen grindstones in the nineteenth century, making flour from grain brought up a narrow channel on barges and later by train. The mill owner, William Catt, lived in a large house next to the mill, and the rest of the village consisted of workers' cottages, a stationmaster's cottage, and outbuildings. You can imagine the bustle and sounds and smells of this place in its prime: the tidal clanking and grinding, the burr of the mill sails; the fish-smelling air; sewage buckets slopping on the way to be dumped into the sea; children sneaking around the back of the boys' hospital built on the edge of the shingle; and the voices of men discussing the day's work.

In 1875, a major storm caused irrevocable damage to the mill as the buckling sea hurled shingle into the millpond and creek. The mill closed in 1883 and was demolished in 1901 but the villagers remained. During the First World War, the beach at Tide Mills had a sea-plane and wireless relay station, and in the 1920s a hospital for boys was built between the village and the beach, providing respite and treatment for young boys. There are wonderful photographs of them doing exercises in the sea and lying on beds rolled outside onto a veranda to soak up the sunlight. One picture shows a boy with an amputated leg being carried down to bathe on a makeshift stretcher. The village was also home to a stable where lame racehorses were sent to recover. The stable owner, David Dale, collected mud from around Sussex and used it as a poultice to heal wounds and lameness, and he swam the horses in the sea to build up their strength and give them exercise. I love how this place, now a source of joy and pleasure for so many walkers and swimmers, has nurtured such a variety of people and creatures through the ages.

The life of the village was short. Under the 1930 Housing Act local councils could declare housing unfit for human habitation. In 1936, Seaford council ordered that houses 8–13 in the village should be cleared, because they lacked sanitation, refuse collection and lighting. An article in the *Daily Mail* in 1937 dubbed Tide Mills the 'Hamlet of Horror' because of the villagers' reportedly squalid living conditions. During the Second World War the site was considered a potential invasion risk, and also an important strategic point from which to observe an enemy approach from the Channel. With only twenty-four hours' notice, the rest of the villagers were ordered to leave and the hospital was emptied. Only one man remained, Stanley Tubb, who convinced the army that his knowledge of the area was useful for creating defences and understanding the tides. He lasted two more months, and then the village was empty. The houses and remaining mill buildings were demolished to give troops a clear view of the sea.

Now, at first glance, it is deserted, save for the passing beachgoers and dog walkers. But look closer, and you will find ghost gardens and thousands of creatures populating this quiet place. From photographs and the accounts of people who lived in the village, we know that where there are now brambles and weeds, there were once gardens. Villagers grew flowers – what look like asters, nasturtiums and chrysanthemums – in their small front gardens, and along the ruined wall of the old stationmaster's cottage sunflowers still grow from seeds left behind all those years ago. One photograph shows a ramshackle garden with a shrimp net leaning up against the house, and an earth closet or wash house in the background. Perhaps this was the shed where one of the villagers hid a shipwrecked corpse he had discovered on the beach, storing it overnight before it was taken to the mortuary. The dangers of the sea would have been a constant presence for the inhabitants of the village.

William Catt trained twelve pear trees against his house, sheltered from the sea winds. It looked as if the house was wearing them like facial hair. Chickens scratched around in his orchard, which was home to fig trees and more pears. Catt was also obsessed with growing pineapples – excavations revealed a sunken 'pineapple pit', which would have been heated with manure to create a tropical environment in this decidedly British landscape. He constructed a large glasshouse in the centre of the village, where he made use of horticultural developments like artificial fertilizers and fungicides to cultivate unusual varieties of plants. In the spirit of Victorian moralistic paternalism, Catt encouraged the villagers to busy themselves growing their own food – potatoes, Brussels sprouts, peas, beans and beets – to keep them out of the pub and live a virtuous life. He also enforced other morally 'improving' restrictions, like a curfew at 10.10 p.m. When he discovered two men flouting the rules and jumping over a wall just ten minutes late, he suspended their privileges and banished them from the village for one month. His power as employer and landlord seemed to extend to curtailing personal freedoms in what seems an almost feudal system.

After Catt sold the mill, it was used as a bonded warehouse. The remaining villagers continued growing fruit and vegetables on allotments on the site of the glasshouse, and today wild roses tangling amidst the weeds are living traces of past gardens. In the village, mill workers were replaced by railway workers and farm labourers. After the clearance in the Second World War, a villager's nephew took a cutting from one of Catt's fig trees and it was said to be bearing fruit into the 1970s. Perhaps it still remains, in a different garden, its origins unknown to the people who pick its fruit every summer.

In the gaps left in this phantom village, nature has taken over. Rewilding is occurring in this rare 'vegetated shingle' habitat, which is now home to long-tailed blue butterflies and 152 species of birds, including stonechat, linnet, sanderling, avocet, great crested grebe, sedge warbler, hobby, dunlin and nesting ringed plover. On the site of cottage gardens, you can see thistle, tufted vetch, yarrow, bindweed, hedge mustard and teasels. The viper's bugloss and red campion that would have brightened up the village two hundred years ago still grow happily amongst the shingle and ruins. In the summer sun, you may find basking grass snakes and common lizards or hear the capriccio of bush crickets against the legato notes of the waves. As you reach the pebbled shoreline, you will see sea kale, yellow horned poppies, grasses, common mallow, sea beet and speedwell. Over forty-six different species of plant thrive in what seems at first glance to be a forlorn, deserted place.

Volunteer groups work hard to clear rubbish from the beach and to protect the ruined site that now forms part of a local nature reserve and the South Downs National Park. Information boards describe how the village used to look, so curious passers-by can stand in front of an old wall and see the lives that flicker around it like a zoetrope that requires us to recalibrate our vision and tune into the light and shadows of the past. A new project to re-establish a garden on the old village allotment site has just been approved. It is not about looking back, awash on a tide of nostalgia, but forward to how this place will live on, for future generations to understand a little more about where they live.

*

I pull up my wetsuit, encasing myself in a sleek second skin, and walk into the water. The cold creeps slowly through the protective layer. There's a sense of release, with a backwash of fear. The pleasure of sea swimming comes partly from this proximity to death – *l'appel du vide*, the call of the void. Though this phrase is usually used in the context of vertigo and being high up, it applies equally to being in deep water. In her dying, my mother taught me that joy and peace come not from forgetting death but through the shared acknowledgement of all our inevitable endings. The ghost gardens beyond the beach are a stark reminder of this – the fact that, however important our lives seem, and however carefully we tend our homes, we are just a fleeting moment in the story of this place. But their persistence, in the seeds that lie dormant under the rubble and the roses that push doggedly through brambles, also speaks of continuity in another form. Each wave collapses in a continuous dance with time. As I swim, always staying close to the shoreline, I look back to the bones of the village, and picture a gaggle of skinny boys hobbling down to the shallows, the shiny flanks of a salt-dipped horse rising from the water, and the snatched grumbles of village wives lugging buckets of slop to the sea. The gap in time closes.

20

DEFIANCE

It seems to me that nothing tastes quite as wonderful as a potato that has just been dug up, boiled and smeared with butter. My peas are sweet and bright, warm ripe tomatoes melt in my mouth, and soft raspberries will always taste of summer, but a fresh potato is something else.

Our leftovers mostly go to the chickens (apart from potato peelings), in one of the pleasing circularities the garden offers up. They turn these scraps into eggs, which we eat almost daily. They currently share the coop with a friendly field mouse, who snatches bits of food the chickens flick away. I watch the mouse in the evenings, her bold, shiny black eyes looking directly at me. Then one day I see a chicken with the mouse in her mouth, playing with it as if she were a cat. I shoo her away and she drops the stiff little body onto the ground. The eyes stare up at me, empty. I scrape the mouse onto my shovel and fling her over the hedge, away from the pecking hens and curious dog.

A pigeon has landed in the apple tree, picking at bugs on the apples. A blue tit joins her, grabbing at the uppermost leaves, and a blackbird flies out from the middle of the branches. It is a temporary resting place, a pit stop, the branches bouncing in an echo of the birds who have just lifted off. I sit at the kitchen table with my laptop, looking out at the sparrows dipping their wings in the bird bath. A peeling piece of chalkboard paper on the wall near the sink catches my eye and distracts me from my bulb catalogue. I pull at it, revealing a painted chalkboard section with our phone numbers written on for babysitters, in case of emergency. Below the numbers is a child's drawing of a person, with four spikes of hair darting from their massive head, which is attached to a stick body with two arms at right angles. It reminds me of a talk I went to where researchers at Peterhouse College, Cambridge, discovered several layers of wallpaper built up over 200 years in one dorm room. They tracked the history of the room through these hidden seams. Each pattern, colour and design spoke of the students' tastes and lives, expressing themselves in lines and flowers. These man-made palimpsests are like the layers of soil that contain old root systems, dormant seeds, the husks of insects, the bones of creatures. The past is tenacious. Dig a little and it is still there.

*

The bulbs I ordered arrive, and I put them out in the shed, where they will wait until I plant them, and then wait some more before they begin to grow. Planting in this garden, projecting into the future, still seems like an act of defiance. But I feel differently about it – the despair and despondency of the winter has shifted. I am no longer raging against the estate agents, or fate, but simply hope to leave a sign that I loved this garden while we were here. The word 'defiance' often comes with negative connotations – disobedience and rudeness – but it also speaks of courage and strength of will.

I think of the gardeners who wrapped seeds in linen to be buried with their rulers in defiance of this mortal life, or secretly braided a seed into their hair to carry a piece of their home into exile.

In the 1970s, the activist Wangari Maathai planted trees across Kenya in an act of defiance against inequality, human rights abuses and the exploitation of the land. Her Green Belt Movement offered women a sense of agency in a society where they had little power. She also encouraged warring tribes to use tree saplings as peace offerings, preventing escalating conflict. Thanks to her efforts, a staggering thirty million trees were planted, and a new model of civil disobedience took root. We see reverberations of this in urban 'guerrilla gardening', where unloved concrete areas and traffic-choked roundabouts are suddenly transformed into reparative places of beauty and life.

Ron Finley lives in South Los Angeles, an area plagued by poverty, violence and drug misuse. He describes it as a 'food desert', the only options for local people being fast-food joints. Fresh produce is hard to come by. Angered by this systemic food paucity, Finley created a garden in the soil between his house and the street. Local authorities tried to remove his 'food forest', but this organic Eden remained. He filled the garden with fruit and vegetables that people could just come and pick, attracting insects and creating a space that locals could feel proud of. As he says in the film *Can You Dig This*, 'If you put beauty into a place that generally doesn't have it, that's a game-changer.'

Finley's defiance not only of the outdated laws governing where people can plant on the land but also of the societal oppression that kept communities like his disempowered and disengaged has inspired community gardens across the city. Each is a political as much as a horticultural act. It seems a world away from the Bloomsbury garden at Charleston, but in fact they share a defiant spirit. Vanessa Bell's move to a secluded farm provided work for the conscientious objectors in her circle, and her garden provided a safe queer space and refuge from society. But the difference lies in Ron Finley's outward-looking ethos. He believes that gardening can be transformational, not just for the land but for the people who inhabit it: 'The garden teaches a system: patience, persistence, care, that things don't happen instantaneously . . . Everything's a process.' Community gardens disrupt, conferring power and resources to those who need them in exchange only for their labour and care. By protecting rather than exploiting the earth, communicating and sharing knowledge, sharing plants and learning to care for it for its own sake rather than for someone else's economic gain, gardening becomes a radical act.

*

But what happens when our defiant acts of faith result in failure? Marguerite Duras tells how her mother, living in exile in Vietnam, spent all her hard-earned savings on what turned out to be a useless plot of land too close to the sea. She tried to grow rice, to be self-sufficient and to root herself in this unfamiliar land, but the sea simply swallowed it up. She built dams and barriers, but the sea kept coming. The despair nearly killed her. Working this garden became an act of self-erasure and futile hope planted in the wrong place. I have learned this, a little – that simply willing something to work does not make it happen. Being furious with probate lawyers for not giving us clarity, or forcing a magnolia tree into soil that will never give it the nutrients it needs and planting it in a position with the wrong light, does not solve anything. I can't use my sheer force of will as a means of coping. I need to think more creatively. In the spaces between the garden and myself there is room for doubts and questions as well as defiance and determination. There is room to think about the life I want, bridging the gap between the woman I wanted to be and the woman I have become; to try different ways of living. Resistance and renewal. Grounding and expanding. I am learning all this from my garden, creating (to paraphrase Vita Sackville-West) a little world, a little perfectly imperfect world.

*

Brambles curl down from the back wall and over the chickens' fence in long, deadly tendrils, as if they are trying to sew themselves into an infinitely looping tapestry between the earth and sky. Cabbage whites falter and shimmer in the hedge, and I spot a pigeon staring at me from the telecoms building roof. I wonder what the garden looks like from up there, with the sparrows and rooks. The pear tree is heavy with fruit. Last year, around this time, my husband, two of the children and I marshalled blankets and nimble climbing limbs to shake down the apples from the tree and catch them before they fell and bruised. I haven't been organized this year, and now most of the apples have been blown down in recent heavy winds. Purple-black elderberries hang in delicate bunches like pin holes punctuating the fading green of the hedge. Colour seems to be draining from everything except the berries tempting the birds, and the glossy red baubles shining from the holly tree – it feels far too early to be thinking about Christmas, but I find myself suddenly looking forward to lighting fires, filling hot-water bottles and wearing woolly socks. Though I am not quite ready to turn my back on the garden for another year. There is still the bulb planting, mulching and seed harvesting to come.

We receive a phone call from the estate agent, telling us the probate dispute will be settled by the New Year – we should know then if we can stay.

*

I think perhaps no garden is ever made in vain. The imagining, the creation, the care and the bounty – these all have value in themselves. But some are more hard won than others. There is something deeply moving about gardens created in the face of war. A few years ago, the photographer and film-maker Lalage Snow travelled to conflict zones in search of gardens. In the midst of the destruction of war, she found oases and flourishing spaces growing in ruins, army bases and on contested lands. She visited a balcony garden in Ukraine, and a kibbutzim at the heart of the Middle East crisis; she met an Israeli woman mourning for her son who explains why she gardens: 'It helps me grieve, and when I am here, I am filled with sunshine, even if it is dark.' Snow describes a paradise created in a Kabul army camp by Brigadier General Shirin Shah, whose garden thrives within a hostile, war-torn place. Dahlias, geraniums and roses bloom in what is regarded as a barren land watered only with blood. She met a 105-year-old man who has made a garden in a ruined palace at an army checkpoint. Sometimes his family only have one meal a day, but he feels rich because of his garden, and is able to grow enough beans, okra and potatoes to keep his family alive. In Islam, the word for planting is *khair*, which translates as 'goodness' or 'peace'.

During the Second World War, a bomb crater in the grounds of Westminster cathedral was planted up as a kitchen garden, the scar tissue turned into a generative space. In a strange circular happenstance, a disused bomb shelter in Clapham is now the site of a hydroponic farm growing herbs and salad leaves. In this unlikely place, 33 metres below Clapham's bustling streets, pea shoots, wasabi mustard, rocket, garlic chives and coriander are amongst the plants grown without soil, on mats made from carpet offcuts. LED lighting creates artificial sunshine, and spigots provide mineral nutrients. The controlled environment underground suits these crops, and there are plans to grow strawberries next. It looks more like a laboratory than a garden, but this innovative farm could provide one solution to changes in climate, requiring far less water to cultivate plants than traditional methods, and staying unaffected by extreme weather. Out of a different kind of destruction – that of our environment and climate – people are finding ways to nurture life.

*

The garden air is fragrant with blackberries – sweet, pungent, earthy, autumnal. Everywhere there is a ceaseless growing and dying, held within the silence of the birds. What can I know of this place as I witness its unpetalling? I know it is on the move, yet will remain here for ever, in some form. I know it is dying, but also that it is regenerating. I know that it holds secrets I will never understand and stories I will only write myself. I know it is made from chalk, flint, earth and memories, and that I am unimaginably lucky to be labouring in it and for it. I know I will leave it for the next tenants to enjoy, better and more beautiful than we found it, and open to new eyes and hands. This is what I know, as I turn my back on the summer and step across another threshold.

SEPTEMBER

21

GATHERING

1 September: the start of meteorological autumn. The garden moves into a new state of gathering, shedding and turning in. It is a time of self-preservation. Where in spring there was a clump of shiny pink rhubarb, there is now a black pulp with an eerie sinkhole at the centre. In the vegetable patch, the leeks and kale are flourishing alongside self-seeded marigolds with their bang of orange. The cabbages are plump and frilly, tangled in the tentacular arms of the squashes, sitting like small buddhas amongst the weeds, which seem more vigorous than ever. It is as if they are summoning every last effort to grow and set seed before the frosts come.

I take dahlia cuttings and collect windfall apples, choosing the best for cooking and leaving the rest in the scrub under the hedge for the birds. My husband comes out to help cut back the wild privet hedge and elder tree. He stands on our wobbly ladder and slashes and chops with an electric hedge cutter. I can't look – it feels too dangerous, but he is confident with heights and loves a challenge. It is good to be working together out here, clearing and opening up our shared space. Sometimes we talk, and sometimes we work in happy silence. With two feet firmly on the ground, I saw up the branches he has cut, working the large and unwieldy wood into a neat pile.

It is an incremental, satisfying job, and the result is a spill of light into the garden, as if we had just pulled back a thick curtain. The hedge shows its ribs. A pigeon watches us warily from a nest on a now-exposed branch, dipping precariously in the wind. I think about baby birds rocked in their nests like this and remember the constant swinging to and fro of trying to settle a crying baby, the way my body would carry on swaying even when the baby was sleeping in their bed. I think about holding my children when they are sad – even the huge teenagers, all limbs and hair – rocking them gently in my arms, and wonder if birds are soothed by the motion in the same way. Does the wind hold them like this? I feel guilty for exposing the pigeon's home so starkly, and then my husband tells me he has accidentally chopped down another nest, and I remember we are destroyers as well as creators.

From the soil rises a musty smell of humus. The word 'humus' comes from the Latin *humilis*, meaning 'low' or 'of the earth'; it is also the root of 'humility', a word that evokes the quiet prostration of the ego. It is easy to find the glory and joy in a garden in the spring and summer; but at this point in the year we have to work harder and look deeper, to the worms and microorganisms turning and enriching the soil, where seeds burrow down for the winter. After the showy exuberance of summer, autumn is the time of introspection and the humble, hard work of dying. Decay has set in, composting the beauty and abundance of the past few months and turning it earthwards. This decomposing matter will improve the soil structure, help it retain water and provide nutrients for the plants.

Since beginning my garden here, I have found I notice the subtle changes, where previously I would just look up from my work and find summer disappeared and the branches bare. Away from the harsh glare of summer sun, the colours seem more vivid, and the softer light makes the perfect backdrop for the fiery reds and oranges that set the trees ablaze. I love the cooler evenings, the way my breath starts to cloud in the air, the stillness before the rains and icy winds of winter. There is energy in the rot. It is the means by which we live forever.

While the outside world turns towards dormancy, at home September is a busy month. New school shoes to buy, lunch boxes to fill, transitions to college and secondary school, early mornings and new daily rhythms. My days are full and there is less time for the garden, but it doesn't need me now. I can harvest, weed and plan its future, but it is perfectly happy shifting seasons without me. I have found my grief, like the plants, getting quieter, not exactly dormant but not as charged and painful. I still weep whenever I hear the music my mother played every night in the hospice, and still sleep with her suitcase under my bed, but there are fewer moments of shocking sadness. I feel less winded by her absence.

*

17 September 2006. After a cold August, September has been warm & lovely. Sadly Wiltrud's Japanese anemones died in the July drought & I miss them. Dug up half the irises & divided them. Planted new Lavatera 'Sulgrave' & onion sets. Pleased with coronilla & sedums. Excellent cucumbers, tomatoes, peppers & courgettes. Beans OK.

*

Autumn has me thinking back to those first numb days in the garden at the spring equinox. As the months since then have unfurled, I have thought deeply about these green, plant-filled places and what they mean. And now the earth is tilting again – through the autumn equinox and into the darkness. Now is a time for reaping, of the Harvest Moon and the Chinese Moon Festival, the sun crossing the celestial equator and moving southwards. The combined pull of the sun and moon at this time of year causes extreme tides, and I head to Tide Mills with two friends to catch the low equinoctial 'spring tide' one evening. The sea is so far back there is a wide stretch of sand that I have never seen before, a new liminal space between the hard, warm pebbles and the water. Above me, the sky is filled with boomerang clouds. The water is deceptively strong, pulling me out, but it is shallow, and I stay in my safe zone, drifting. The vast indifference of this sea makes all my concerns and thoughts seem irrelevant and tiny. These waves will roll in and out regardless of what currents shape my life.

I always supposed that in some imagined future crisis, I would be one of those mothers who attain superhuman strength and lift a car off a trapped baby. But I have been struggling to cope with plain, everyday life, afraid I will go under. A memory: a few years ago, on holiday in France with friends. We are at a lake. Some of the children have swum across to the other side, where they can jump off a rope swing into the water. I begin a gentle breaststroke towards them, happy to be at surface level, moving slowly and deliciously through the lake. A boy – not one of ours – is swimming towards me, shouting. On his back, he has a younger boy, maybe six or seven, and he is trying to swim from the rope swing back to the shore. I realize he is in trouble, the younger boy slipping from his shoulders as his shouts get more frantic. I swim as fast as I can towards them, my French vocabulary abandoning me like pigeons flapping up from a town square, and I just grab the smaller boy. The older one swims off towards his mother, who is lying on a towel smoking on the shore, seemingly unaware of the potential disaster that is unfolding. I hold the boy and tread water. I remember that in films people flip drowning people onto their backs and hook them with an arm, but I can't remember the French word for 'back' and time has gone strange and I realize that I can't hold him like this. The water is so black and so deep. I know that if I let go, he will be gone. I see his mother swimming towards us and when she reaches me, I pass the boy to her, relieved that he is safe. But then I see that she is a weaker swimmer than I am, and she can't hold him either. For a terrifying moment, I think they will both drown. Luckily, two men have seen what is happening and are front-crawling their way towards us. One takes the boy and lifts him onto his back, swimming strongly to the edge of the lake. The other man, my friend, takes the woman on his back to safety. I swim behind them and stand shaking on the shore.

It was so frightening, and all I can think of that night, and for days to come, is how close I was to letting go. Since then, I always have to battle my fear in deep water. I learn that drowning is one of the most frequent causes of accidental death – what kills most people is the cold shock. By swimming outdoors all year round, I am exposing my body to extremes and stress, which makes it more adaptable and resilient. Changing our environment can help us get used to new challenges. We can train ourselves to cope better with change. I love the sensation of being in a completely different element, and observing the changes in the flow, waves and sea temperature. But I stay close to the beach and resist the tug of the tide.

22

TRACES

My flowering Japanese quince has arrived in the post. The planting label says it is 'nearly indestructible', which sounds promising. I plant it next to the long wall, where I will try to espalier it, behind the empty potato patch.

I take stock of the garden, aware that soon I will be spending even less time out here. The cabbages are big but have been badly nibbled, their leaves punctured like doilies. The squashes are swelling and ready for eating. Bindweed has taken over once again, entwining itself on every surface like a living net cast over the garden. Asters, cosmos and gaura keep the flower beds looking alive, their fresh bursts of pink a welcome sight amongst the receding growth elsewhere. The leaves on the raspberry canes are browning and crispy. I remind myself to pick the remaining fruit before it is furred with mould. Tiny rudbeckia valiantly battle on in the cutting patch, for some reason only reaching about 10 centimetres tall, the flowers like small yellow yolks.

I pick a dandelion head, cupping it carefully so as not to release the seeds. It is a beat in time, a childhood cry, 'Just five more minutes, please!' In the autumn garden, everything is calling for five more minutes. The spiders have come out, stringing their lacy webs from leaves, branches and the washing line. These homes that are also traps unspool around me. In the morning dew, the webs glimmer with pearls, a glorious adornment in this fading place. I have been watching a garden spider in my studio, captivated by her efforts and focus. She dangles from a silken thread, poised above my head as I sit at my desk, engaged in less bodily toil. Suddenly, she reels the thread back in and retreats to safety, as if my presence has alarmed her. She struggles with the angled rafter, slipping off, but catching herself with her very own lifeline, retrying, gingerly making her way to a more stable geometry. I wonder what calculations she is making, what space she perceives and what her goal is. Perhaps she is looking for a safe place to lay her eggs. She will then wrap them in layers of silk and keep watch over them until they hatch in the spring. Her front legs start moving frantically, as if plucking an invisible harp, and then she is still again, simply suspended.

How miraculous to have a home that is created within your body; how wondrous for a creature to have developed spinnerets that spool forth delicate yet steely-strong tendrils, to be able to balance, ballerina-like, in the air and build yourself a house that will also be your hunting ground. The next day she is completely still, curled up, dead-looking. I wonder if the hot air from my heater has somehow killed her. For three days I don't see her, but then, one morning, I notice a web right next to the doorway and am filled with happiness that she found the right place to construct a home for herself and her family. When her eggs hatch, the tiny baby spiders will float on the air currents, held by silk threads, 'ballooning' to their new home. The empty web will be a gossamer trace of her labour.

*

I have heard it said that a garden dies with the gardener. I disagree. I believe that the hands of those who planted, dug and pruned before us are always visible in what remains. I think of my mother's garden, and how when we eventually sell the house and its new owners move in, they will see her beloved primroses every spring and enjoy the running water plinking in the well. I think of Charleston and the mosaics pressed into the garden terraces, of Sissinghurst and the extraordinary White Garden, of the tropical plants at Monk's House, and the santolina at Prospect Cottage, the herb garden at Farleys. Every present custodian has had to grapple with how much of the past should be allowed to remain, and how much the garden should be evolving. The place where this seems most striking is the wonderful garden at Great Dixter, near Northiam in East Sussex. The ghosts of its original creators loom large here, but the garden embodies separation and transition at the same time.

The house at Great Dixter is a patched-up amalgamation of a medieval property and a Tudor house rebuilt on the site, joined together by a Lutyens centrepiece. Yet the creation looks seamless, a hulking, skulking beauty of a building, crouching at the centre of the most wonderful garden. The six-acre garden wraps around the house, which is visible from every point, a constant as you move through the different 'rooms'. Nathaniel and Daisy Lloyd bought the property in 1910, and raised six children at Dixter. Like Harold Nicolson and Roland Penrose, Nathaniel Lloyd was interested in the architecture and structure of the garden. He installed rippling yew, and cut box topiary into huge peacocks and coffee pots. He created a sunken garden with a pond, while

Daisy presided over the planting of the long flower border, rose garden and vegetable garden. By all accounts, she was a strong, often domineering woman, known as 'The Management', who insisted on serving lunch at 12.27 p.m. precisely. She liked to wear an Austrian dirndl and Quaker clothing in recognition of her Puritan Cromwell ancestry. Her youngest son, Christopher, was interested in the garden from an early age, and together they conjured a magical space that was to shape and form the whole of Christopher's life.

When Christopher Lloyd was twelve years old his father died, and he was sent away to Rugby School. It was an odd choice for a child who hated sport, and he never really fitted in, but he was a good pianist and found solace in music. After serving briefly during the Second World War as a young bombardier, he went to study horticulture at Wye College, eventually teaching there. He was happy and loved the job, but was sacked for challenging one of the professors about his laziness. This questioning of authority and outspokenness is a feature of Lloyd's later life. At the age of thirty-three, he returned to Great Dixter and remained there for the rest of his years, gardening with his mother, and establishing a clematis nursery. He wrote columns and articles on gardening in his bombastic, enthusiastic voice, and became one of Britain's most respected gardeners and garden writers. He filled the borders with plants of different heights and textures, mixing colours in an innovative, surprising way. He brought a sense of adventure and experimentation to the garden, and encouraged readers and visitors to do the same: 'We do not all want to float endlessly among silver, greys and tender pinks in the gentle nicotiana-laden ambient of a summer's gloaming. Some prefer a bright, brash midday glare with plenty of stuffing.'

Lloyd was fifty-one when his mother died and he became sole keeper of the Dixter estate. Much remained from his childhood – his family were known to never throw anything away, and the cupboards are still filled with their belongings – but he also began breaking from his past, expressing himself freely in his planting. The garden became a place for him to show his individuality, stepping out from Daisy's shadow and finding new ways to be creative. He ripped up the old formal rose garden and replaced it with an audacious tropical garden – a lush, dramatic place full of wild abundance and juicy life. His garden is vibrant and bold, a great joyful song belting out across the Wealden countryside.

After his mother's death, Lloyd opened up the house to his friends, holding weekend parties and creating strong bonds with younger people, whose energy he found invigorating. As a closeted gay man, this was now a chance have fun, and he embraced it. He gardened as he lived, wanting 'the plants to look as if they're enjoying themselves'. He taught himself to cook, serving lavish meals made with seasonal produce from the garden, and seemed to squeeze every last drop of happiness from life. His outspoken columns and open criticism of other horticulturalists ruffled plenty of feathers, and he was well known for being irascible and infuriating. But he somehow got away with it.

In 1992, he was joined at Dixter by Fergus Garrett, who has been head gardener there ever since. It was a perfect partnership, the two men understanding each other's vision and respecting their mutual knowledge and expertise. Garrett knew exactly what inspired Lloyd, he shared the joy in what Lloyd describes as 'that intangible something which immediately proclaims that behind the scenes there is an original whose guiding hand has created something ephemeral, yes, but with the magic of a sunset'.

Together they planted meadows filled with buttercups, dandelions, *Camassia quamash*, yellow rattle, common spotted orchids, cranesbill, vetch, bird's foot trefoil and ox-eye daisies. These wild, beautiful areas are home to rare orchids, a hugely diverse range of creatures, and 180 types of spider. Dixter itself attracts 140 species of bees. They tinkered, improved, plotted and nurtured mixed borders that played with shape and height, and encouraged plants to self-seed. They achieved a divine balance between control and allowing the garden space to breathe, eschewing manicured perfection and pristine paths in favour of crevices stuffed with creeping thyme and erigeron. Lloyd tells us to mistrust those who fill in all the cracks in the pursuit of perfection: 'How you deal with cracks in your paving reveals quite a lot about the sort of person you are. If they are cemented in and the slabs are all square, that's the sort of person you are too, square and cemented in, no cracks showing!' I feel better about my wonky, weedy, homespun paths, reading this. His desire to create beauty in in-between places, to leave room for life to burst through rather than create an entirely uniform, controlled space, mirrors his own blossoming in later life.

Lloyd died in 2006, but Fergus Garrett remains at Great Dixter. The property is run as a trust, ensuring that the garden will be enjoyed by visitors for years to come. Horticulture students stay at the house to learn from Garrett and his team. They are guided by Lloyd's spirit rather than replicating exact planting schemes from the past. Garrett intuitively knows what will work and what the garden needs, retaining its essence and honouring the traces of its forebears with four-season successional planting and plenty of hard toil.

*

I drive down the shady lane to Great Dixter on a misty autumn morning. At this time in the year, the main spectacle of the garden is finished, but thanks to Lloyd's and Garrett's skills and imagination, it still looks stunning. I have arranged to meet my father and stepmother here to visit the garden. We buy tickets from a small hut and I have a quick nose around in the sheds where photographs and displays tell the story of the house. As we go through the gate into the garden, I am struck immediately by the *rightness* of it all – the central pathway leading your eyes to the low, timbered house, and the wild grassy areas to the edges, culminating in a collection of pots by the front door. These are like a still life composition, a moveable feast that plays with colour and shape. We turn right and step down into the sunken garden, still rich with flowers and foliage, even in autumn: cannas, dahlias the size of footballs, amaranthus and *Arundo donax*. I am squeezed on all sides by plants, and flowers tower over my head. It is the kind of place that leaves me a little breathless, not knowing where to look, wanting to drink it all in.

We enter the tropical garden through an old cowshed, as if we were stepping through the wardrobe and into a jungle. I lose sight of my father and stepmother in the lush canopy, but I can hear the rattle of yucca leaves as they walk. The sun snaps through the foliage, and if it weren't for the yew hedge enclosing us, I would feel slightly worried that I might get lost and be wandering here for ever amongst the banana plants, bamboo, *Begonia luxurians*, dahlias and *Verbena bonariensis*. It is a giddy, extraordinary place in the middle of quiet, rural Sussex.

Passing round the back of the house, we have a moment to pause, eyes alighting on a gentle lawn sloping down to some trees, and then we are at the long border. This strip is bursting with a heady mix of perennials, shrubs, annuals, climbers and biennials. It is cramped and full of colour, uninhibited and clashing, exuberant yet carefully considered. Lloyd instinctively knew which plants would work together, amassing herbaceous plants, dotting them with bulbs and annuals, and 'leavening' them with evergreens. Garrett describes this as 'organized (and magical) chaos', and I have a disappointing sense that Lloyd would have found my garden colour scheme 'tasteful and cowardly'. Here, the enclosed 'rooms' are entered through clipped hedges shaped like ramparts, and blowsy foliage laps the paths (made from London paving slabs, reclaimed when the roads were tarmacked), leaving little space for the curious visitor. It is as if the garden is hurrying us along, encouraging us to look, yes, but to *feel* more, to allow our senses to be overwhelmed by its beauty. There is nothing contrived about this beauty; it is more that every inch of soil serves up a feast – even the compost heap is covered with pumpkins. The meadows have been cut, revealing a medieval ridge-and-furrow field, another trace of those who worked the land before. And in the corner of every scene sits the house, looking on, a guardian spirit, the one continuous presence in this shifting landscape.

My stepmother offers to buy me some plants from the nursery as an early birthday present. I choose two brightly coloured salvias, determined to add some Great Dixter clashing colours next year.

*

I have neglected to pick the pears, missing that crucial moment just before they ripen. Some have gone mushy, others have fallen to the ground. There are a few left, but they are not quite ready. I give them a twist and they stay firmly attached to their stems. I will try another day. Christopher Lloyd had strong feelings about pears. His words, 'crisp pear is anathema, bearing a horrid affinity to raw turnip', ring in my head. He describes the lyrical-sounding diseases my pears have so far avoided: pear rust, fireblight, blossom wilt; and quotes Edward Bunyard's *The Anatomy of Dessert*: 'there are but two classes of pears – those that taste of hairwash and those that do not'. Thankfully, mine are the latter. But only if I time it right.

At Dixter, it is easy to see how gardeners carve their stories in the soil. Lloyd's story was one of love for his mother, devotion to his home place, and a late-blooming zest for life. What stories will remain traced in my small garden? Future inhabitants might find springs from the trampoline buried in the ground, the crocheted corner of a blanket in the hedge, a small herb garden (I will keep trying), the roses grown from cuttings from my mother's garden, haphazard pathways that only make sense if you know what they were leading to, undiscovered Easter eggs. Perhaps there will be more imprints to come.

As well as leaving traces of our pasts, we are also haunted by the futures we never had – the babies that were never born, the houses we could have lived in, the conversations I could have had with my mother as I navigate this next phase of motherhood, the neighbours we didn't meet, the people we would have become. I realize now that what is important is to recognize these phantom lives but not to let them cloud the present. I have been living in a land of *what ifs* for a long time, and I can see it is time to let them go. *What if* we lose the house? It will be difficult and sad and possibly lead to a huge upheaval, but we will survive, and someone else will come to love it as I do. *What if* I can't be the mother or wife I wanted to be? My children will thank me for my flaws and imperfections that mean they don't have to live up to some idealized notion of parenthood, and hopefully my husband will forgive me. *What if my work is a failure?* I will know I tried. There will always be other seasons.

23

FAITH

Michaelmas, 29 September – in folklore the last day before the blackberries are claimed by the Devil. Most of ours have been claimed by the sparrows, the chickens or by me, placing them on trays in the freezer until solid, and then bagging them up for winter puddings. In the garden, the swifts and goldfinches have been replaced by fat magpies, who thump from hedge to grass, cackling and cocking their heads. Inspired by my mother's garden journal and Leonard Woolf, I order a 'Paul's Himalayan Musk' rose to plant near the front door. At Monk's House, this rose clambered around Virginia's window, and I want the same cloud of pink and scent to embrace people as they enter our home.

Crane flies skim at the windows, reminding me of school playtimes when cruel boys would catch them and pull off their legs. My nickname (thanks to my height and gangliness) was 'Daddy Longlegs', and I feel an affinity for these fleeting visitors. I am busy with work and family life, and spend little time in the garden. My stepfather, amazingly, is still alive. Each week we think it will be his last, but he keeps on going. His body, once a towering bulk, is thin, and his skin hangs from his arms like scalded milk.

I have been told he doesn't have long left, so I go to say my goodbyes.

The front door at my mother's house is sticking. It is getting harder to open and close; and now the back door refuses to open. The house is either trying to keep us out, or keep us in – I can't decide. My stepfather asks me what I've been doing and I tell him how my daughter and I have been harvesting our potatoes, and how it never fails to seem like magic – the scalp of a scraggy patch of mud and leaves lifted to reveal golden nuggets. I tell him how I love sliding my fork down, pressing beneath the roots of the plant and easing it skyward. I tell him how I discard the leaves and send my fork back down, oh so carefully, so as not to spear the potatoes, turning and pushing at the same time. My daughter (the lookout) spies one, then another, lying complacently – casually – in the ground; it is as if they are roused from a deep slumber and wake to find the mud sky replaced by a yellow-blue infinity, a whole new world filled with light and air and motion. I tell him how we scrabble for these soil-dwellers, thrusting them into the day from the underworld, carrying the secrets of their growth within their knotty skin. What I am really telling him is that I will miss his huge, muddy hands dropping freshly dug lettuce into the washing-up bowl; that I love him.

We talk about his last book, and he manages to laugh at one of my jokes. Mostly I just sit there, sweating in the blast from an electric heater. Occasionally he drifts into sleep and I feel relieved that I don't have to think of anything to say, but also guilty that there seems so much I should be saying. He hates any expression of emotion, so instead I tell him that in Denmark stepfathers are known as 'bonus fathers', and let the love behind this statement just sit there unspoken. I hope he knows what I am saying. I get up suddenly and tell him I had better be going, and he twists his head in a strange kind of lurch, as if he is crying out, but no words come. I should hug him or pat his hand or something, but I know he would find that awkward, so instead I scuttle too quickly out of the room and close the door. Soon he will join my mother in her grave, as they wanted, reunited and separated only by thin strips of wood and a layer of clay. Half the world's dead are buried in coffins and half are not. I am not sure what use this information is, but my brain has noted it. My mother and stepfather believed they would see each other in the afterlife, but, with no faith in God, I am left to wonder if eventually their bones will find their way to each other in some everlasting entanglement.

*

30 September 2010. Came back from ten days in Portugal & Spain to find grass & weeds at their highest ever. Making attempts to tidy up for autumn. Moved conservatory plants inside today. Good tomatoes & rocket & courgettes, beans disappointing, beetroot, carrots, spinach, chard all good. Leeks getting on slowly, sprouts OK, having been covered with netting till today.

*

I put away my garden notebooks, tidy up some of the pots and remove the now-rotten netting that supported the beans. I leave most of the plants as they were, to provide food for the birds and winter homes for insects. I like seeing the architectural outlines of dead alliums and sedums, marking time until the earth warms again next year. There will be work to do – manuring, pruning, covering, discarding – but there is so much more time for all this now the frenzy of the growing season is over. All the garden requires of me at this point is to have faith, to hold my nerve, until we have news about our eviction, or until the seasons turn, whichever comes first.

What I want to say is that autumn is not an end, it is a beginning. It brings skeletons, but at the core of these husks the roots are renewing, preparing for a sleep that will bring new life at the end. Right now poppy seeds are sprinkling onto damp soil; worms are scribbling their maps in the earth depleted by the potatoes; a cosmos seed sticks to a cat's fur and is shaken off further down the garden; roots gather water and nutrients to sustain them through the cold months; and the trees throw their leaves to the wind so they can conserve their energy. The apple and pear trees in the garden slowly strip back to knuckled branches, and it looks like nothing is happening. But beneath the soil, they are talking to each other, to my neighbours' trees, and the sycamores in the car park, along mycorrhizal networks, just as the operators in the telecoms building next door once connected people with each other. Through these impossibly intricate filaments, they tell each other about the weather, the air and looming threats, in ways we don't fully understand.

The Jewish festival Tu B'Shevat (New Year of the Trees) at the end of January celebrates the rising of the sap in the trees, an 'invisible spring' where people encourage the sap by eating only fruit and nuts. They honour the importance of this moment for providing the food that will come later, summoning the hidden spirit and force of the trees. I wonder if trees feel this awakening, like the electric tingle of a numbed limb when the blood starts flowing again. Do they feel a warm tide surging in their bones? What heart is pumping this energy around them? These majestic beings show us how nature can be not just a palliative but a potent cure – they can prevent floods, clean our poisoned air, create and support ecosystems.

Trees are striving in two directions – up to the light to expand, and down into the earth for stability. Like me, they are yearning for the space and freedom to grow, yet also need to feel secure and grounded. Like me, they are a living contradiction. But, unlike me, they will be here for many years. They will remake themselves out of blossom, green shoots, sap, leaves and fruit. They will dance through cycles of rebirth and reimagination. The wisdom of plants allows them to form a connection with, or root themselves into, something else in order to ensure their survival. They can re-sprout leaves after being cut, send up vigorous new growth after a frost has scorched their outer leaves. They will always try to find ways to stay alive. Humans also have this innate capacity for regeneration. Our bodies create clots and calluses to protect new bone cells that heal fractures, stretch fresh skin over wounds, and grow hairs from follicles devastated by poisons. We forget this, in our rush to discover *who we are*. We are constantly changing, our identities in flux and our bodies renewing even as they are decaying. Imbedded within this mutability is the potential for growth.

How will I remake myself? I will practise gratitude instead of worrying about the future. I will acknowledge the sheer, glorious privilege of witnessing my garden grow, my children grow; of being alive. I will tend to my hardy perennials, and those precious things I take for granted – my marriage, friends and community – so that our strength feeds each other. By working with local refugee projects, offering support to writers whose voices may not be heard, and through political and climate activism I will try to look beyond these walls and this messy hedge, beyond the boundaries of nations and continents, to help create spaces where people can make themselves at home, and where they can belong. What can I give back to the garden that has rewarded me with so much? My attention and care, my labour. This is what I can offer.

In some British villages, church bells peel to 'ring home the dead'. This 'nostos', a return to dust, is given a sonic reverberation, the air clanging with stories of a life passing through. If we can make peace with this inevitable homecoming, perhaps all the other home-leavings will not have such a sting. Perhaps we can ring out our life too, creating choruses in the houses and gardens we tend and leave behind, pulsing beats through the bodies of our children or the things we create, making echoes with our words. I think that the root shock I have feared so much is both a real threat and a misunderstanding. Before a plant is uprooted, we can take cuttings or collect seed. If the roots do not hold, we can find ways to grow new ones. Homesickness comes from a yearning for a past that is lost yet still exists within our imagination; we need to divert its energy, call up the sap and give it somewhere else to take root. 'Home' is not where the heart is – our heart can be scattered in many places and many people. But 'home' does exist, as much a state of mind as an actual place. It is, quite simply, where we are. We must pin our soul-stars to this place and, where we can, connect to the earth around us so that, like Rilke's trees, we can rise up rooted.

POSTSCRIPT

Much of the final draft of this book was written during the Covid 19 pandemic – a time that highlighted injustices and inequalities in so many areas, including in relation to people's access to outdoor spaces. I would like to acknowledge here how lucky I have been, and how hugely grateful I am for my garden. At this time of enormous uncertainty and fear it has been even more of an anchor for me, as I know gardens were for many of us during this crisis.

Just after I finished writing the book, I had an email from the executor of our late landlord's estate. After four years' acrimonious dispute, the settlement had finally been agreed, and the house was going to the person we had hoped it would. Our new landlady called me soon after, saying not only that we *could* stay in the house, but that she *wanted* us to stay. I took the call out in the garden, under the apple tree, and the relief was immediate and visceral. I felt like someone had offered to take a heavy load I'd been carrying for so long its weight had begun to shape me. I could fully and deeply breathe. I am filled with gratitude that we get to spend more time in our home, and with excitement for the flowers and plants to come – a sprinkling of ox-eye daisies by the raspberries perhaps, a circle of meadow with scabious, sorrel and crested dogstail grass . . .

ACKNOWLEDGEMENTS

With heartfelt thanks to my editor Laura Barber for her expertise, encouragement and belief in this book; and to my agent Natalie Galustian for her wise words and constant support. Thanks also to the team at Granta Books who have made the publishing process a joy, especially Christine Lo, Lamorna Elmer, Simon Heafield and Daphne Tagg. It is a privilege to work with all these talented people, and this book is very much the result of a collaborative effort.

Deep thanks to my friends, many of whom have lost much but given more. I couldn't have written this without you. Thank you to those who read early versions of the book and offered invaluable advice. I am grateful to Anna Green for the cover design and to Neil Gower for his beautiful illustration.

Thanks to the gardeners and curators who helped in my research – Harry Hoblyn at Charleston, and Antony Penrose at Farleys House in particular. And to the long-dead growers and planters whose inspiration lives on in their gardens. I am grateful to the people who shared their stories of homes lost and gardens created (especially Ahmed Masoud, Melissa Harrison, Julian Bell and Kamin Mohammadhi). And to all those in my community and beyond who have offered gardening advice, seeds, plants and wisdom.

Thanks to my family for their faith in me, for cheerleading my work and for being surprised that I knew something about gardening. Love always to my mother and stepfather. Huge thanks to my husband Mark for believing I could do it and keeping the home fires burning. And to my children – home will always be wherever you are.

*

I am grateful to be granted permission to include the following lines of poetry:

Philip Larkin, 'The Trees', *High Windows*, 1974. Reproduced by kind permission of Faber and Faber Ltd
Amy Lowell, 'Lilacs', *What's O'Clock*, 1925. By kind permission of the Trustees of the Estate of Amy Lowell
'Full Moon' © Vita Sackville-West, 1933. Reproduced with permission from Curtis Brown Group Ltd on behalf of the Estate of Vita Sackville-West

I have also quoted from the following works, with gratitude and respect:

Robert Adler, consultant ed. *Penguin English Dictionary*, 2002
Quentin Bell and Virginia Nicholson, *Charleston: A Bloomsbury House and Garden*, 1997
Ronald Blythe, *Word from Wormingford*, 2007
Jorge Luis Borges, *The Garden of Forking Paths*, 1941
Ami Bouhassane, *Lee Miller: A Life with Food, Friends and Recipes*, 2017

Roald Dahl, *Roald Dahl: From the Inside Out – the Author Speaks*, roalddahl.com

Charles Dickens, *Great Expectations*, 1861

Emily Dickinson, 'Letter to Cornelia Sweetser, May 1883', archive. emilydickinson.org

Joan Didion, *Blue Nights*, 2011

Tove Ditlevsen, *Childhood*, 2019

Patricia Dwyer, 'On Elizabeth Bishop, Loss, and Coming Out after 20 Years in a Convent', lithub.com, 7 May 2019

Angelica Garnett, *Deceived with Kindness*, 1995

Renee Gladman, *Houses of Ravicka*, 2017

Susan Goodman, 'A House for Life, Love, Art and Inspiration', *New York Times*, 31 March 1994

Adam Gopnik, 'Voltaire's Garden', *New Yorker*, 7 March 2005

Tove Jansson, *Moomin: The Complete Tove Jansson Comic Strip, Vol. 1*, 2006

Derek Jarman, *Modern Nature*, 2018; *Derek Jarman's Garden*, with photographs by Howard Sooley, 1995

E. Alex Jung, *Michaela the Destroyer*, vulture.com, 6 July 2020

Charles Lamb, 'Letter to Thomas Hood, 1827', *Letters of Charles Lamb*, ed. William Carew Hazlitt, 1886

Lemon Tree Trust, '100-Year History of Supporting Refugees with Seeds', lemontreetrust.org, 20 May 2018

Christopher Lloyd, *In my Garden*, 2010; *The Well-Chosen Garden*, 2021; obituary, *Telegraph*, 30 January 2006

Katherine Mansfield, *The Collected Letters of Katherine Mansfield, Vol. 5, 1922*, ed. Vincent O'Sullivan and Margaret Scott, 2008

Thomas Marks, 'Guests and Gadgets: In the Kitchen with Lee Miller', *Apollo Magazine*, 1 June 2020

Adam Nicolson, *Sissinghurst: An Unfinished History*, 2009

Mirabel Osler, *A Breath from Elsewhere*, 1998

Alice Oswald, 'On Behalf of a Pebble', TORCH lecture, streamed 4 March 2021

Oxford English Dictionary, oed.com

Michael Pollan, *The Botany of Desire*, 2003

Elizabeth W. Pomeroy, 'Within Living Memory: Vita Sackville-West's Poems of Land and Garden', *Twentieth-Century Literature*, Vol. 28, No. 3, Autumn 1982

Sophie Radice, 'Surreal Lives', *Guardian*, 13 July 2002

Mary Ruefle, 'Observations on the Ground', *Granta*, 20 November 2013

Vita Sackville-West, *In Your Garden*, 1997

Vita Sackville-West and Sarah Raven, *Vita Sackville-West's Sissinghurst: The Creation of a Garden*, 2014

Helen Simpson, *Hey Yeah Right Get a Life*, 2000

Lalage Snow, *War Gardens*, 2018

Sue Stuart-Smith, 'How Gardening is Good for Us', *Gardens Illustrated*, 6 April 2020

Katherine Swift, *The Morville Hours*, 2009

Terry Tempest Williams, 'A Disturbance of Birds', *Ecotone*, Vol. 6, No.1, Fall 2010

Claire Tomalin, *Katherine Mansfield: A Secret Life*, 2003

Anne Truitt, *Daybook*, 2013

Shaun Usher, *Letters of Note: Love*, 2020

Alice Walker, 'In Search of Our Mothers' Gardens', *Within the Circle*, ed. Angelyn Mitchell, 1994

Leonard Woolf, *Downhill All the Way*, 1968

Virginia Woolf, *A Change of Perspective: The Letters of Virginia Woolf, Vol. III, 1923–28*, ed. Nigel Nicolson and Joanne Trautmann, 1977; *The Diary of Virginia Woolf, Vol. II, 1920–1924*, ed. Anne Olivier Bell with Andrew McNeillie, 1980; *The Diary of Virginia Woolf, Vol. III, 1925–1930*, ed. Anne Olivier Bell with Andrew

McNeillie, 1980; *Moments of Being: Autobiographical Writings*, ed. Jeanne Schulkind, 2002; *A Writer's Diary: Events Recorded from 1918–1941*, 2017

Dorothy Wordsworth, *The Grasmere Journal*, 1990

Ann Wroe, *Six Facets of Light*, 2016

Caroline Zoob, *Virginia Woolf's Garden*, 2013

An Interview with Dennis Potter, with Melvyn Bragg, *Channel 4*, 5 April 1994

Blue, dir. Derek Jarman, 1993

Can You Dig This, dir. Delila Vallot, 2015

Derek Jarman: A Portrait, dir. Mark Kidel, BBC Arena, 1991

Rivers and Tides: Andy Goldsworthy Working with Time, dir. Thomas Riedelsheimer, 2001